Shifting Sands

Shifting Sands

*The Rise and Fall of
Biblical Archaeology*

THOMAS W. DAVIS

OXFORD
UNIVERSITY PRESS
2004

OXFORD
UNIVERSITY PRESS

Oxford   New York
Auckland   Bangkok   Buenos Aires   Cape Town   Chennai
Dar es Salaam   Delhi   Hong Kong   Istanbul   Karachi   Kolkata
Kuala Lumpur   Madrid   Melbourne   Mexico City   Mumbai   Nairobi
São Paulo   Shanghai   Taipei   Tokyo   Toronto

Published by Oxford University Press, Inc.
198 Madison Avenue, New York, New York 10016

www.oup.com

Oxford is a registered trademark of Oxford University Press

Library of Congress Cataloging-in-Publication Data
Davis, Thomas W, 1956–
Shifting sands: the rise and fall of Biblical archaeology /
Thomas W. Davis.
p.   cm.
Includes bibliographical references (p.   )
ISBN 0-19-516710-4
1. Bible—Antiquities.   2. Bible—Evidences, authority, etc.
3. Excavations (Archaeology)—Palestine—History.
4. Palestine—Antiquities.   5. Albright, William Foxwell, 1891–1971.
6. Wright, George Ernest, 1909–1974.   I. Title.
BS621 .D38 2004
220.9'3'09—dc21   2003006652

9 8 7 6 5 4 3 2 1

Printed in the United States of America
on acid-free paper

To my wife, Jenny
Proverbs 31:10

Preface

The current generation has witnessed great changes in the archaeology of Palestine. Before the 1970s, biblical archaeology was the dominant research paradigm. Today, biblical archaeology has been "weighed in the balance and found wanting." Although not all American archaeologists in Syria/Palestine rejected the earlier terminology (Lance 1982), most now prefer "Syro-Palestinian archaeology," or a similar, specific political/geographic term (Dever 2003).This is not just a nominal shift, but reflects a major theoretical and methodological change that has been labeled a revolution (Dever 1981). A new consensus has formed around principles articulated by the anthropological archaeologists working in the United States. The clearest sign of the change in Palestine is in the current research designs, field projects, and preliminary publications of American archaeologists in Palestine. A thorough evaluation of the new theory and method will occur when all the new projects are published.

Why, then, look at the old? No revolution is ever complete, particularly a scholarly one. The new paradigm of Syro-Palestinian archaeology carries the stamp of its parent, biblical archaeology. The senior figures in the field, those who brought about the change in paradigm, are all products of biblical archaeological training. In the popular mind, the biblical archaeology paradigm is still alive and well, as witnessed by the success of the *Biblical Archaeology Review*. I believe the reason for this dichotomy is a failure to recognize the changing nature of biblical archaeology through time. This study elucidates the changes that did occur during the lifetime of biblical archaeology, following a chronological framework.

This study traces the interaction of biblical studies and archaeology in Palestine. Archaeology carries the connotation of fieldwork, and this study highlights the field aspect of biblical archaeology. An immense amount of data was gathered under the paradigm of biblical archaeology. This study enables that data to be more useful for current research by clarifying the theoretical and methodological framework of the original excavators. Until the 1920s, biblical scholars remained on the sidelines, although they were actively supporting archaeology and using the data gained from excavation. William Foxwell Albright brought biblical archaeology into the mainstream by conducting field research to ultimately aid biblical scholars. Biblical archaeology gained its prominence in Palestinian archaeology due to Albright's brilliant breakthrough in field methodology. Ironically, Albright's student, George Ernest Wright, would bring about the demise of classic biblical archaeology by continuing the tradition of methodological experimentation.

Biblical archaeology was, in simplest terms, a search for realia. It was an attempt to ground the historical witness of the Bible in demonstrable historical reality. Throughout its history, it was linked to this aim. Only when the archaeological data themselves became recognized as dependent on interpretation for their meaning (in other words, no longer seen as purely objective data) did biblical archaeology lose its positivist foundation, and collapse.

The history of classic biblical archaeology is ultimately a history of an aspect of biblical studies, not archaeology. As will be shown below, the theoretical base for the archaeology lay in the field of theology. This is why biblical archaeology was almost exclusively an American endeavor. American Protestantism strongly resisted the inroads of continental biblical criticism, and research in the ancient Near East became a potential source of support for the conservative opponents of critical study. Biblical archaeology became a weapon in theological debate, ultimately being very closely linked to the biblical theology movement by George Ernest Wright. The practitioners of biblical archaeology believed, albeit in different ways, that biblical faith, both Christianity and Judaism, depends on the historical reality of the events that displayed the Hand of God. If the events that the Bible interprets as the intervention of the divine have no basis in reality, then there is no basis for believing in the biblical witness. Thus, any evidence that might help to buttress the hope of faith is welcome. Here is the ultimate drive for realia. The archaeology of Palestine, the Land of the Bible, became biblical archaeology.

Biblical archeology still has validity as a name for the sphere of interaction of archaeology and the Bible. The new biblical archaeology is currently racked by fierce polemics (e.g., Dever 2001; I. Finkelstein and Silberman 2001). Ironically, archaeology is once again a weapon to be used to further particular biblical perspectives. The "maximalists" accept a certain level of validity to the historical witness of the Hebrew Bible; the "minimalists" reject any historicity associated with the Hebrew Bible and consider it to be a product of later Judaism. As will be explored below, both sides in the debate employ archaeology in the same way, as did Albright and Wright, as a source of objective data.

This book is a revised version of my Ph.D. dissertation at the University of Arizona, first prepared in 1987. I give my very special thanks to Dr. William G. Dever, teacher, advisor, and friend, for without his belief in this topic the study would not have been completed. Thanks are also due to the late Professor James A. Sauer, formerly of the University of Pennsylvania, for permission to use the library and archives of the University Museum in Philadelphia; Douglas M. Haller, chief archivist of the Museum archives, and his assistant, Georgianna Grentzenberg, for their aid in researching C. S. Fisher; and the Committee of the Palestine Exploration Fund and the secretary of the Fund, Dr. Rupert Chapman, for their permission to examine and use the archives of the Fund. Many scholars generously gave of their time to read and review various stages of this manuscript: Dr. Steven Falconer of Arizona State University, Dr. Peter Machinist of Harvard University, Dr. Bonnie Magness-Gardiner of the U.S. Department of State, Dr. Michael Schiffer of the University of Arizona, and my first editors, Chris and Linda Hulin. A special thank you is given to Dr. James K. Hoffmeier of Trinity International University, who reawakened my interest in the topic when he invited me to join him on an excavation in Egypt, after I had been a long time away from the Levant. My deep personal thanks to my brother, Dr. Edward B. Davis, for his practical suggestions and encouragement in the dissertation process; my parents, for their belief in my ability; and most of all to my wife, for her unending patience, love, and support.

Winston Churchill, while paying tribute to his predecessor, Neville Chamberlain, described the perspective that history can bring to an endeavor:

> It is not given to human beings, happily for them, for otherwise life would be intolerable, to foresee or to predict to any large extent the unfolding course of events. In one phase men seem to have been right, in another they seem to have been wrong. Then again, a few years later, when the perspective of time has lengthened, all stands in a different setting. There is a new proportion. There is another

scale of values. History with its flickering lamp stumbles along the trail of the past, trying to reconstruct its scenes, to revive its echoes, and kindle with pale gleams the passion of former days. What is the worth of all this? The only guide to a man is his conscience; the only shield to his memory is the rectitude and sincerity of his actions. It is very imprudent to walk through life without this shield, because we are so often mocked by the failure of our hopes and the upsetting of our calculations; but with this shield, however the Fates may play, we march always in the ranks of honour. (1949: 550)

Biblical archaeology as understood by Albright and Wright is no more. Today, the field and its practitioners are often vilified. I hope that this study will allow a more sober, reasoned judgment of the achievements and the failures of biblical archaeology to be made. It is not the final word on the subject, for we are still too close for such surety. For biblical archaeology, the hopes failed, the calculations were upset, the realia were lost, but surely, it belongs in "the ranks of honour."

Contents

Shifting Sands

I

The Beginnings

The explorations of the biblical world that culminated in biblical archaeology found their source in the pilgrim impulse. For more than
two millennia people have traveled for religious reasons to Palestine.
Whether to fulfill the hope expressed in the Passover prayer "Next
year in Jerusalem" or to "walk where Jesus walked," the pilgrims
came to a specific place out of a belief that their faith was grounded
in events having a historic reality and that the arena for those events
was Syria/Palestine. The religious aura of the land of Palestine, "the
Holy Land," created a ready market for the tales of pilgrimage. The
listener, and later the reader, could become a vicarious pilgrim
through the accounts of the returnees.

As a result of its biblical connection, Palestine remained
uniquely in the forefront of the historical consciousness of the West.
The medieval pilgrimages to Palestine, exemplified by the great cru-
sades, were one element of Catholicism rejected by Protestants. John
Bunyan's *Pilgrim's Progress* demonstrated the belief that the true pilgrimage was an inner, spiritual one, rather than an external, physical journey to an earthly city. For a time, interest in the physical (as
opposed to the metaphysical) Palestine faded. The metaphor of Palestine remained very powerful in the common mind, particularly in
views of the New World. Certainly, the Atlantic Ocean was seen by
some Protestant divines as a new Jordan that had to be crossed to
get to the Promised Land—a new Promised Land, where God's
Kingdom would be built according to His guidelines. Still, interest

in the physical Palestine was only dormant, waiting for revival. Despite the fading of the medieval pilgrimages, there remained a strong core of interest in "biblical antiquities." From this core came the pioneers of biblical archaeology.

Although occasional travelers returned with descriptions of the Levant, the impetus for a revival of Western interest in Palestine came from the international rivalries of late eighteenth- and early nineteenth-century Europe. Napoleon Bonaparte, seeking to cut the British off from India and give France a colonial empire, attacked the weak Ottoman Empire in 1798. He landed in Egypt, where his army was eventually stranded by Nelson's victory at Aboukir Bay. Napoleon, echoing Alexander the Great, brought a team of draftsmen and scholars to study the geography, resources, and antiquities of Egypt. Under the auspices of the French Egyptian Institute, scholars fanned out all over Egypt, recording and measuring the various monuments. While engaged in fortification work in Alexandria, Pierre Bouchard, a young army officer, discovered a basalt slab embedded in a wall. It became known as the Rosetta Stone and ended up in London as spoils of war. In 1809, the French began publishing the results of their research and so brought ancient Egypt before the scholarly public (Adkins and Adkins 2000).

Edward Robinson

Surprisingly, the first systematic exploration of Palestine was the result of the combined efforts of two Americans: Edward Robinson and Eli Smith. Robinson was the prime mover in the enterprise, but without Smith's linguistic abilities, their aim of a scientific geography of the Holy Land would have failed. Robinson stood at the threshold of scientific exploration, yet he also looked back to the days of pilgrimage. He combined biblical interest and a strong personal faith with an attempt to be as "scientific" as possible in his research. This combination of characteristics would often be repeated in the practitioners of biblical archaeology. Any study of the field must begin with Robinson, for all later archaeological research in Palestine is in some way indebted to him. His geographical study marked a new era. "In Robinson's footnotes," wrote the biblical geographer Albrecht Alt, "are forever buried the errors of many generations" (1939: 374).

The only major biography of Robinson is by Roswell Hitchcock, the president of Union Seminary at the time of Robinson's death in 1863 (Hitchcock and Smith 1863). Written with W. B. Smith, Hitchcock's work is more hagiography than biography. All later treatments of Robinson, such as Albright's (1937) and King's (1983a, 1983b), are derived from this first work. The reader of Robinson's journals can discern the varied influences of his training and background.

Born in 1794, Robinson was the son of a clergyman who had turned his energies to farming. He went to Hamilton College, where he graduated in 1816 with the highest scores in mathematics and linguistics. He had a lifelong love for mathematics, which undoubtedly contributed to his meticulous eye for detail—very helpful on his journeys.

In 1821, Robinson went to Andover Seminary to publish an edition of the *Iliad* with Latin notes. This was a watershed decision. At Andover he came into contact with Moses Stuart, "the father of modern biblical study in America" (Williams 1941:17). Stuart had introduced the results of German biblical scholarship to the United States, predominantly its linguistic aspects. Robinson quickly mastered Hebrew at Andover and by 1823 was helping Stuart with an edition of Stuart's *Hebrew Grammar*. Stuart's biblical scholarship was at heart conservative, although he had serious reservations regarding the accepted doctrine of verbal inspiration (Williams 1941: 17), the belief that God inspired the Bible and directly gave every word in the original texts to the human authors. From the perspective of current biblical scholarship, the rejection of verbal inspiration does not seem very radical, but in the third decade of the nineteenth century it was. Andover was an unlikely place for such an approach, for the Congregationalists had founded it as the conservative counterweight to Harvard, which had become dominated by the Unitarians.

Pursuing philological interests, Robinson went to Germany in 1826. There he encountered a freer atmosphere of inquiry. He met Gesenius at Halle, a man he considered "the first Hebrew scholar of the Age" (according to Hitchcock and Smith 1863: 50). Gesenius was the author of a Hebrew grammar that was the basis for Stuart's work in the United States. Robinson would later translate Gesenius's work into English. Robinson's eyes were opened to more than just philology when, traveling on to Berlin, he met the German geographer Ritter. A pioneering scientific geographer, Ritter must have made a profound impression, because at this point, Robinson began to plan a systematic work on the geography of Palestine (60).

Robinson returned to the United States and in 1831 began the first scholarly series on biblical and theological topics in this country, the *Biblical Repository*. His name spread beyond the conservative world of Andover, and he was offered a post at the newly formed Union Seminary. In 1837 he accepted this offer with the provision that he be allowed to make a journey to the Near East.

Robinson in Palestine

Robinson set out in the fall of 1837 for Cairo, where he teamed up with Eli Smith, a Beirut-based missionary who had visited Andover. Robinson (1841) kept a daily journal of his trip, which retained its original format when it was published in three volumes. This format was intentional, chosen by Robinson to show the "process of inquiry" that he pursued on the course of his journey. The journals are fascinating reading, containing detailed information on the country he passed through. He wrote in them every night, often battling with fatigue to record the events of the day. An excellent observer, he reported on the flora and fauna of the land, the social customs of his guides and of the Arabs they encountered, as well as detailed geographical notes. His reports of the variety of social customs are becoming more and more valuable today as the way of life he recorded is almost gone from living memory. On occasion, Robinson exhibited a rather typical Western contempt for the "indolence and procrastinating habits of the Egyptians and Arabs [which are] well known" (1: 22). He also evidenced the classic traveler's trait of immortalizing himself by defacing certain monuments with his name (3: 520)! He attempted to be as fair as possible with his guides and servants, recording minute transactions and expenses incurred by them. Eli Smith was fluent in the local Palestinian Arabic, which eased the difficulties of the journey considerably.

Robinson professed to three motivations for the trip: personal gratification (a motive not generally confessed by New England Congregationalists for any undertaking), a desire to increase his biblical knowledge, and the preparation of a scientific geography (1841, 1: 46). He brought a new approach to the location of biblical sites: He believed that the key to locating ancient sites was "the preservation of ancient place names among the common people" (1: 376). As a linguist, Robinson was aware of the scholarly views on the breakdown of human languages into families. He believed the ancient Semitic place-names were likely to be continued in the Arabic of the local fellahin. Robinson does not explain how he arrived at this idea, but it is quite likely that his own observation of the tenacity of American Indian place-names in his native Connecticut may have led him to expect the preservation of Hebrew names in the colloquial Arabic, despite the Roman and Byzantine interregnums.

Robinson's first success with his new approach was the recovery of his first "lost" site, Elusa, in the southern Negev (1841, 1: 296–98). First he noticed that there were ruins visible adjacent to a well where he and Smith had stopped. In the name of the ruins (ascertained by Smith from the local bedouin), el-Khalsa, Robinson recognized an echo of Elusa. Next, in his journal, Robinson listed historic accounts of the site, such as that of Ptolemy, to check that all the details were in agreement. Finally, he accurately plotted the site and determined its distance from Jerusalem as a means of checking the historical accounts. This same procedure of discovery, ascertaining the current name, checking historical, biblical, and travelers' records, and the accurate plotting of the location was followed throughout his travels.

When Robinson entered Palestine proper, this methodology bore rich fruit. He correctly located more than thirty-five previously "lost" ancient sites. A typical example is the ancient site of Gibeon, prominent in the biblical accounts of Joshua and David (Robinson 1841, 1: 455). Robinson located it at the modern village of el-Jib, which he thought was an echo of Gibeon. (That same day, 5 May 1838, he located four other biblical sites.) In the 1950s, excavations conducted by a team from the University of Pennsylvania confirmed the identification through ostraca found at the site (Pritchard 1962).

Robinson was not dogmatic in his assertions. Sometimes, when he was sure of identification but did not have proof of habitation, he would make only a tentative placement. The location of the site of Ai, which the Bible describes as "a ruin heap" (Joshua 8:28), is an example of his caution. Two possible sites were acceptable to him on philological grounds: Et-Tell and Khirbet Haijah. Robinson preferred Khirbet Haijah because it was the only site with visible ruins. As for Et-Tell, "the position would answer well to that of Ai; and had there been traces of ruins, I should not hesitate to so regard it" (1841, 3: 312–13).

One of the ironies of Robinson's work is illustrated in the problem of the location of Ai: He did not grasp the nature of the tells that dot the Palestinian landscape (figure 1.1). He has been criticized for this, perhaps unfairly (Abel 1939). But the laws of superposition and stratigraphy were still being hammered out in geology and were not yet totally accepted. Without an understanding of stratigraphy, Robinson did not realize that tells were essentially artificial in nature. As a result, on occasion, he made faulty identifications or refrained from a correct identification, as in the case of Tell el-Ful, "a high conical hill near the Nablus road . . . with a large heap of stones upon the top" (1841, 3: 114). In the vicinity of the tell, he was looking for the biblical site of Gibeah, capital of Israel's first king, Saul. He had already located two sites in the vicinity, Jeba and er-Ram, which he had identified as ancient neighbors of Gibeah: "Did there exist any trace of an ancient site between Jeba and er-Ram, I should have no hesitation in regarding it as the site of Gibeah" (3: 114). He did not consider Tell el-Ful a candidate, despite its location between Jeba and er-Ram, because the only visible ruins were a Turkish tower. Also, his own methodology may have misled him in this case, because the name of site is "hill of the bean," a name unconnected to the supposed ancient name of Gibeah. W. F. Albright

FIGURE 1.1 A classic Near Eastern tell site, Tell el-Husn in Jordan. Photo by author

(1922b) would later excavate Tell el-Ful, demonstrating its antiquity as a site of habitation and the most likely candidate for Saul's capital.

A clear clue to the nature of tells was presented to Robinson in Egypt. The explorer noticed that many villages were built up on mounds, and he recorded this as a passing observation: "Mud hovels . . . built on mounds from the ruins of former dwellings" (1841, 1: 28). Robinson can be faulted only for not applying the same reasoning to the tells in Palestine. It is a curious and rare failure of an otherwise brilliant observer. Yet, fault is not the word; it is no failure to be ahead of one's time only most and not all of the time.

Prior to Robinson, the main source for the location of biblical sites had been church tradition. Robinson was highly suspicious of the locations of biblical sites and events put forward by the religious establishments of Palestine: "All ecclesiastical tradition respecting the ancient places in and around Jerusalem and throughout Palestine is of *no value*, except so far as it is supported by circumstances known to us from the Scriptures or from other contemporary testimony" (1841, 1: 374; emphasis in original). His distrust of the ecclesiastical, particularly Roman Catholic traditions was so strong that he has been accused of anti-Catholic bias (Bliss 1907; Stinespring 1939). The harsh, judgmental tone of Robinson's observations in Jerusalem does reflect a strong antagonism toward the Roman Catholic rites that he saw there. He was in Jerusalem during Holy Week and was clearly offended by the noisy ostentation of the services

(1: 329–31). He saw the "annual mockery" of the Greek fire, the Latin priests "enacting their mummery" (figure 1.2). "The whole scene to a Protestant was painful and revolting." One cause of his strong feeling was the reaction of the Moslem inhabitants of Jerusalem, who, according to Robinson, "look on with a haughty scorn" (1: 331). This produced "a feeling too strong to be borne, and I never visited the place [the Holy Sepulchre] again" (1: 331). However, Robinson did not judge all Catholic ceremonies in the same way; for example, he called the celebrators at St. Peter's in Rome "intelligent and noble" (1: 331). Nor can he be accused of a blanket condemnation of all Eastern rites. He attended a service at St. Katherine's in the Sinai and found it "dignified and solemn" (1: 142). His harsh comments at Holy Week are probably due to his own height-ened awareness and the deep emotion he felt on being in Jerusalem for that season. In addition, his interest in missions led him to be very disturbed by the Moslem reaction to the rites in the Sepulchre. He was very mission-minded on his journey, as evidenced by his repeatedly expressed interest in the various missions in Palestine and by his involvement as a courier for various mission-aries (1: 25).

The pilgrim impulse was not very far below the surface in Robinson. It was an unspoken fourth reason for his trip. Occasionally in his diary, the re-ligious excitement breaks through his scientific façade, and he records in-

FIGURE 1.2 The Holy Sepulchre in Jerusalem, where the rites of worship offended Edward Robinson. Photo by author

stances of deep emotion, such as first seeing Jerusalem or crying at a service at St. Katherine's monastery (1: 326). Personally, he was a very devout man. He closed his preface to his published accounts of his travels with a prayer: "May He who has thus far sustained me, make it useful for the elucidation of His truth" (1: vii). Robinson always broke his travel for the Sabbath, except for one occasion that bothered him considerably (1: 94). He strongly supported the full inspiration of the Bible, accepting its historical claims as accurate (Brewer 1939: 361). This was in clear contrast to his view of tradition and marks him as solidly Protestant in attitude.

Robinson combined a profound respect for the historical accuracy of the Bible with what was meant by "science" in his day. This is apparent in his refusal to accept unverifiable claims made by church tradition. Of course, it must be pointed out that Robinson treated the biblical text as the standard by which to judge other evidence. He considered it already verified, hence usable in a scientific inquiry. Sometimes this caused him problems; on occasion, his geographical observations ran counter to a literal interpretation of the Bible, as occurred in the Sinai desert. Robinson had decided to go overland to Palestine from Cairo to check the route of the Exodus (1841, 1: 76). Recording his thoughts at the Sea of Reeds, he pondered the nature of miracles, concluding that miracles are supernatural applications of natural laws. The one item that gave him pause was the lack of water in the Sinai, considering the number of people listed in the Exodus accounts. Troubled, caught between his own observations and the biblical numbers, Robinson took refuge in declaring the solution "a mystery" (1: 106).

Edward Robinson is the prototype biblical archaeologist. Underlying his approach is the search for solid demonstrable evidence of the accuracy of the biblical witness; it is a search for realia. Providing the Bible with a scrupulously accurate geographical framework was the fulfillment of Robinson as scientist and theologian. He saw unity between what Kepler called "the finger and the tongue of God" (Hitchcock and Smith 1863: 8), and he approached the geography of Palestine with this in mind.

Robinson came to Palestine expecting to find support for his conservative views on the Bible. He came with a closed mind regarding the accuracy of Scripture, and despite evidence to the contrary, as in the Sinai, he did not change his views. This did not cause major problems for him, because nothing was known to contradict him. Only later would the tools of archaeology be honed enough to check his results. Also, questions of site location are of a different nature than questions of event or date. Even if a suspected identification is shown to be accurate, it does not follow that the biblical date or event connected with the site is also accurate.

Robinson's belief that ecclesiastical tradition was of no historical value did cause problems in some of his work (Stinespring 1939). His disgust for the rites in the Church of the Holy Sepulchre prevented him from making an unbiased evaluation of the claims put forward for the church as the location of Calvary. He dismissed the stations of the Via Dolorosa as absurdities (1841, 1: 344), including the Church of the Holy Sepulchre. In his desire to avoid being "contaminated" by supporters of Church tradition, Robinson stayed with Protestant missionaries (1: 378). Because the aim of these missionaries was to "reawaken the Oriental Church to the purity and simplicity of original form[s]" of the gospel (1: 322), one can be sure that his hosts reinforced his antitradition stance. Because he had no feasible alternative for the location of Calvary and the tomb (he wrote more than forty years before General Gordon's [1885] suggested alternative), Robinson was unable to dismiss totally the traditional claims. Today, most scholars, even conservative Protestants (McRay 1991), accept the identification of the Church of the Holy Sepulchre as the place where Jesus was buried (Barkay 1986; Biddle 1999; Wilkinson 1978).

Robinson did indulge in a little of what might be called archaeology while he was in Jerusalem. He went all over the ancient city, measuring and comparing the holy sites with his knowledge of the biblical accounts and the ancient historians. He correctly identified what is now known as Robinson's Arch as a pier for one of the bridges leading to the Herodian temple (1841, 2: 425). He also crawled through Hezekiah's Tunnel, but missed the inscription found later in the century on the walls of the watercourse (1: 505–7). On his second trip, he met Dr. James Barclay, an American missionary in Jerusalem. Barclay had explored various areas of the city, including beneath the Haram. Robinson (1852) was grateful for his assistance and praised his maps. Barclay published an account of his investigations in Jerusalem in 1858 (Lewis 1988).

Robinson demonstrated to both scholars and the general public that scientific exploration could benefit the study of the Bible. As a mark of his achievements, the Royal Geographical Society awarded him a gold medal. In 1852 he returned to the Levant with Eli Smith, wishing to concentrate on the areas to the north of Palestine (Robinson 1852). He wanted to publish the definitive biblical geography, combining the results of both trips. When he died, the historical and topographical portions of the study were unfinished. This led to Hitchcock's lament: "There lives no man to finish it; and when one shall be born to do it, God only knows" (Hitchcock and Smith 1863: 97). Robinson's work has been properly recognized as one of the most important contributions of the preexcavation era to archaeology in Palestine. Frederick Jones Bliss (1907: 207), one of the pioneer excavators in Palestine, called Robinson one of the giants. On the hundredth anniversary of his trip, the Society of Biblical

Literature honored Robinson by devoting an entire issue of its journal to his career (Abel 1939; Alt 1939; Brewer 1939; Stinespring 1939). Before Robinson, geography in Palestine was hearsay and travelers' tales; after him, it was well on its way to becoming a science.

Following Robinson's Lead

After Robinson's journals were published from his first trip, two expeditions to explore the Dead Sea were organized. A British expedition came to grief through attacks by Adwan Bedouin and fevers (Silberman 1982), but an American attempt had more success. William Lynch (1849), a U.S. Navy lieutenant, commanded the expedition. Lynch was interested in the possibilities of opening up U.S. trade in the Levant, using the Jordan basin. One of the people he consulted before leaving for Palestine in 1847 was Edward Robinson.

After many trials, Lynch's expedition reached the Sea of Galilee, where he launched the boats that had been carried overland from the Mediterranean. The entire length of the Jordan River was accurately mapped for the first time and the Dead Sea circumnavigated. On his return to the United States, the trade route proposal was not pursued, but the accounts of his trip (Lynch 1849) aroused a great deal of interest among the biblically minded. The results of the Lynch expedition were rapidly taken up by the popular religious literature, and he continued to be quoted as an authority up to the end of the nineteenth century (Smith 1884).

The Growth of the Societies

The 1840s saw interest in the ancient Near East increased by the first excavations in Mesopotamia. Paul Emile Botta, the French consul in Mosul, dug among the ruins at Khorsabad and was the first to recover the remains of the Assyrians. Henry Layard (1891), an Englishman who excavated at Nimrud, quickly followed him. Layard was concerned by the rapid deterioration of the objects that he uncovered but was unable to do much about this due to his very limited budget. Both Layard and Botta were primarily looking for museum display pieces. Layard was rewarded by the discovery of the famous Assyrian reliefs now in the British Museum. He found it necessary to cut off portions of the sculpted panels to ship them to London. The excised portions included inscriptional material that Layard felt was duplicated on the preserved portions; of course, because the cuneiform script was as yet unread, he could not be sure. Layard also worked at Kuyunjik, a site that Botta had given up on as not yielding enough antiquities (Cleator 1976). At this site, he uncovered a royal library. Later work brought the total number of tablets recovered to nearly twenty thousand.

The French-English national rivalry in Mesopotamia carried over into Palestine. French interest in the potential gains to be had in the decaying Ottoman Empire led to military intervention in 1860 in what was to become Lebanon. A theologian, Ernest Renan (1864), accompanied the military expedition. Napoleon III wished to emulate the scientific success of his uncle's expedition to Egypt in 1799, and Renan was given a free hand to excavate. He dug at Byblos, Sidon, and Tyre, looking for museum-quality material. The French never relinquished their primary archaeological role in the area.

This French activity aroused great indignation in England (Silberman 1982). This increased when it was reported in 1863 that a Frenchman was the first to excavate in Jerusalem! A quixotic adventurer named de Saulcy, who had earlier led an expedition to the Dead Sea, decided to excavate at the supposed tombs of the kings of Judah in Jerusalem. The British response to all this French activity was not long in coming.

The Palestine Exploration Fund

On 22 June 1865, the Palestine Exploration Fund (PEF) was born (Grove 1869b: 10). Its leadership included the archbishop of York, the president of the Royal Geographical Society, and millionaire industrialists. Royal favor was procured, and Queen Victoria donated £150. The Fund aimed for the scientific investigation of the "Archaeology, Geography, Geology, and Natural History of Palestine" for its own sake and for the purpose of biblical illustration (Grove 1869a: 1–2). By the time the PEF was founded, "archaeology" had come to mean "excavation," not just "antiquities," as in the past. This was a result of the work of the first pioneer excavators such as Layard in Mesopotamia.

The Fund began its work in Palestine by sponsoring the explorations of an officer of the Royal Engineers, Charles Wilson. He had begun surveying Jerusalem in 1864, and the first secretary of the Fund, Sir Charles Grove, suggested that Wilson be authorized to survey sites for excavation (figure 1.3). In 1867, another officer of the Royal Engineers, Charles Warren, was sponsored by the PEF to investigate Jerusalem. Both of these expeditions depleted the Fund financially and demonstrated that a full survey of Palestine would require

FIGURE 1.3 Jerusalem, where the PEF began their research in Palestine. Photo by author

an immense expenditure of time and energy. Warren's work was more successful, raising public interest in Palestine, which the Fund decided to tap.

By 1869 the PEF was facing serious difficulties. In the first *Quarterly*, an appeal was made for more funds (Grove 1869b). This appeal was directed to "the full body of the clergy of the Church of England; to the whole body of the non-conformist ministers; to students of the Bible of whatever opinions" (8). It is typical of Victorian England that neither the Roman Catholic nor the Jewish clergy were considered likely candidates. A clear statement of the Fund's appeal to its supposed audience followed: "Those who know the value of the removal of difficulties from the right understanding of the sacred text should be foremost in helping a society which has no other aim than to remove them, and no other reason for existence" (9). The appeal very carefully avoids any theological stance; followers of every school of thought regarding the Bible (as the PEF nowhere makes clear what approach it considers to be correct) could accept the "right understanding of the sacred text." This is in keeping with the Fund's aim of biblical illustration as opposed to apologetics. The mandate to illuminate the Bible was interpreted in the broadest terms, with no fear of undercutting the Bible. Therefore, any field of inquiry that expanded knowledge of ancient Palestine was welcomed; the focus was geographical, not biblical.

R.A.S. Macalister, from the perspective of the 1920s, criticized the initial aims of the PEF. He felt the focus on Jerusalem was "a premature assault . . . a fundamental mistake" (1925: 31). The excavations, primarily conducted by tunneling, destroyed much more information than they provided. Macalister felt another site should have been chosen for the initial explorations by the PEF. When the problems of excavation were recognized and solutions field-tested, then Jerusalem could be approached without the irreparable loss of information. His criticisms were well founded, but he did not take into account the state of excavation in other areas besides Palestine. Warren's work was in keeping with the approach of Layard in Mesopotamia and actually more advanced than what Renan was doing in Lebanon. He tried to destroy as little as possible and kept good records of what was attempted. He was conscientious in reporting to the PEF what he accomplished. By tunneling through more than 130 feet of debris, he was able to prepare the first survey of the original rock levels of the city. No one in the late 1860s appreciated the potential of pottery for dating purposes, and Macalister criticized this aspect of the Fund's early work in Jerusalem. Yet, there is no guarantee that the excavation of a different site would have discovered the chronological use of pottery. Macalister did not take into account the nearly absolute ignorance of scholars in these early days about the nature of a tell. The planners of the Fund had no idea of the complexity of the task they set for Warren. Undoubtedly, the popular interest in Jerusalem was a major factor in the decision to begin there. After Warren's results were made public, the PEF found itself able to make ends meet financially. Beginning in Jerusalem may have been a mistake archaeologically, but it was a resounding popular success. To the Fund's credit, it must be pointed out that once financial stability was achieved, the PEF turned away from excavation and pushed for exploration of the entire country. They correctly saw this as a necessary prelude to excavation anywhere else in Palestine.

The financial report of the annual general meeting of the PEF in 1870 demonstrates the success of the subscription drive (Grove 1870b: 142). Twenty-five local societies were operating by that time, covering the British Isles and including a local branch in Chicago (Grove 1870a: 112). American interest was also documented in a letter from the Long Island Historical Society, which appeared in the *Quarterly* (Grove 1869d: 63–65). The letter mentioned the avid interest of American readers in reports of the Fund and pointed with pride to the efforts of Robinson and Lynch to explore Palestine. With that heritage in mind, the letter expressed a desire for a distinctly American society, which would work with the Fund in exploration.

The Palestine Exploration Society

The desire for an American society was attained with the formation of the Palestine Exploration Society (PES) in 1870 (King 1983a; Moulton 1928). Among its members were J. Henry Thayer of Harvard and Roswell Hitchcock of Union Seminary. Hitchcock was Robinson's biographer and the second president of the Society. Although the PEF was the model for the new endeavor, the stated aims of the PES were profoundly different: "The work proposed by the Palestine Exploration Society appeals to the religious sentiments alike of the Christian and the Jew; it is of interest to the scholar in almost every branch of linguistic, historical, or physical investigation, but its supreme importance is for the illustration and defense of the Bible. Modern skepticism assails the Bible at the point of reality, the question of fact. Hence whatever goes to verify the Bible history as real in time, place, and circumstances is a refutation of unbelief" (King 1983a: 8).

To the PES, the needs and interest of the scholar were followed only if they aided in the defense of Scripture, a direct reversal of the priorities of the PEF. The Society placed itself solidly in the search for realia. The presence of Hitchcock among the founders may explain this orientation. In expecting to find "the point of reality" in the dirt of Palestine, the U.S. organization followed the lead of Edward Robinson. Clearly, the results of the investigations of scholars in the Society were to be judged acceptable only if they were usable for the defense of the Bible. Robinson's investigations were an acceptable guide, as they had supported the basic reliability of the conservative viewpoint. The apologetical reasoning of the PES was fruit of the success of Robinson and reflected no fear that any discoveries would challenge Orthodoxy. Indeed, the exploration of Palestine was viewed with the expectation of gaining ammunition for debate.

James R. Moore's (1979) study of the Protestant reactions to Darwinism documented the various attempts to reconcile the new science with theology. These attempts characterized the immediate post–Civil War generation in U.S. science and theology. Much of the religious community in the United States saw a threat to the Bible "at the point of reality." The founders of the PES evidently wished to counter the scientific attacks on biblical veracity with demonstrable support for biblical history. The linkage of biblical history with biblical theology was made explicit in the constitution of the Society. This was a reflection of the connection of biblical science to biblical theology made by some in the post-Darwin debates. Certain leading natural scientists such as Asa Gray and George Frederick Wright advocated a synthesis called Christian Darwinism. The members of the PES were not so sophisticated, and clearly expected their beliefs to be upheld by their investigations. I suggest that the attacks on the Bible generated in the scientific community helped lead to the founding of the PES. If the theology of the Bible could be attacked through its science, then perhaps demonstrating its historical accuracy could defend its theology. The apologetical use of archaeology would become a recurring element in U.S. archaeological thinking in Palestine.

Only the American PES felt the need to justify the exploration of Palestine with an appeal to the Bible. The British PEF used the biblical connection as a fund-raising technique, but it was never presented as the primary focus of inquiry. The British agenda reflects the fact that the PEF was not just a religiously sponsored group. As Neil Silberman has pointed out in his study, *Digging for God and Country* (1982), the PEF functioned in an atmosphere of imperialism. The opening of the Suez Canal, with its obvious benefits to British India, and national rivalry with France added to the attractions of Palestine in British eyes. In light of the Great Powers rivalry for influence in the Ottoman Empire, it comes as no surprise that the first two PEF-sponsored explorers were British army officers (Wilson and Warren). The great survey of Palestine, to which the PEF is forever linked, was first proposed by Capt. Wilson and carried out by the Royal Engineers. The resulting map not only provided a tremendous resource for exploration in Palestine, but it could also be used by the military. This combination of religious interest and imperial ambition was very appealing in late Victorian England and gave the PEF the advantage of official backing.

The PES quickly became involved in partnership with the PEF. As part of the grand survey of Palestine that the PEF was undertaking, the Americans took on themselves the task of surveying Transjordan. This appealed to the American desire to perpetuate the work of Edward Robinson (Moulton 1928). Although originally opposed to the idea, the PEF realized the potential benefits to its own project and an agreement was reached. The Fund attempted to ease the problems for its "sister American society" in terms of firmans (official documents giving permission to work in the Ottoman Empire) and the antiquities laws (PEF/WS/21). The first expedition, led by a U.S. Cavalry officer, Edgar Stevens, was a failure due to lack of funding and training. "Nothing will be done, east of the Jordan, by the Americans if they continue to organize their expeditions as they do," wrote a knowledgeable British observer to the PEF (PEF/WS/120). A second expedition of the PES produced a map, but it was a failure: When the British later tried to link it to their own survey results, they discovered the Americans had not properly surveyed their base points, preventing effective use of the survey results. Col. Lane, who had accompanied the second expedition along with Selah Merrill, recommended that the Society contribute $25,000 for a long-term project if they wanted to achieve anything of significance (Moulton 1928: 65). The directors balked at this prospect, and, financially drained by the abortive expeditions, the PES came to an end in 1884. It left little mark on later scholarship.

The failure of the PES was the fault of its own aims. By emphasizing the gathering of information of apologetical value, the Society was not paying due regard to the limited state of knowledge about ancient Palestine. The survey of Palestine, a necessary first step before any real excavation could take place, was not an activity designed to provide apologetical data. Thus, the expectations of its subscribers were bound to be frustrated. The attempt at a survey failed because of a lack of expertise in the staff of the expeditions. Although a U.S. Cavalry officer led the first expedition, the War Department did not provide any support beyond granting Stevens leave (Moulton 1928: 60). One can only speculate that the uncompromising apologetical approach of the PES kept the U.S. military from becoming officially involved in the surveys. Of course, the same strategic interests were not present either. Lacking the technical resources and constrained by its own agenda, the Society was unable to go on alone. It would have been much better advised to take a subordinate, supportive role to the PEF's survey.

Society of Biblical Archaeology

In 1870, a private meeting "of a few gentlemen" was held in London to explore ways of filling a gap in the burgeoning ranks of scholarly societies that studied the ancient Near East (Birch 1872a: i). A new association was seen as necessary to pull together the data from current investigations that related to the Bible. The founders felt that such data had been put into an interpolated position, peripheral to the main areas of interest in the various geographically oriented societies active in Britain. This proposed association "would investigate and systematize the Antiquities of the ancient and mighty empires and primeval peoples whose records are centered around the venerable pages of the Bible ... to accumulate data and to preserve facts—to give a voice to the past, and permanence to the efforts of all students in Biblical Archaeology" (ii).

In the familiar pattern of Victorian societies, a public meeting was held on 9 December 1870. The following resolutions were proposed and adopted:

I.   That a society be initiated, having for its objects the investigation of the Archaeology, Chronology, Geography, and History of Ancient and modern Assyria, Arabia, Egypt, Palestine, and other Biblical Lands, the Promotion of the study of the Antiquities of these countries, and the preservation of a continuous record of discoveries, now or hereafter to be in progress.

II. That the said Society shall be called the Society of Biblical Archaeology. (Birch 1872a: ii–iii):

The inaugural address of President Birch (1872b), entitled "The Progress of Biblical Archaeology," presented the aims and goals of the Society. The Society was to pull together material relating to the Bible from the different branches of "Semitic Archaeology." Birch made it quite clear that this was not an organization dedicated to apologetics. The Society was not to shy away from investigations that might bring biblical interpretations into question: "There is nothing to alarm the exegetical critic in the slight discrepancies that always present themselves in the world's history when the same fact is differently recorded by the actors in the same national struggle. For truth, the whole evidence is required, and the same monuments of antiquity too often reach our hands as broken pieces of an imperfect puzzle" (2). In conclusion, Birch wrote, "Its scope is Archaeology not Theology; but to Theology it will prove an important aid" (12). This is a marked change from the viewpoint of the Palestine Exploration Society.

To President Birch and his colleagues, biblical archaeology was interdisciplinary. There is no provision for the sponsoring of excavations by the Society. This was to be an "armchair" brand of inquiry, drawing from the results obtained by fieldworkers sent out by the various societies who were geared to actual excavation, such as the PEF. The entire realm of Near Eastern studies was the area to be mined for biblical data, with special attention paid to the translation of new texts. Birch was keenly aware of the importance of philology for understanding the past: "The truth of history depends on the accuracy of philology" (1872b: 12). In the program he outlined, the known inscriptions of Egypt, Assyria, Cyprus, and Arabia figured prominently. Birch had played a leading part in the decipherment of Egyptian hieroglyphics, being the first in England to support Champollion (Adkins and Adkins 2000). With a philological orientation, the Society was able to fulfill its mandate at least initially. Two series of publications were produced by the Society: the *Proceedings* and the *Transactions*. The early issues of the *Proceedings*, first published in 1879, contain articles on a wide variety of subjects, including falconry, Dilmun, chronology, geography, Old Testament articles, New Testament subjects, and Islam. Articles reflecting the philological orientation of the Society cover an amazing spread of languages: Etruscan, Coptic, the Cypriote syllabary, Akkadian, Egyptian, Altaic, Hittite, Aramaic, Carian, and, of course, Hebrew and Greek. The Society's membership included leading names of Near Eastern scholarship, such as

Rawlinson, Layard, Petrie, and the two explorers of the PEF, Warren and Wilson. The Society was international in its appeal, including in its membership list for 1893 many foreign scholars and institutions: Paul Haupt, the Johns Hopkins University Orientalist who would later make an immeasurable contribution to biblical archaeology by teaching William Foxwell Albright; D. C. Lyon of Harvard, later to head the work at Samaria; and George Barton of Bryn Mawr. The American names first appear in any number in the early 1880s, probably a result of the demise of the PES. Supporters of the Society included Prime Minister Gladstone.

The philological orientation of the Society eventually proved to be its undoing. When excavation began in Palestine in the 1890s the Society did not pay much attention. It was too oriented to literary study to properly appreciate the value of nonliterary remains. After the turn of the century, appeals for funding become more and more common in the *Proceedings*, as the interests of the Society failed to keep pace with the new discoveries. By World War I, the Society was in trouble. The last issue of the *Proceedings* came out in 1918. It was symptomatic of the dying Society; for example, there was no meeting in May because no lecturer was available.

Although ultimately a failure, the Society of Biblical Archaeology did recognize one very important principle: that research on the ancient Near East can be of great value for biblical studies. Often, professional biblical scholars, particularly on the Continent, did not recognize this.

Biblical Archaeology: A Change in Meaning

The orientation of the Society of Biblical Archaeology reflects the understanding of biblical archaeology that was current in its day. This understanding had undergone modification since the terminology had first been used. When Edward Robinson was conducting his geographical research in Palestine, biblical archaeology meant biblical antiquities. Johan Jahn (1839) followed this common interpretation in a study entitled *Biblical Archaeology*. Originally in Latin, this is a study of the ancient Near East in connection with the Bible. Archaeology is defined as the "knowledge of Antiquity reduced to a system" and biblical archaeology as "everything in the Bible worthy of notice and remembrance" (i.e., everything worthy of notice for the antiquarian; 1). In this view, the Bible is seen as a reliable source for information about ancient life, which Jahn divides into three areas: sacred, political, and domestic. Jahn went beyond the bounds of Scripture to illuminate ancient life. He used as many sources as he could gather, both written and nonwritten. For the written sources, he

lists the Bible, the Mishna and Talmud, Philo, Josephus, classical pagan authors, and Church Fathers. In addition, Jahn used coins, ancient monuments,
and travel literature. In a surprisingly modern note, the author warned scholars
to be careful when using travelers' accounts, "lest we assign to antiquity what
belongs to a more recent period" (4). Jahn recognized the potential value of
biblical archaeology for apologetical purposes, answering the objections of "op-
posers of Revelation" (2). The apologetical approach was an element of continuity in the understanding of biblical archaeology, even when the perspective
shifted.

The newly formed societies interested in the ancient Near East produced
a new approach to biblical archaeology. Rather than using the Bible as a source
for information about the ancient world, scholars hoped to use the wealth of
new knowledge available to put the Bible in perspective. The entire ancient
Near East was seen as prospective territory for biblical archaeology. The wide
geographical spread of the mandate of the Society of Biblical Archaeology illustrates this. The supporters of biblical archaeology saw the newly emerging
disciplines of Egyptology and Assyriology as part of their own field. Biblical
archaeology, as conceived by the society of that name, was a supradiscipline,
providing a rationale for research. That this research was predominantly linguistic in orientation is the result of the combination of the state of research
in the 1870s and the perceived nature of the Bible. Palestine, where the potential impact of nonliterary remains was the greatest, had been as yet untouched
by systematic excavation. Egypt and Mesopotamia had both yielded voluminous
texts, which could now be read, and the study of these texts overshadowed
other research. Because the Bible is a literary text, the newly gained linguistic
knowledge was a clear aid to its study. Linguistic investigation would remain
a primary focus of biblical archaeology well into the next century.

Biblical Higher Criticism and Archaeology

Archaeology was overshadowed in biblical scholarship in the nineteenth century by the revolution in approaches to the Bible that had been wrought in
Germany. The new orthodoxy was known as "higher criticism," or the study
and analysis of the formation of the text of the Bible. John Rogerson (1984)
has ably traced the development of higher criticism in nineteenth-century
Germany. This approach rejected the literal historicity of the Old Testament,
replacing it with a developmental model that owed much to Hegel. Conservative reaction was fierce, but by the 1870s the new views were dominant in
Germany.

The penultimate statement of higher criticism was the work of Julius Well-hausen. Wellhausen was born in Hameln, Westphalia in 1844. He studied at Gottingen and taught there for two years. In 1872 he went to Greifswald as a professor of the Old Testament, resigned after ten years, and became a professor of Oriental languages, eventually returning to Gottingen.

Wellhausen published a series of articles that culminated in the full treatment of his *Geschichte Israels I*. This book was reissued in a second edition as *Prolegomena zur Geschichte Israels* (1883, English 1885). Many of the elements of Wellhausen's scheme were already in place when he wrote his treatment (Rogerson 1984), but he gave these elements a coherent unity, simple and comprehensive, very much in keeping with the evolutionary element in nineteenth-century thought. In the popular mind, he personified the critical approach, and the system was called "Wellhausenism."

In the *Prolegomena*, Wellhausen gave classic expression to the "documentary hypothesis." The Pentateuch, the major focus of critical study, was regarded as a composite account in contrast to the biblical ascription of the books to Moses. Critical scholars before Wellhausen had isolated four major sources for the Pentateuch. Wellhausen took these sources and supplied them with what had been lacking: a coherent historical context for their development and final formation. He saw an evolutionary progression from animism and polydaenomism to monotheism. He rejected the historicity of the accounts of patriarchal religion, as well as the early dating of ritual and legal texts ascribed to Moses, and concluded that the development of monotheism was the work of the Prophets. The culmination of the editing process occurred in the post-exilic period, with the final form of the Pentateuch being the product of priestly hands.

Although higher criticism was dominant in Germany at the time of Wellhausen, it had a rougher road in Britain. The Victorian Church felt threatened by the many crossovers to Catholicism following the Oxford Movement (Chadwick 1970), which began as a conservative Anglican reaction to the growth of liberalism in the early nineteenth century. The scholars associated with the movement strongly opposed Wellhausen. A part of the movement led by J. H. Newman returned to orthodox Catholicism. Any yielding to liberalism on the part of the Anglican establishment was felt to be a further opening of the door that would unleash a flood of defectors (Rogerson 1984). Not until Samuel R. Driver, a Hebrew professor at Oxford, published his *Introduction to the Old Testament* (1891) was full-blown, higher critical study acceptable in English academic circles.

Archaeology as Response: A. H. Sayce

Archibald H. Sayce (1890, 1894, 1895, 1904), the president of the Society of Biblical Archaeology, wrote a series of responses to Wellhausen, both before and after Driver's publication. Sayce was an Assyriologist, and thought the results of recent research in Oriental archaeology were being ignored by the followers of Wellhausen. The studies undertaken by Sayce tested the main points of Wellhausen's thesis against the evidence of archaeology. The titles of Sayce's works are clear indications of his approach: *Fresh Light from the Ancient Monuments* (1890); *The "Higher Criticism" and the Verdict of the Monuments* (1894); and *Monument Facts and Higher Critical Fancies* (1904).

Despite his position in the Society of Biblical Archaeology, Sayce did not label himself a biblical archaeologist. He considered himself an archaeologist with no modifiers, and spoke only of "oriental archaeology" (1894: 1). He followed the principles laid out by the Society, seeking "to follow archaeology wherever it leads" (v). For Sayce, archaeology led him to test the results of Wellhausen.

Sayce (1894: 12–21) was encouraged in this approach by the success of Heinrich Schliemann at Troy. Before Schliemann, Homer's work was considered to have little if any historical basis. Homeric literary criticism had pioneered the techniques later used by biblical critics. Schliemann, a self-made millionaire, set out to prove that there was a firm historical basis to the stories and legends set down by Homer. He excavated Hissarlik, which he believed was ancient Troy, then Mycenae and Tiryns, both cities mentioned in the Homeric epics. Schliemann (1880) demonstrated that these were actual ancient cities, not figments of the poet's imagination. As Sayce makes clear, Schliemann's discoveries led not only to the beginning of the recovery of the Mycenaean civilization, but to a reevaluation of the historical worth of Homer: "It has similarly been reserved for the excavators and archaeologists of the last twenty years to restore the lost pages of the ancient history of civilisation, and to make it clear that the literary tradition, imperfect though it may have been, and erroneous in its details, was yet substantially correct" (18).

Sayce aided in spreading the results of Schliemann's work, writing the preface to the English edition of *Troja* (1884), the report on Schliemann's return work at Hissarlik in 1883. Sayce argued that "theories that were the product of the literary, and not of the scientific, imagination [are] houses of straw upon a foundation of sand" (xxx). He contended that as a result of Schliemann's work, literary critics must yield place to archaeologists, with dilettante antiquarianism no longer possible.

Sayce reasoned that if archaeology functioned as an independent test on the conclusions of Homeric criticism, then it could function in the same way in biblical criticism. Basic to his case is the necessity of placing an incident or personage from the Bible into its proper cultural setting:

> Old Testament history has been unfairly treated alike by friend and foe. They have both sought to defend a thesis instead of endeavoring to discover what it actually has to tell us . . . Commentators have been more anxious to discover their own ideas in them, than to discover what the statements contained in them really mean. It is indeed strange how seldom we think of even trying to understand what a passage of Scripture must have originally signified to the author and his readers, or to realize its precise meaning. (1894: 27)

The test of Oriental archaeology could cut both ways. Sayce did not reject critical results on a priori grounds: If the facts of archaeology supported critical claims, then he was willing to accept such claims:

> It must not be supposed that oriental archaeology and "higher criticism" are irreconcilable foes . . . The same evidence and the same arguments which have demonstrated that the skepticism of the higher criticism was hasty and unfounded in certain instances have equally demonstrated that it was well founded in others. We cannot accept the evidence in one case and refuse it in the other. If once we appeal to the judgment of oriental archaeology, we must abide by its verdict, whatever it may be. (27)

Although Sayce was an ordained clergyman, he carefully separated historical from theological questions. He envisioned a common approach shared by archaeology and higher critical studies: "Both alike are seeking for the truth, and this truth is historical and not theological. It is as historians and not theologians that we must investigate the records of the Old Testament" (1894: 25). In terms of archaeological research, he thought the Old Testament should be treated as any other fragment of ancient literature, subject to the same tests as any other historical text. Here he parted company with the "apologists," who, in his words, "had recourse to arguments which sinned against the first principles of common sense . . . arguments which would not have been admitted in the case of any other literature" (22). Sayce's study displeased his publishers, the Society for Promoting Christian Knowledge; in an introduction to his work, the Society cautioned that they did not endorse all of his views (1894: xiii).

Sayce (1894: 31–283) accepted one fundamental belief of biblical higher criticism: the composite nature of the Pentateuch. He found this idea to be in full agreement with the results of archaeology, pointing to the composite nature of both Egyptian and Mesopotamian religious documents. But Sayce broke sharply with Wellhausen on the dating of the various documents and their consequent historical worth. He argued from the abundant evidence of scribal schools and the widespread international use of Akkadian that the age of Moses was a literate age; therefore, a historian of that age could have had access to written documents of earlier periods. Sayce found support for this thesis in the newly discovered Amarna letters, an Egyptian royal archive of the fourteenth century B.C. dealing with Egyptian international relations, including the rulers of Palestine (54). He was willing to concede that the initial writing of the Pentateuch may not have occurred until the time of Samuel, but he believed the author(s) had access to written materials from which they framed the Patriarchal narratives. Sayce contended that evidence of early literary activity removed a major objection to the historicity of the accounts: "That primary assumption of the late use of writing for literary purposes in Palestine, which, consciously or unconsciously, has done so much to wreck the belief of the critic in the earlier narratives of the Bible, has been shown to be utterly false" (561).

Archaeology as true realia is the basis for Sayce's approach. He had a very sophisticated view of "facts." "We must not forget," he wrote, "that in a fact of history and archaeology is included its interpretation by the archaeologist and the historian. The conclusion he draws is, in short, part of the fact itself" (1894: 556). Sayce believed that the introduction of philosophy into the interpretation process of the "facts" led higher criticism astray: "Philosophy and archaeology or history are wholly separate things, and the attempts to introduce the terms and conceptions of philosophy into history have led only to bad philosophy and still worse history" (556). According to Sayce, the archaeologist, dealing only with realia, was not under the sway of philosophical or theological presuppositions. Hence, archaeologists can obtain "true" results that can act as a check on views distorted by a priori approaches. He recognized the inherent difficulties in approaching the Bible in such a dispassionate manner: "It is difficult to altogether escape from our surrounding, and to regard the sacred books of one's own faith with precisely the same equanimity as the sacred books of some other religion" (563). Despite seeing archaeology as realia, he recognized that archaeology often failed to provide "assured results." This was due to the fragmentary nature of the archaeological record, which produced "facts," not the character of the "facts" themselves. Neither apologists nor higher critics can take refuge in the fragmentary record produced by archaeology, for as Sayce cautions, "facts have a way of revenging themselves" (562).

Sayce's judgments in The "Higher Criticism" and the Verdict of the Monuments are even-handed. His study was an attempt to measure different views on the Bible by an unbiased yardstick. He considered both supporters and opponents of higher criticism to be blind to the facts of archaeology. Their interpretations were predetermined by their theological positions. "The facts of oriental archaeology," he wrote, "have nothing to do with theology. The archaeologist writes for the historian, not for the homilist or the defender of dogma" (1894: 562).

The facts of archaeology used by Sayce are nearly all derived from textual material, with the exception of the excavations at Tell el-Hesi undertaken since 1890 by the PEF, first under Flinders Petrie, then under F. J. Bliss. Field archaeology was in its infancy in 1894, and Sayce does not discuss possible problems with excavated evidence. There was no way he could have foreseen such problems; there was no experience to guide him. Sayce is somewhat cautious in dealing with his written sources, being aware of possible bias in the records, both biblical and nonbiblical (e.g., his discussion of the Assyrian attacks on Jerusalem in the eighth century B.C.; 1894: 389–456). He is not concerned with internal biblical problems, avoiding, for example, any discussion of Isaiah's unity or authorship. Only where external evidence speaks on such questions does he deal with them. Looking back on this work, Sayce wrote, "There I have written purely as an archaeologist, who belongs to no theological school" (1895: iv).

In a later study, *Patriarchal Palestine* (1895), Sayce revealed his theological concerns about critical claims:

> For those who "profess and call themselves Christians," however,
> there is another side to the question besides the archaeological. The
> modern "critical" views in regard to the Pentateuch are in violent
> contradiction to the teaching and belief of the Jewish Church in the
> time of our Lord, and this teaching and belief has been accepted by
> Christ and His Apostles, and inherited by the Christian Church . . .
> It is for the individual to harmonize his conclusions with the imme-
> morial teaching doctrine of the Church, not for the Church to recon-
> cile its teachings with the theory of the individual. (iv)

Although Sayce went on in this study to write of "the Palestine of the Patriar-chal Age, as it has been disclosed by archaeological research, not the Palestine in which the revelation of God's will to man was to be made" (16), his theo-logical position was becoming more dominant in his writings. However, he retained the view of archaeology as the final arbiter. For example, he rejected the use of "Philistine" in the book of Genesis because the historical records of Egypt were unanimous in rejecting the presence of the Philistines so early in Palestine (17). Sayce did write one unabashedly apologetical work, *Monument*

Facts and "Higher Critical" Fancies (1904), and an apologetical strain was present in much of his work, including articles on purely archaeological topics.

The hopes of the now defunct Palestine Exploration Society regarding the apologetical use of archaeology were sustained by the work of Sayce. He clearly demonstrated the possibilities in such usage. Many conservative scholars (e.g., Uruquart 1915) ignored Sayce's earlier approach and used archaeology as a weapon, not a neutral yardstick. The conservative understanding of Scripture became the yardstick, with only supportive archaeological data cited. Sayce's willingness to follow archaeology "wherever it leads" was overshadowed by the apologetical tone of his later works, although his view of archaeology as realia would resurface in the circles of biblical archaeology. An endeavor that can be labeled "apologetical archaeology" ultimately developed out of this approach.

Pioneers in the Field

The late nineteenth century saw the change from treasure hunting to true scientific inquiry in Palestinian archaeology. The excavation of Palestinian sites was part of the mandate of the Palestine Exploration Fund. The great survey undertaken by the Fund had located many potential sites for excavation, but work did not begin immediately due to the tight financial situation of the PEF (a result of the expenses incurred by the survey). The delay was beneficial for Palestinian archaeology, for when the first excavation began in 1890, it was led by an excavator who had gained experience during the previous decade in Egypt.

Egypt Produces a Genius: Petrie

The British challenged the French domination of research in Egypt by founding the Egypt Exploration Fund in 1883 (later renamed the Egypt Exploration Society). The organization of the new society was modeled on the PEF. The new society was international in its appeal, calling itself the Egypt Exploration Fund of England and America. Perhaps the demise of the American Palestine Exploration Society helped garner American support for the new group. American subscribers to the Egypt Exploration Fund eventually included President Theodore Roosevelt, who, in 1902, gave $25.00.

The Egypt Exploration Fund was clearly aware of the importance that research in Egypt could have for other branches of archaeology. The objective of the new society was "to organize excavations in Egypt with a view to the elucidation of the History and Arts of Ancient Egypt and the illustration of the Old Testament narrative, so far as it has to do with Egypt and the Egyptians; also to explore sites connected with Greek history or with the antiquities of the Coptic Church" (Egypt Exploration Fund 1883: 86).The reference to Old Testament illustration in the agenda demonstrates the power of biblical motivations in the research of the ancient Near East. In turn, the Egypt Exploration Fund would aid (albeit unwittingly) its sister society, the PEF, by providing employment for the first excavator of Palestine, William Matthew Flinders Petrie.

PETRIE IN EGYPT. Petrie caused a revolution in archaeological technique in the Near East (Albright 1942b; Callaway 1980; Fargo 1984; King 1983a). He was a self-trained surveyor who began his career with a study of Stonehenge. He was hired by the Egypt Exploration Fund as its first field director, starting with a survey of the Delta (Petrie 1932). The ransacking of antiquities that he encountered in Egypt appalled Petrie. He realized the tremendous loss of information that occurred when an object was torn from its context without proper recording. "Our museums are ghostly charnel-houses of murdered evidence," he wrote (1904: 48), and proceeded to challenge the prevailing museum mentality.

Petrie (1904) realized a basic characteristic of archaeology: It is destructive. Thus, the excavator has the duty to record what he excavates as faithfully as possible. The present has a responsibility both to the future and the past to preserve as much as possible. Either the excavator must make as faithful a record as possible, or he must leave it for the future.

Petrie's ethical attitude regarding recording had concrete results. In paying attention to material normally overlooked by excavators who were interested only in museum-quality antiquities, Petrie made a major advancement for archaeology: He discovered the value of ceramics for dating purposes. The excavation of a vast prehistoric cemetery at Diospolis Parva provided Petrie (1901) with the material that enabled him to illustrate the principles of sequence dating. He observed various changes in the pottery vessels that accompanied the burials in the cemetery and he grouped the pots into various "types" on morphological grounds, with subcategories within each type. He postulated that various minor changes within the types were indicators of chronological change. Petrie was guided in his view of sequence dating by his belief in eugenics (Silberman 1991). He saw a rise and decline for each pottery type, which he correlated with ethnic groups. The equation of ceramic types to specific ethnic types remains problematic in Syro-Palestinian archaeology today (Dever 1995b).

Petrie (1901: 4–12) organized a typological sequence for a specific style of jar handle called a "ledge handle," which best demonstrated his ideas. He could show in this sequence the development of the ledge handle and therefore could group the pots having ledge handles into a relative chronological sequence. The principle of sequence dating when combined with the stratigraphic context of a site should make any site datable, at least in general terms (1904: 127–30). This was the Petrie revolution.

PETRIE IN PALESTINE. In 1890 Petrie had a disagreement with the Egypt Exploration Fund, and he made himself available to the PEF for an excavation in Palestine. He was interested in testing ideas about Egyptian chronology and desired to excavate in the south of Palestine to check the date and extent of Egyptian influence there (Petrie 1891). The only pre-Roman site he could find was Tell el-Hesi (PEF/Petrie/13). The tell is cut by the Wadi Hesi, and in the cutting Petrie was able to discern the layering of the strata. He recognized typological change in the pottery of the exposed strata and realized the potential of the fortuitous wadi: "If I do nothing else, I shall at least have established a scale of pottery which will enable any future explorer to date all the tells and khirbets" (PEF/Petrie/13). In six short weeks, that is exactly what he did.

Petrie's espousal of complete recording was flatly contradicted by his field methodology. "Duplicate pottery is of no value to us for fresh information," he wrote in a letter to the PEF (PEF/Petrie/13). In consequence, he published only types in his various catalogues, not individual pieces (Petrie 1891, 1894, 1901, 1931–34). He defended his method in *Method and Aims in Archaeology* (1904). The massive amount of pottery produced by a tell excavation needed rapid recording; publishing a corpus of the pottery types from the site could do this: "Now the excavator merely needs to look over the corpus of plates and writes down on the plan of the tomb say, B 23, P 35b, C 15, F 72, thus the whole record is made, and not a single piece need be kept unless it is a good specimen" (125)! He paid his workers by the piece, rather than a daily wage, as this saved the trouble of constant supervision. Petrie believed the "bakhshish system" was the best way to protect the portable antiquities whose acquisition was one of the aims of excavation (1904: 33). To make sure that work continued on the site while he was away examining the finds, he devised many different stratagems, including oblique approaches and the use of a telescope! Some later authors (Fargo 1984: 221; King 1983a: 19) have overlooked this negligent field methodology because of a facile acceptance of Petrie's own statements that everything has a value and every artifact must be recorded.

Petrie revealed his surveyor's orientation by including the acquisition of top plans and topographical information among the goals of excavation. To achieve this aim, he advocated a method of wide exposure and the use of trenches to follow walls: "In the case of tracing a building, trenches cut along the lines of the walls are a good beginning; and then if more is wanted the plan is clear and the rooms can be emptied with foresight" (1904: 41). The entire site could be so excavated, chamber by chamber. Petrie was concerned with the preservation of the buildings once they had been uncovered. To protect them, and to facilitate the removal of the covering debris, he advocated a system he called "turning over" (43). When the excavator began a new section of the tell, he should backfill the previously dug section (once it had been fully planned) with the debris from the new digging. This would preserve the walls as well as unexcavated material in the rooms. To aid in the recording of the plans, Petrie made avid use of photography, a tool he felt was invaluable for the archaeologist. His emphasis on planning was in deliberate opposition to the sondage method: digging a long deep trench in the hope of finding something interesting. He believed the resulting deep cut in a tell prevented the archaeologist from accurately drawing a top plan of the various phases the trench cut through.

From Petrie's writings one can deduce his understanding of the nature of the tell as an architectural product, and his method was geared toward this. Trenching along walls removes the stratigraphic record of the various construction phases, but it is the quickest way to gain a total plan. Petrie envisioned a tell as a series of datable architectural phases, the product of a succession of destructions and reconstructions. Therefore, the various town plans were the most important information recoverable from a tell; pottery was treated only as a tool for dating the individual phases, or as objets d'art.

PETRIE'S LEGACY. After finishing his fieldwork, Petrie returned to London and prepared his results for publication. *Tell el Hesy* was published the following spring (1891), and this enviable record continued after every field season. Petrie was aware of the lack of in-depth understanding of the material in his books, which was a result of the speed of publication. However, he believed that publication was the best possible way of ensuring the preservation of knowledge (1904). Unfortunately for later scholars, his publications are very difficult to use. The publication of pottery by type rather than by individual piece makes the pottery plates in his volumes useless for anything other than general chronological questions. Nevertheless, despite their weaknesses, Petrie's publications were quite influential in spreading his breakthrough of sequence dating.

Petrie's demonstration of ceramic typology at Tell el-Hesi was the foundation of Palestinian archaeology. Later practitioners in the field acknowledged their debt to him. William Foxwell Albright (1942b) called him the "Nestor" of

Palestinian archaeology and labeled him a genius. In a memorial note, Nelson Glueck wrote, "All of us who are engaged in archaeological pursuits stand on the shoulders of men like him who pointed the way which we follow today" (1942: 6). In recognition of his valuable contributions to archaeology, Petrie received a knighthood.

Although his work was revolutionary in 1890, Petrie never advanced beyond it. When he returned to Palestine in the late 1920s, his methods had been surpassed. He never changed his style, as is clear from the Tell el-'Ajjul volumes (Petrie 1931–34). Sir Mortimer Wheeler (1954), while paying homage to the positive aspects of Petrie's career, roundly criticized his method. He rebuked Petrie for being outdated in the 1920s, and also contended that he was behind in the 1890s! Wheeler (25–28) correctly blamed Petrie for not keeping a full record of what was excavated, pointing out that in 1887, retired British general Pitt Rivers published an example of meticulous recording in archaeology. "It is abundantly apparent," wrote Wheeler, "that between the technical standards of Petrie and those of his older contemporary Pitt Rivers there yawned a gulf into which two generations of Near Eastern archaeologists have in fact plunged to destruction" (15). I think the success of Petrie's sequence dating obscured the disadvantages of his recording system. Petrie also greatly influenced the students who came under his spell. They would have been loath to break with his approach, as it appeared to be successful. "I left him for the last time," wrote Wheeler, "with a renewed sense of the devotion which he inspired in the hearts of his pupils and friends" (16). Wheeler felt "almost a sense of guilt" as he criticized Petrie's method (figure 1.4).

Bliss and Macalister

Petrie's methods were carried on in subsequent excavations sponsored by the PEF. Frederick J. Bliss (1894, 1907), an American, was the PEF's choice to continue work at Tell el-Hesi. Bliss was born in Lebanon, the son of Protestant missionaries. His father was the founder of what is now American University of Beirut. He was a graduate of Union Theological Seminary with no formal training in archaeology. He went to Egypt and worked with Petrie for a few months before starting work at Tell el-Hesi in 1891 (Blakely 1993).

Bliss made a great cut in the center of the mound and provided a stratigraphic framework for the ceramic sequence established by Petrie. He observed the superimposed layers, recognizing them as remnants of distinct occupations. He kept much better records than Petrie and took a personal interest in the excavation. His report was well received, but his insights into tell formation never bore fruit (Blakely 1993).

FIGURE 1.4 Tombstone of Petrie in Jerusalem. Photo by author

After becoming the archaeological director of the PEF, Bliss moved in 1894 to Jerusalem, where he teamed up with A. J. Dickie to continue the investigations begun thirty years before by the PEF. Bliss did not impress the American consul in Jerusalem, Selah Merrill. Merrill wrote a private note to George Armstrong, the secretary of the PEF, complaining that Bliss "is a mere infant in regard to all questions pertaining to the antiquities and topography of Jerusalem" (PEF/Schick 33/1–3). In 1898 Bliss teamed up with Robert Alexander Stewart Macalister, an Irishman who had his first archaeological training in England. They turned to the Shephelah region of Palestine, where they hoped to excavate the Philistine city of Gath (Bliss and Macalister 1902). Four sites were probed, but the PEF was unsatisfied, and Bliss was replaced by Macalister with a new goal: the excavation of biblical Gezer (Dever 1967, 1978; Dever, Lance, and Wright 1970; Macalister 1912; Thomas 1984). Bliss never returned to the field. Jeffrey Blakely (1993) notes that Albright was impressed with Bliss and called him the "Father of Palestinian Archaeology" in an *American Biography* article in 1958, although Albright never defined his reasons for that label.

MACALISTER AT GEZER. Following the training he received from Bliss, Macalister decided to follow the Petrie method at Gezer. Confronted by the large, 30-acre mound, Macalister believed that only the trench method would provide him with the ability to gain a large exposure in a reasonable amount of time. Beginning at the eastern end of the sizable tell, he dug down to bedrock in wide (40-feet) trenches. When one trench was being excavated, the backdirt would be thrown into the excavated trench to the east. Macalister excavated two-thirds of the tell in this way.

The Gezer excavations presented many new problems. Macalister had to contend with a great number of varying stratigraphic phases and he was unable to link up the strata in his different trenches in any coherent fashion. Although the field method used at Gezer was a vertical one, Macalister approached the tell as a horizontal question. He did not make use of the vertical exposure presented by the successive trenches, which would have duplicated the natural cut at Tell el-Hesi from which Petrie worked. Instead, he used the trenches at Gezer as a means of uncovering successive plans. The method did not match up to the goals of the dig, and Macalister was unable to overcome the problems this tension produced. When Gezer was reexcavated in the 1960s (Dever 1967), the new team was unable to make sense of the work done by Macalister, and much of his information is now seen as unusable.

An additional cause of problems in the fieldwork at Gezer was the huge scale of the work. The excavations were vast, employing up to two hundred workmen at one time. For most of the excavation, Macalister was the only archaeologist on site. This was far too large for one man to handle, and he lost control of the work in the field. The success of Petrie at Tell el-Hesi may have misled the PEF into thinking one man could successfully run a major excavation. After the Gezer excavations were completed, teamwork became the rule in Palestinian archaeology.

The final publications of the Gezer excavations reflect the failure of the field methodology employed by Macalister (1912). The finds are published by category, shorn of all contexts, a paper example of one of Petrie's "charnel-house[s] of murdered evidence." The architectural plans combine elements from several strata, the result of both Macalister's loss of control over the excavation and the trench method he chose to uncover the plans. In his defense, Macalister did make full use of Petrie's ceramic chronology, although his results often varied from the Tell el-Hesi sequence. Gezer was only partially occupied in the later Iron Age, and Macalister tried to bridge this unrecognized gap by pulling down the ceramic chronology. His resulting dates were often several hundred years off, but he did publish individual pieces, not just types, which permits partial reworking of his material (see Dever et al. 1970). Macalister believed the excavator of a site should not have a set program: "A true excavator will choose his site with but one intention—to find out what it contains" (1925: 32). Even when measured against the excavation's own aim— finding what is there—Gezer must be considered a failure of methods and execution.

GEZER AND THE BIBLE. The vastness of the Gezer excavations and the abundance of recovered finds aroused a great deal of interest. The excavation was highly praised, being "universally regarded as one of the best examples extant of how such work should be carried out" (Baikie 1923: 324). The discoveries at Gezer attracted the interest of biblical circles, which Macalister encouraged. The excavations became a stop for Sunday School tour groups; Macalister would escort them around the site and then ask for donations (PEF/Macalister/ 135). In 1907 the *Sunday School Times*, an American publication, asked Macalister to write two articles for their adult readers: "Were There Giants in Canaan?" and "On Cities Founded by Israelites" (PEF/Macalister/250). He gladly obliged.

To tap the biblical market for Gezer material, Macalister wrote a popular account of the work entitled *Bible Sidelights from the Mound of Gezer*: "[It is] impossible to assert definitely that any given scientific truth, stored up in the Quarterly Statement of the Society, will not prove of importance even to the non-scientific reader. But . . . the Society and its officers are by no means blind to the immediate claims of the Bible student" (1906: 2). Macalister satisfied these claims by presenting the Gezer material historically and using it to illustrate various biblical customs and events. Taking a central place in this presentation is the Gezer High Place (figure 1.5), which Macalister discusses in a chapter entitled "The Iniquity of the Amorite" (53–79). He defined a "High Place" as having (1) an altar, (2) standing stones and Asherah, (3) a laver, (4) a sacred cave, and (5) a depository for refuse. At Gezer, the suspected High Place consisted of a row of ten large upright stones with a laver. Macalister considered a nearby cave as the location for oracular utterances. Following a long series of surmises, he makes the following startling conclusion about one of the standing stones of the High Place: "It is quite admissible to believe that at the foot of this stone in its original position the author of Genesis located the attempted sacrifice of Isaac by Abraham" (62). Interspersed with the discussion of the Gezer material are numerous biblical quotations of judgment on Canaanite rites, echoed by Macalister in the moral tone of his analysis of the discoveries: "Outside the High Place other discoveries were made throwing a lurid light on the iniquity of the Amorite. One of these may be briefly alluded to here: a cistern at the bottom of which were fourteen skeletons, one of them that of a young girl who had evidently been sawn asunder . . . Evidently some savage tragedy here took place, though of its precise nature we are ignorant"

FIGURE 1.5 The Gezer "High Place" first uncovered by Macalister.
Photo by author

(75–76). The chapter closes with a quotation from a speech given at the annual meeting of the PEF by George Adam Smith, which contrasts the "high spirituality" of the religion of Israel to the cruelty of the Canaanite rites.

The emphasis on biblical illustration in this popular study, which led on occasion to dubious connections, such as the linking of the Gezer High Place stone to Abraham, was essentially mercenary: Macalister wanted money to be given to the PEF to enable excavation to continue. In the epilogue, he included a "teaser" to get more money from biblical society sources:

> In the very last week of the excavation when the permit was on the point of expiry, a few graves of a very remarkable cemetery were discovered. The stature of the bodies in the tombs was unusual for Palestine, where men of great height are exceptional . . . We seemed almost on the point of coming into contact with the Philistine giants whom David's men slew at Gezer. But the government permit ex-

pired, and we were regretfully compelled to leave this suggestive field of work unexamined. (197)

What lover of the Bible could resist an appeal to uncover cousins of Goliath?!

Macalister's shrewd fundraiser is the first study of biblical archaeology to depend on the results of fieldwork in Palestine. As befit the product of the field director of the PEF, this is a study that follows the mandate of the Fund to illustrate the Bible. Macalister is not in the business of apologetics and does not discuss it in *Bible Sidelights*. There the emphasis is on archaeology as the best source for illustrating biblical life, in contrast to the contemporary practice of reading current peasant life back into the Bible. He is aware of the distortion the reliance on archaeology may induce: "The picture will necessarily be incomplete; for it is impossible that any antiquities of perishable material could survive the damp earth and climate of Palestine" (99–100). Still, this is certainly better than earlier studies, which Macalister dismisses as "idealistic reconstructions . . . both profitless and misleading" (97).

German Excavations in Palestine

Following the visit of Kaiser Wilhelm to Jerusalem in 1898, the Germans became very active in Palestinian archaeology. They received official backing and were soon launched in the field. The German Oriental Society was founded the same year and began working at Baalbek in Lebanon. The Baalbek mission was a treasure hunt, with the Germans carting off carvings and mouldings by the boatload to Berlin (Silberman 1982). Another German society, the Deutscher Palastina Verein, had been in existence since 1877 but had not conducted any excavations. With the improved relations between Berlin and the Ottoman government, a firman was obtained for survey work, which was conducted east of the Jordan under the direction of Gottlieb Schumacher, a trained architect who lived in Haifa. After the survey, Schumacher was invited to join the work of the University of Vienna, which was planning to excavate Tell Ta'annak, a site the excavators believed to be the biblical Ta'annak (Sellin 1904). The excavations were under the direction of Austrian theologian Ernest Sellin, who had been trained at the classical excavations on the island of Samothrace begun by the Austrians in the 1870s. He brought with him an epigrapher, a surveyor, and a new methodology, a methodology pioneered in the burgeoning excavations of classical archaeology. Ta'annak was its first test in Palestine.

THE CLASSICAL CONNECTION. German excavators, inspired by the success of Schliemann, were leaders in the new excavations in Greece during the late nineteenth century. Their showcase was Olympia, the major testing ground for government-sponsored excavation. The expedition to Olympia mounted five campaigns in the first series (Curtius and Adler 1897; Gardiner 1925). The agreement to excavate the site, the Olympia Convention, was a government-to-government contract designed to protect the antiquities of the site. The convention marks the beginning of the end for museum treasure hunting in Greece, designating that all of the finds from the excavations were to remain in Greece. This was in reaction to Schliemann, who had spirited away the "Treasure of Priam" from Hissarlik. Olympia was to be a scientific excavation with the only reward for Germany being scientific knowledge and prestige.

The excavators came to Olympia with the intention of uncovering the remains of the Temple of Zeus described by Pausanius. Trenches were used to uncover the temple, which lay beneath sixteen feet of debris. Along with the recovery of the temple plan, the excavators hoped to recover the sculpture associated with the temple. The findspots of architectural elements and sculptural fragments were meticulously planned, enabling reconstruction to be undertaken. The excavators had chosen Olympia because of its cultic significance and the previous recovery of metopes from the suspected temple. Because it was a cult site, domestic life was not as visible at Olympia and was essentially ignored by the excavators.

The questions asked by all of the excavators working at Olympia were art historical and literary, and this was the pattern at other classical sites. Stephen Dyson (1981), a classical archaeologist who has broken with this old approach, has aptly described the traditional role of classical archaeology in this way: Its "basic job is to provide an illustrated Herodotus, Thucydides, or Pausanius for a classical world that is already well known from the literary text and to add to the repertoire of beautiful objects in museums" (8). The name of Homer should be added to Dyson's list, as it was the challenge of "proving" Homer that led Schliemann to Troy.

The choice of sites for initial excavation reflects the literary/artistic bias. They include known cult sites such as Delos, Delphi, and Olympia, and sites of previous artistic finds such as Samothrace. The excavators—Hirshfeld, Botticher, and Dorpfeld—were trained architects, products of a classical education. Although some of these pioneers changed in the field (Dorpfeld recognized the value of pottery while working with Schliemann at Troy), the majority remained classicists first and archaeologists second. They were at home with the elements of architecture and knew their Pausanius, but they were woefully ignorant of pottery and stratigraphy.

The trench method fulfilled its function of discovering and laying bare architectural plans. It enabled the excavator to make the best use of the available resources. The trench told the excavator where the most fruitful areas for clear-ance excavation lay. If the area trenched yielded only fragments of walls and pottery, the area would not be uncovered. However, if a major wall or building was touched, the walls would be cleared on that level. Once the plan of a monumental structure was clear, the probable locations of the architectural elements could be predicted and the area probed for them. Thus, energy would not be wasted on material ungermane to the excavation.

TA'ANNAK. Sellin did not consider the accurate recovery of pottery a high pri-ority and instead focused on the recovery of architecture and the defense sys-tem. To achieve this goal, he decided to use a series of trenches as had been done on Samothrace. When a building was located, the trench would be ex-panded to allow the full clearance of the structure. At Ta'annak, Sellin found no fortification walls and no major buildings, so from the architectural stand-point the dig was not a success. (He did find twelve tablets in Akkadian, which aroused a great deal of interest.) The excavators separated the stratigraphy into four main phases. Pottery was published, but it was secondary to the plans. Even these were sparse, because Sellin (1904) presented plans only for five small structures, which he considered "fortresses," as there were no circuit walls. No clearly domestic architecture was portrayed, betraying Sellin's mon-umental orientation.

MEGIDDO. After the first season at Ta'annak, Schumacher left to direct a series of excavations at Tell el-Mutesillim, biblical Megiddo. From 1903 to 1905 Schu-macher (1908) worked on the massive 15-acre tell. The focus was on the re-covery of a series of architectural plans. The major excavation was a 20- to 25-meter-wide trench running across the mound in a north-south direction. Schumacher separated the architectural remains into six phases, accompanied by a wealth of small finds (Watzinger 1929). The small finds were for the most part accurately located on the plans, but the plans often did not reflect the reality of the excavation (Albright 1949). Schumacher, like Macalister at Gezer, was a "lone wolf," and the excavation had the same problems of supervision that Gezer did. The stratigraphic recording was minimal, and the later reex-cavators of Megiddo, the University of Chicago team, were unable to correlate their levels with the phases of the German excavation (Lamon and Shipton 1939; Yadin 1977).

JERICHO. Following the excavations at Tell Ta'annak, Sellin teamed up with an Olympia-trained archaeologist, Carl Watzinger, to excavate the suspected site of Jericho, Tell es-Sultan (Sellin and Watzinger 1913; figure 1.6). Sellin had

FIGURE 1.6 The Neolithic Tower at Jericho (Tell es-Sultan). Photo by author

no worries about financing the dig, as he was ably supported by the Vienna
Academy of Sciences (Ruby 1993). Watzinger brought a trained staff of architects with him, providing enough personnel for adequate supervision. The
recording of the Jericho excavation was of a much higher standard than that
of Megiddo or Ta'annak. The trench system was used, exposing the fortification
system and some of the architectural phasing. However, the dating of the material presented many problems. Despite this, W. F. Albright, the great figure
of the next generation in Palestine, considered the dig to be of great value due
to the quality of the publication: "The German excavators surpassed all their
predecessors in the precision and completeness of their engineering treatment,
and the published account of the successive fortifications of the town is a model
of scientific method" (1932a :31).

CONCLUSION. The German trench system fit a specific view of the nature of
a tell. This system was designed to reveal monumental buildings and defense
systems and to recover architectural fragments and objets d'art. In such an

approach, a tell is understood as the product of activity and action of an elite class. Pottery, for the most part the utilitarian product of the commoner, held little importance in this schema (unless it was an art object in its own right). A tell site, the place most likely to reveal the remains of elite activity, is the place of choice for excavation. It is archaeology of the elite.

The Ecole Biblique

The first scientific institute to open its doors in Palestine was the Ecole Pratique d'Etudes Bibliques, under the guidance of the Dominicans. The Ecole opened in 1890 under the direction of Father Marie-Joseph Lagrange (Viviano 1991). Lagrange was an Orientalist and established a record of linguistic scholarship that remains a hallmark of the Ecole. Edouard Paul Dhorme, a later director, was on one of the original Ugaritic translation teams. The Ecole gathered numerous ancient inscriptions, making squeezes and conducting critical research. The linguistic approach at the Ecole culminated in the publication of the Jerusalem Bible in 1956.

Fortunately for Palestinian archaeology, Père Louis-Hugues Vincent became one of the first staff members. Vincent visited all of the active excavations and assiduously collected sherds. He became the first true master of Palestinian pottery, and Albright (1932b: xiv) feely acknowledged his great debt to Père Vincent.

The American School

The new century saw a new society dedicated to Palestinian archaeology: the American Schools of Oriental Research. Despite the demise of the Palestine Exploration Society in the mid-1880s, U.S. interest in Palestinian research remained strong. U.S. scholars and institutions were members of both the Society of Biblical Archaeology and the Palestine Exploration Fund. In 1895, practical steps were undertaken to reestablish an official U.S. presence in Palestinian archaeology. The president of the Society of Biblical Literature (SBL, founded in 1880), J. Henry Thayer of Harvard University, pushed for the establishment of a school in Jerusalem, similar to the American School of Classical Studies in Athens. The Athens school had been founded by the Archaeological Institute of America (AIA), whose members were primarily interested in the classical world. Together with the American Oriental Society (AOS), the SBL and the AIA became the parent organizations of the new American School of Oriental Study and Research (or the American Schools of Oriental Research,

ASOR). By the end of 1900, ASOR's first overseas director was in residence in Jerusalem.

In his institutional history of ASOR, Philip King (1983a), a past president of the Society, highlights its strong initial biblical interest. The SBL provided many of the early officers of ASOR, including Charles C. Torrey, the first director in Jerusalem, and J. Henry Thayer, who became the first chairman of ASOR's managing committee. The SBL championed higher critical study in the United States, and its academic approach to biblical studies is reflected in ASOR's nonapologetical approach to archaeology. The following resolutions became the basis for ASOR's work in Palestine:

1. The main object of said School shall be to enable properly qualified persons to prosecute Biblical, linguistic, archaeological, historical, and other kindred studies and researches under more favorable conditions than can be secured at a distance from the Holy Land.
2. The School shall be open to duly qualified applicants of all races and both sexes, and shall be kept wholly free from obligations or preferences as respects any religious denomination or literary institution. (King 1983a: 27)

The resolutions clearly show that although a biblical orientation existed, it was not a religious orientation. No theological burdens were placed on ASOR. The new society was not in the business of apologetics, unlike its predecessor, the Palestine Exploration Society. ASOR's philosophy was more in keeping with the Palestine Exploration Fund, which put the focus on Palestine, not the Bible.

The secular nature of ASOR was a vital element in its success. ASOR's stance encouraged the support of a wide variety of institutions, ranging from major universities such as Pennsylvania and Yale to small theological schools such as the Episcopal Divinity School in Philadelphia. The joint sponsorship of the AOS, AIA, and SBL ensured the continuation of this orientation. When ASOR entered the field, secular archaeologists who might have rejected an overtly biblical society made themselves available for ASOR-sponsored excavations. By rejecting the defense of the Bible as a goal (contra the PES), ASOR could only gain from excavation. Even if excavation results challenged the historicity of the biblical accounts, the purpose of ASOR would not be undercut. Therefore, archaeology in Palestine did not need a biblical justification. This mandate gave ASOR a great deal of flexibility, which enabled it to weather the theological storms of the 1920s and the increasing secularization of archaeology in the 1970s.

Samaria and the Reisner Method

The first fully American excavation in Palestine was at Sebastia, biblical Samaria (Reisner, Fisher, and Lyon 1924). Harvard University sponsored the excavation, having obtained the assistance of David Lyon, the director of the American School in Jerusalem (King 1983a: 39). The dig was first proposed in 1905 when Jacob Henry Schiff offered $50,000 for excavation work in Palestine. This was an astronomical amount for the day, and the plans for Samaria were ambitious. The aim of the work was to "recover every particle of historical evidence" from the site. "It has long been recognized," wrote Reisner, the major excavator, "that a site should be excavated as a whole" (Reisner et al. 1924: 34). This boundless confidence and optimism characterized the spirit of this first American dig in Palestine. It is reminiscent of the first expedition mounted by the PEF, which had as its mandate the solving of all the problems of Palestinian archaeology!

A long series of negotiations ensued between the hopeful Americans and Turkish officials in Istanbul. After numerous delays and setbacks, work was scheduled to begin in 1908. The original investigator was to have been George A. Reisner, a professor at Harvard who gained his archaeological training in Egypt. But due to the long delays in gaining a firman for the excavation, Reisner had committed himself to a season of fieldwork in Egypt, so he was not able to exert full control until 1909. The organizers turned to David Lyon in Jerusalem and obtained the aid (for a short period) of Gottlieb Schumacher. Macalister, still involved at Gezer, had the opportunity to visit Samaria during the first season of excavation; he was unimpressed with what he found. In a postscript to a letter to the secretary of the PEF, Macalister wrote, "Entre nous, I fear they [Lyon's team] are making a mess of things: they have worked barely 3 months, so far as I can make out, and have spent 50,000!!!" (PEF/Macalister/282). He later wrote (PEF/Macalister/299) that he found an article by Lyon unintelligible, and that Père Vincent, the French archaeologist, shared that view. Macalister reports that Père Vincent found the U.S. team "obsessed with finding something sensational—either a big epigraphic monument, or a portrait bust of Jezebel or a full sized golden calf—and did not appreciate the importance of the things they did find, nor take the trouble to examine them properly." Lyon did a very poor job of controlling the excavation. He was a substitute for Reisner and should not have started the excavation without him. Even Macalister had high hopes for Reisner: "I understand Reisner is to be in charge this year [1909], so we may hope for something better" (PEF/Macalister/299).

Reisner was finally free to direct the second season at Samaria. He brought trained Egyptian workmen with him to help control the large workforce. Samaria was to be a showcase excavation, and the workforce was huge, averaging over 200 men at a single time, on one memorable occasion numbering 450 (Reisner et al. 1924: 6). The professional staff also included experienced personnel, such as Clarence Stanley Fisher, an architect, who had worked with the University of Pennsylvania's pioneering excavations at Nippur. Thanks to the increased number of supervisory personnel, Reisner was able to exert much better control over the site than Lyon had been able to do. As a result of his trained staff, Reisner was able to achieve a great deal in the two years he excavated at Samaria.

In keeping with the original aim of excavating the entire mound, the trench method of "backfilling as you go" was the intended technique. Fortunately, as it would turn out, the rather wasteful season under Lyon had used up a large portion of the finances of the excavation, and Reisner had to narrow his sights and use the method of expanding probes. He first dropped a trench to bedrock "in order to discover the nature of successive strata" (Reisner et al. 1924: 5). He tried to trace the natural floor levels in the strata he encountered in the various probes. While attempting to follow the varied surfaces his workmen found, Reisner became aware of the problems that intrusive material brings for the archaeologist.

As a result of the mixture of material present on a tell, Reisner developed a revolutionary concept: The key to understanding a tell lies in the thorough analysis of nonarchitectural debris—the material that makes up over 90 percent of a tell. "The attention given to the study of debris is one of the most important features in our method of work" (Reisner et al. 1924: 36). He isolated five varieties of debris: geological (that not deposited by human activity, such as eolian sands); mason's debris (i.e., stone chips, in which Reisner recognized on-site activity); decay debris; silt; and dump debris (i.e., refuse materials such as food remains and dead animals). This material was often intrusive into earlier or later strata, and as a result the excavator of tell debris must pay particular attention to the stratigraphy. Only with a clear understanding of debris formation can intrusive material be separated out.

Reisner foreshadowed the contemporary focus on formation processes (see Schiffer 1983). He did not use the terminology of formation processes, but he was astonishingly prescient in being aware of their importance. He noticed the effects of postdepositional activity on the material of a tell, and he noted the unnatural smoothness of a surface, which he suspected was the result of trampling; therefore, the surface was a pathway, a conclusion worthy

of modern anthropological archaeology (Reisner et al. 1924: 35). He wrote of
the importance of recognizing "sweepings in the corners" of rooms and included a long discussion of "dump formation" (38–39). He was aware of the
possibility of postdepositional disturbances, which can occur in the course of
later "building operations, plundering and agriculture" (40). All of these various activities come together to produce the landmark of Palestine, the tell.

The truly revolutionary aspect of Reisner's archaeology was his belief that
a tell is the product of human activity and that the archaeologist's role is the
analysis of this activity. He believed that the destruction archaeology unavoid-
ably produces has as its goal "to untangle the series of human actions which
have left their mark on the place" (Reisner et al. 1924: 34). This was a radical
change from previous approaches, which saw a tell as a series of artifacts, or
architectural phases. With this theoretical understanding, Reisner was way
ahead of his time. Only in the 1970s would Palestinian archaeology rediscover
this.

Reisner made a classic statement regarding archaeological ethics: "No
pains in recording work are excessive . . . the deposits are gone forever. The
only justification that a man can offer for this destruction is a record as un-
prejudiced and mechanical as the technical means of his day permit" (Reisner
et al. 1924: 43). In keeping with this Calvinist approach to recording, the publication in 1924 of the results of the excavation was all it should have been.
There are section drawings showing wall interrelationships and, in a few cases,
stratigraphy of nonwall areas such as dumps. The plates are beautifully colored,
and the building plans can be followed. Unlike Macalister at Gezer or Schumacher at Megiddo, Reisner was able to partially connect the strata revealed
in the various probes. His major problem was the heavy construction undertaken by the Romans, which seriously disturbed the underlying strata. (The
second expedition to Samaria in the 1930s had the same problems.) The second
section of Reisner's final report, entitled "Principles, Methods, and General
Results," presented the methodology of the excavation.

Amazingly, Reisner's work was almost forgotten. His emphasis on stratigraphic digging was followed, but only as a "bag of tricks," not as an element
of a complete method and theory package. The questions he asked about human activity and tell formation were not restated in Palestinian archaeology
until the current generation. Mortimer Wheeler (1954) acidly attacked Palestinian archaeology for its poor methodology, and correctly so, but his treatment
would have been more accurate and balanced had he included a treatment of
Reisner at Samaria. Reisner's career was one of the great "if onlys" of Palestinian archaeology, because he never dug again in Palestine.

Summary

World War I brought a halt to active fieldwork throughout the Near East. Although the lost time was keenly felt, the enforced hiatus permitted needed assessment and analysis. Unfortunately, the war also interrupted some publications that were under way, such as the Samaria volumes, which were delayed until 1924. Understandably, contacts between German scholars and the English and French were cut off for the duration of the hostilities. The inability of the various scholars to compare their results either in print or in person prevented attempts to unite the first thirty years of excavation into a coherent whole.

In this early period, the societies that sponsored field excavation in Palestine—the PEF, ASOR, the Deutscher Palastina Verein—set their research parameters geographically, not biblically. Biblical interest remained a strong motivation in these groups, but it was in all cases subsidiary. With such an approach, the field archaeologists of Palestine avoided becoming subsumed under biblical studies. The majority of early field pioneers came to Palestine already experienced in archaeology. Their methodologies were borrowed from Egypt and the classical world. When the war began, Palestine was in the forefront of archaeology, having benefited from its supraregional connections. The biblical connection encouraged public support and interest, but it did not dominate the research interests of the societies or the field archaeologists. (The only society that tied itself to a particular theological approach, the PES, had long since disbanded.) Biblical information did have a strong influence on the choice of locales for excavation; Jericho, for example, was chosen because of the famous biblical account of its capture. The Society of Biblical Archaeology remained aloof from fieldwork, content to assimilate the information gathered by fieldworkers. Therefore, despite a generation of excavation in Palestine, biblical archaeology remained an armchair endeavor, a subdiscipline of biblical studies.

Encouraged by the success of Schliemann in rehabilitating Homer, conservative biblical scholars eagerly embraced the discoveries of archaeology. The umbrella of biblical archaeology covered Egyptology, Assyriology, Palestinian archaeology, and elements of Classical archaeology. Biblical archaeology remained a part of the biblical, rather than the archaeological, world. The illumination of the Bible provided a rationale, a framework, and an interpretive key for archaeological research. The conservatives used the results of archaeology in an attempt to demonstrate the historical accuracy of the Bible, to support their theological positions. The writings of A. H. Sayce are a good example. Like his fellow conservatives, Sayce sought realia in archaeology. This approach was strengthened by the positive results (in conservative terms) so far produced by archaeology. By 1914, the general outline of biblical history appeared to be historically accurate. Archaeology was well on the way to becoming a potent weapon in the battle against higher criticism.

Mainstream biblical scholars tended to ignore the results of archaeology. W. F. Albright wrote of the adverse effects the confused state of Palestinian archaeology had in biblical circles: "Small wonder that historians and Biblical scholars turned away from this chaos of conflicting views in despair, convinced that the main purpose of archaeology was to unearth inscriptions and occasionally to elucidate the arts and the crafts of the ancient inhabitants" (1932a: 36). Albright does not give the full picture. The close embrace of archaeology by their opponents discouraged higher critical scholars from seeking their own answers from the data of archaeology. A new critical approach, form criticism, sharpened the focus of biblical scholars on internal biblical issues that drew attention away from possible uses of archaeology. The result of these various influences was to devalue the importance of archaeology for biblical studies and the yielding of the field to the conservatives.

World War I delayed the first trip of a young Oriental studies scholar to Palestine. That unfortunate young man was William Foxwell Albright. His impact on biblical archaeology and Palestinian archaeology would be of such magnitude that all previous research in Palestine might be properly termed the praeperatio Albrightiae.

2

The Albright Watershed

Seen through the eyes of archaeologists, Palestine changed radically
following the defeat and collapse of the Ottoman Empire in World
War I. The country had been an active theater of war, conquered by
the British under General (later Field Marshall) Allenby. The British
army controlled the new administrative apparatus, which functioned
in a bureaucratic vacuum until Palestine gained official status as a
Mandate, a territory being prepared for self-rule. The divided tree of
the mandate would soon bear bitter fruit, but for archaeology, British rule ushered in a golden age (so christened by a later archaeologist, G. Ernest Wright, 1970).

William Foxwell Albright profoundly changed the nature of biblical archaeology (figure 2.1). When he first arrived in Palestine, it
was a nebulous supradiscipline more interested in Assyrian texts
than Palestinian pots. Yet, when Jewish-Arab tensions exploded in
violence during the late 1930s, effectively ending excavation in Palestine, biblical archaeology was intimately linked with Palestinian
excavation and his name, and was in a position to become the most
viable model in Palestinian archaeology. The new biblical archaeology that would emerge from the golden age was a field-oriented
endeavor that subsumed the old name of biblical archaeology. The
prototype was Albright's, and the depths of his scholarship and
achievements ensured that no longer would a biblical archaeologist
reside only in an armchair.

Albright grew up in Chile, the son of Methodist missionaries.

FIGURE 2.1 W. F. Albright (center) visiting Gezer with William Dever (pointing at left) and Joe Seger (right). Courtesy of William G. Dever

In an autobiographical article, he noted the similarities between the Chile of his boyhood and the Palestine of his scholarly life (Albright 1964a). After his family returned to the United States, Albright went to Upper Iowa University, a small Midwestern Methodist college, where he obtained what he called "a good education in Latin, Greek, and mathematics" (306). He taught himself Hebrew and "Assyrian," and after a year as principal of a German-language school, he was accepted into Johns Hopkins University for a Ph.D. in Oriental studies.

At Johns Hopkins, Albright studied under Paul Haupt, a brilliant Semitic linguist. Haupt espoused a view known as pan-Babylonianism. This school of thought emphasized the importance of Babylonian thought on the Old Testament, and his emphasis on the cultural continuum of the ancient Near East led to a dismissal of Hebrew thought as derivative (Sasson 1993). Although opposed to the Wellhausen reconstruction of Israel's development, Haupt was a supporter of source-critical studies of the Bible, publishing a polychrome Bible that had all of the different critical sources (such as J, E, D, P, etc.) color-coded.

The program of study Albright followed was entirely linguistic in orientation, and linguistics was Albright's strength. He was a highly successful student and, with Haupt's backing, won ASOR's annual Thayer Fellowship in

Jerusalem. Originally intending to stay just one year, he became the director of the American School, remaining there until 1929 (Running and Freedman 1975).

Albright came to Palestine with no firsthand knowledge of archaeology and no set methodology: He was free to plunge into the pool of varied archaeological approaches that characterized the 1920s. However, in spite of the successes of biblical archaeology under Albright (and, as we shall see, they were many), the model was fatally flawed: It lacked a solid theoretical base; its research agenda was too narrow; and, most important, biblical archaeology was the mirror of the man. Only Albright could meet the standards he set; lesser mortals would be unable to do so and would require a different paradigm with which to approach the data. However, none of these flaws was apparent in the golden age of the 1920s and 1930s, when there were giants in the land.

Archaeology in the 1920s: The Options for Albright

Palestinian archaeology was in a ferment of excavation and experimentation under the British Mandate. The close nature of the community of archaeologists centered in Jerusalem and the geographical proximity of the various excavations ensured that new methods and interpretations were widely shared. Also, the small pool of archaeologists passed from dig to dig (e.g., Clarence Stanley Fisher, who directed excavations in Syria/Palestine for five different institutions), providing a broad range of field experiences for the various excavations to draw on. From the competing field methodologies being explored in Palestine, Albright fashioned the methodology of biblical archaeology.

The Department of Antiquities

The British Mandatory government introduced a new set of antiquities laws in October 1920 (*Official Gazette of the Government of Palestine*, no. 29). They provided for much easier access to potential sites for excavation than had been permitted under the old Turkish firman system. The newly formed Department of Antiquities was given the power of expropriation of property as a last resort when dealing with recalcitrant landlords or village associations. The new law defined an antiquity as "any object or construction made by human agency earlier than 1700 A.D." However, the British authorities were well aware of the dangers of tampering with the delicate balance of the various ecclesiastical parties in Palestine. Article 8 of the new act specifically excluded religious or ecclesiastical movable material from the protection (and limitations) of the act, and Article 23 permitted changes to religious buildings on approval by the Department. The Antiquities Ordinance set up an advisory committee consisting of the three annual directors of the British, American, and French Schools in Jerusalem, with a representative from the hoped-for Italian School to join later (until that point, the Italian interests would be represented by the high commissioner or his deputy). The defeated Germans were allowed no voice in archaeological affairs. Four members of the local communities (two Jews and two Arabs) rounded out the committee, along with the director of the Department of Antiquities, who was an ex-officio member. This committee was to protect the interests of the various national schools, act as a clearing house for information on policy changes, and facilitate excavation by encouraging the pooling of resources and preventing duplication of effort.

The Palestine authorities permitted museums that had sponsored excavations to gain title to a greater share of the antiquities discovered in the course of the sponsored excavations than the French authorities did in Syria. This was a result of the wide, multinational interest in Palestine that had been clearly demonstrated in the Turkish period, and the British believed that international access to the archaeological heritage of Palestine was in keeping with their mandatory responsibilities. The Antiquities Ordinance made provision for this by including guidelines for the division of material between the sponsoring institution and the Department of Antiquities. The Museum of the University of Pennsylvania quickly took advantage of this liberal attitude and was the first U.S. institution to approach the new department for a permit to excavate.

The Department of Antiquities needed an individual with both archaeological and administrative abilities. At this crucial time, this need was met by the appointment of John Garstang of the University of Liverpool to the post of director. Garstang encouraged field archaeology with enthusiasm and dedication (Albright 1932a: 15). He actively supported non-British excavations, continuing Palestine's record of multinational archaeology. As a result of this open bureaucratic attitude, Palestine was a popular place to dig in the 1920s.

British control over Palestine ensured an active British effort in archaeology. The Department of Antiquities directed many soundings and small-scale salvage work throughout the country. They also sponsored larger projects in conjunction with the British School in Jerusalem and the Palestine Exploration Fund. These larger projects were directed by both young archaeologists trained in the new department and by older, established prewar excavators, who employed a wide variety of methodological approaches on the major projects. Unfortunately, the usefulness of the results, a product of the diverse methodologies employed by the different excavators, was similarly variant.

The British Mandate caused a major change in the activity of the PEF. While maintaining a working relationship with the Fund, the Department of Antiquities quickly moved to the forefront of the British archaeological effort in Palestine. The PEF could not rival the financial and technical resources of the Department, nor did they wish to. They were content to support work of the Department and function primarily as a channel to disseminate information to the British public. In his capacity as director, Garstang gathered together a remarkable number of archaeologists who would make their mark in many different branches of archaeology. Ernest Mackay would receive a great deal of field experience in Palestine before going on to work in Mesopotamia (Kish) and mainly in India. One of the great names in archaeology in the 1920s, C. L. Woolley, was a staff member with Garstang. On occasion, archaeologists trained in the Department remained in Palestine, working for non-British excavations; for example, P.L.O. Guy left the Department to dig with the University of Chicago team at Megiddo. This cross-fertilization helped at least some of the British stay abreast of archaeological developments in other areas.

Albright observed the Department-sponsored excavations firsthand and commented on them in the *Bulletin of the American Schools of Oriental Research* (*BASOR*), the new journal that he edited. Phillip King (1983a: 57) relates that Albright considered Garstang and W. J. Phythian-Adams his first teachers in method. The excavations at Ashkelon (Garstang and Phythian-Adams) and Jerusalem (Macalister) and the work of Petrie in the south provided Albright with a cross-section of British methodological approaches. He observed the trials and triumphs of the experienced excavators working with the Antiquities Department and established a cordial relationship with the Department that proved beneficial in his own excavations.

The archaeological professionalism of the Department of Antiquities continued the tradition of the PEF, which in its prewar years had hired professionals, such as Petrie and Macalister. Under the British system, nonprofessionals could influence Palestinian archaeology but only on the interpretative level. However, if a biblical scholar was also a trained archaeologist, then there was no barrier to working in Palestine.

ASHKELON. Appropriately, the British directed the first excavation to take place in the new Mandate. As soon as the Versailles Treaty was signed, the PEF and the Department of Antiquities mounted a small-scale dig at Ashkelon directed by Garstang (1920–21) and W. J. Phythian-Adams (1923). A classically trained archaeologist, Phythian-Adams was also on the staff of the Department of Antiquities. The Bouleuterion of the classical city was cleared, but most important, a graded section was cut along the beach. The sections were drawn and published. They are rough and unsophisticated, yet the evidence can be examined and the conclusions of the excavators evaluated (Phythian-Adams 1923).

The original excavators of Ashkelon are to be commended for digging within their means. Their intention was to get a wide exposure of the Philistine occupation phases. According to the Bible, Ashkelon was a member of the Philistine pentapolis at the beginning of the Iron Age. Shrewdly, the PEF desired their first postwar work to be at a clearly biblical site, yet one that would answer an archaeological question: What are the material characteristics of the Philistines in Palestine? Unfortunately, the amount of material remaining from the later Roman and Byzantine city prevented Garstang and Phythian-Adams from gaining this exposure. However, due to the beach erosion along the west side of the site, the excavators were able to get a sense of the cultural sequence of the site without a great deal of expense. Like Petrie at Tell el-Hesi, the British excavation team took advantage of a natural cut to expose the stratigraphy of Ashkelon.

Ashkelon introduced section drawing to postwar Palestine. However, the potential of this technique remained unfulfilled, partly because of the publication record of the dig. No final report ever appeared, so the impact of the dig on scholars who were not on the ground in Palestine was minimal. Although Phythian-Adams and Garstang are to be commended for recognizing the potential of the beach erosion, the stratigraphic section that resulted was not part of the methodological package of the original plan. A vast amount of Roman/ Byzantine material overlay the Philistine layers, which were the original target of the excavation. The use of the beach cut was the only economical way that the Philistine material could be sampled by the expedition. The vertical exposure provided by a section was of little value to archaeologists who approached a tell as a horizontal construction. It is no surprise that the British excavations at Ashkelon stopped in 1921, as the horizontal exposure of Philistine material was impossible without massive amounts of money and effort. The excavation had not met its goals, and in the general disappointment the potentially revolutionary section drawings were ignored.

Ashkelon was the first dig that Albright (1921a, 1922c) observed at close hand. Although he examined the section with Garstang and Phythian-Adams, its impact on him was minimal. As is evident from his first work at Tell el-Ful, Albright did not grasp the tremendous aid that the use of sections could provide in unlocking the secrets of a tell. What he did gain was experience handling a ceramic collection in the field.

JERUSALEM. Jerusalem had been the first site in Palestine to be examined by the nascent Palestine Exploration Fund in the 1860s. Not surprisingly, the first

British expedition after Ashkelon investigated Jerusalem. The new PEF-sponsored effort at Jerusalem was under the primary direction of a highly respected veteran of work in Palestine, the Irish archaeologist R.A.S. Macalister. Macalister (1926) and his assistant, J. Gerrow Duncan, employed the same methodology at Jerusalem as had been used twenty years earlier at Gezer. Lacking a stratigraphic methodology, the excavators could make little sense of the remains on the Ophel, the ridge running south from the city walls, where they concentrated their efforts. When any walls were uncovered in the excavations, the excavators would dig a trench along the wall to uncover its length and enable its plan to be drawn. By trenching along a wall, all the chronological evidence for that wall was destroyed. Because the wall remains uncovered by the British in 1923–1925 were for the most part fragmentary, no solid dates could be assigned to the remains. Kenyon (1974: 32) considered this to be a result of the inability of Macalister to recognize the stratigraphic indicators of a wall that had been mostly robbed out. Being in the hill country, the ancient inhabitants of Jerusalem naturally used a great deal of stone in their constructions. As Kenyon pointed out, the robbing of stone from earlier walls for later construction is endemic to sites where the use of stone is heavy. The only remaining evidence for the existence of robbed-out walls are the trenches dug by the later inhabitants for the removal of the stone. Because Macalister was looking for walls that he could trench along in an effort to gain a top plan, the few remaining stubs and discarded stones would not have made much impression. He cut right through the robber trenches, not recognizing what they were. The Macalister method was not suited to Jerusalem, nor was it abreast of the more stratigraphically oriented work being done elsewhere in Palestine (such as by Fisher at Beth-Shean [modern Beisan]; see below). Macalister's ceramic chronology, established at Gezer, also was faulty, and as a result, his dates were off by several hundred years. He may have been an archaeological pioneer before the war, but he was woefully out of date by the 1920s.

The PEF sponsored further work at Jerusalem in 1927 under the new director of the British School of Archaeology in Jerusalem, John Crowfoot (1929). George Fitzgerald assisted him when Fitzgerald was not working with the University Museum at Beth-Shean. Aware of the difficulties experienced by the previous expedition, Crowfoot dug a trench at an angle to the suspected line of fortification to avoid separating the walls from their associated remains. He also had problems reading the stratigraphy (see Kenyon 1974: 50), but he was aware of the importance of preserving the stratigraphic record, even if he did not have the ability at the time to utilize it fully. Crowfoot would later direct a seminal excavation at Samaria.

PETRIE RETURNS. Macalister was not the only old hand to return to Palestinian archaeology during the Mandate. Sir Matthew Flinders Petrie, the director of the first scientific excavation in Palestine (at Tell el-Hesi), had not worked in the country since his short season in 1890. Still primarily concerned with Egypt, Petrie (1931–34) wanted to clarify the chronology of the Egyptian First and Second Intermediate periods, particularly its relationship to South Palestine. To this end, he investigated three sites in this area: Tell Jemmeh, Tell el-Far'ah (which Petrie called Beth-Pelet), and Tell el-'Ajjul (which he believed was ancient Gaza).

Although Petrie had been a brilliant young pioneer in 1890, introducing the principle of sequence dating to archaeology, he had failed to stay abreast of new developments. The work of Petrie (1931–34) at Tell el-'Ajjul was reviewed negatively by Albright: "On the debit side are his habits of hasty generalization, lack of expert knowledge of many ancillary fields from which he draws material, complete indifference to the results of other archaeologists, sketchy and often inaccurate plans and drawings of objects, and inadequate description and classification of pottery" (1938a: 339). Still, Albright acknowledged the debt owed by archaeology to Petrie: "Sir Flinders Petrie remains the greatest archaeological genius of modern times, whose work stands alone in originality and quantity. His fame rests secure, whatever lesser men may think of the quality of his last few campaigns" (339).

Archaeology and the French Mandate

At Versailles, the victorious French gained a mandatory control over a sizable portion of the former Ottoman Empire. Nineteenth-century French interest had been focused on the Levantine coast and the Syrian interior; this became the new French Mandate. Although French archaeological activity in Palestine continued under the direction of the fathers of the Ecole Biblique in Jerusalem, the major French archaeological effort was north of Palestine, but in the same milieu archaeologically and culturally. The French antiquities laws followed the Turkish laws, and with rare exceptions, forbade the export of archaeological material out of the country. Albright (1921b) felt this was scientifically preferable to the Palestinian arrangement. However, he saw a practical problem, as tight control over acquisition "greatly reduces the incentive to give money for excavation." Albright believed strongly in international access to archaeology, particularly in Palestine: "The Holy Land and its antiquities are the possession of the whole world, and all should collaborate in their recovery, and share in their ownership" (10).

The first large French excavation under the Mandate began at the coastal site of Byblos (modern Jebail). It offers an instructive example of French methodology in the 1920s (Dunand 1939, 1954, 1958, 1973; Montet 1928). Byblos is relatively close to Palestine, even by the transport standards of the day, and Albright (1923b) and American scholars in general did not allow the political boundaries to limit their archaeological interests. The annual American School survey tour usually included southern Syria and Byblos in its itinerary. Thus, Albright, although based in Jerusalem, gained a complete picture of French field methodology from his observations at Byblos.

BYBLOS. The site of Byblos lies on a slight promontory some twenty-five kilometers north of Beirut. Two natural bays make the site an ideal port. Byblos had been identified with the tell immediately to the south of the modern village of Jebail by the 1860 expedition of Ernest Renan (1864). After much stone robbing in the late nineteenth century, Pierre Montet (1928) began organized excavations in 1921 (figure 2.2). Echoing Schliemann, Montet initially aimed at substantiating the strong Egyptian presence at Byblos presented in the classical versions of the myth of Isis and Osiris. Later, the government purchased the site to create an archaeological park. Once started, the excavations built up a momentum that kept the dig going after the original aim had been satisfied.

FIGURE 2.2 Byblos (Jebail) in Lebanon. Photo by author

Maurice Dunand became the director in 1924. He excavated for at least forty-two seasons, usually twice a year. In this way, approximately 85 percent of the tell was excavated. Dunand (1939: 6) excavated Byblos in "rigorously horizontal" layers called levees. At Byblos, each levee had a depth of 20 cm. Ultimately, a total of fifty levees were followed on the tell. This was done by careful measurement from an established base point located on a slight rise in the northwest area of the mound. Large squares (25 m. × 25 m.) formed a grid over the tell, with each divided into 5-meter subsquares. The function of these squares was purely to give horizontal boundaries for the recording of material finds; they did not function as limited areas for excavation. Montet, Dunand, and their colleagues aimed at total excavation of the site, and realized this by peeling off each levee across the entire mound.

Dunand (1939) defended his method strongly. He believed it provided the only means of understanding the mass of walls. Most important, the location of each find could be precisely located within the grid. With this in mind, the plans of the publications are presented in meter levels, with the five levees making up that level indicated on the plans by different colors (Dunand 1939, 1958). Thus, a find was horizontally placed on the plan with its vertical location given in exact figures. Dunand believed that the Byblos publications enabled the reader to reconstruct the site exactly without any "false linkages" made by the excavator. However, in the presentation of the finds to the scholarly community, he ignored the stratigraphic relationships between the recorded objects. This is very different from the physical relationship. The reader of the Byblos reports has no way of determining if two objects from the same subsquare and levee are contemporaneous in usage, or if one or both are material from an intrusive feature, such as a pit or burial.

The Byblos methodology implies certain theoretical approaches. Dunand understood an archaeological "fact" as an entity separate from its interpretation. This is demonstrated by the elimination of the stratigraphic context from both the field approach and the final publication. In the hope of easing the interpretative process, Dunand actually made it nearly impossible. Only a very painstaking study of artifact depositional patterns can provide some stratigraphic understanding. Excavation by arbitrary levels can be very valuable in sites that have a relatively short occupation history or lack visible cultural stratigraphy. Very successful excavations carried out in the American Southwest at the same time as the Byblos excavations utilized similar methodologies (Willey and Sabloff 1980: 91–93). However, its application to the complex stratigraphy of a major tell site reflects an incorrect picture of tell formation.

If the tell is understood as the compilation of a series of architectural phases, then the Byblos plans are excellent aids to that understanding. The

Byblos method does enable walls and buildings to be grossly phased by comparing the heights of the surviving walls, which the plans clearly present. However, the artifact subassemblage of the buildings can be only partially determined (e.g., Saghieh 1983). The Samaria volumes containing Reisner's
revolutionary focus on tell debris were published the year before Dunand began at Byblos, but they clearly had no impact on the Frenchman's thinking.
Like so many other scholars before and since, Dunand approached the tell with
a preconceived idea of its structure, and he did not let the material dissuade
him.

As an example of complete control over the actual excavation, Byblos is
praiseworthy. However, the intelligibility of the results is the true test of any
method, and by that standard the excavations at Byblos were a failure.

American Archaeology under the Mandate

Clarence Stanley Fisher, an excavator of great experience and prestige, dominated American archaeology in Palestine in the 1920s. Albright (1925b: 12)
considered Fisher "the ablest field archaeologist in America," an opinion
shared by the popular press. Despite his popular image, Fisher was clearly a
difficult man to work with, suspicious and autocratic. He repeatedly resigned
from excavations that he was directing, ironically helping to spread his methodology. His awkward temperament eventually left him professionally isolated,
dependent on an appointment as professor of archaeology at the Jerusalem
School, where he influenced the young director, Albright.

Fisher worked as an architect with the first American excavation in the
Near East at Nippur, in 1898. He then went to Egypt, where he worked for the
Museum of the University of Pennsylvania, which had sponsored the Nippur
excavations. While there, he met George Reisner, from Harvard, who invited
Fisher to accompany the Samaria expedition. Fisher did so in the capacity of
architect and had his first archaeological experience of Palestine. After the
seasons at Samaria, he returned to Egypt and worked at Bra Abu el-Nuja and
Mit Rahineh. He remained in Egypt throughout World War I in the employ of
the University Museum.

BETH-SHEAN: ORGANIZATION AND ADMINISTRATION. Fisher had very strong
views on method in archaeology. He emerged from the shadow of people like
Reisner when he directed his first excavation in Palestine at the huge site of
Beth-Shean. There, he consolidated his own method, which would influence,
directly or indirectly, all of the American digs between the wars in Palestine
and many in Syria. Beth-Shean is also important because it was always a

museum-dominated excavation. As a consequence of the University Museum's control, the goals of the Beth-Shean excavations were very different from the goals of the PEF or the French at Byblos.

With the war over, Fisher feared the Egyptian authorities would be much less encouraging of foreign museum work. The last straw came in a letter to George Gordon, the director of the University Museum, in which Fisher accused Sir Flinders Petrie of undercutting other digs in Egypt by hiring all of the skilled workmen (UMA Beisan/Box 1: 1/2/20). Fisher, with the approval of Gordon, turned to Palestine, where archaeological officialdom appeared more amenable to museum excavation. He had made many friends among British officialdom by offering his services in the restoration of the Dome of the Rock in Jerusalem. As an experienced archaeologist, he expected little trouble in getting a permit.

Fisher wanted to dig at Tell el-Husn, a large mound at the southern end of the Jezreel Valley, near the Jordan River, believed to be the ancient city of Beth-Shean. The tell had been the private property of the sultan before World War I and had not been excavated or even sounded, nor did the usual surface cemetery, an endemic feature of Palestinian mounds, encumber it. The University Museum, the sponsor, put certain constraints on the excavation. In their eyes, Fisher's main job was finding museum display pieces that would enhance the standing of the Museum in the academic community. Long, drawn-out negotiations occurred with the Palestinian authorities over the division of the recovered material at the end of each season. Fisher uncovered inscriptional material referring to a number of different Egyptian pharaohs. Excited by the discoveries of Howard Carter in the tomb of Tutankhamun, the general public was very interested in anything Egyptian, and Gordon's staunch advocacy of the University Museum's claims to the various stelae reflects this growing public interest. The Museum director saw a potential moneymaker, and he wanted it!

The desire of the sponsors to gain museum-quality material coincided with the prewar methodological goal of total excavation of a site. This would, of course, ensure that no object of museum quality would be missed. Therefore, despite the expense, Fisher's plan for the total excavation of Beth-Shean was fully supported by Gordon (UMA/Beisan/Box 1; CSF to Gordon 1/2/20). The budget reached the figure of $14,000 for the four-month season of 1922, a sizable investment for the day (UMA/Beisan/Box 1; CSF to Gordon 1/8/22. Albright would spend only $1,000 for his first season in 1922 at Tell el-Ful). Beth-Shean was to be a showplace excavation, and the Museum was willing to provide Fisher with a budget to match.

FISHER'S METHODOLOGY. The Fisher method (1925, 1929) grew out of his architectural training. It focuses on the recovery of the architectural sequence and associated material. Albright succinctly summarized the Fisher method as follows: "The main points are: systematic and careful planning, surveying, and leveling; excavation of areas rather than trenches; full and exact drawing of pottery forms on millimeter-ruled paper; systematic recording and card-indexing, with the use of a large record book for the detailed entry of all objects discovered" (1932a: 67). Fisher took his system of record keeping from the excavations at Samaria. The emphasis on accurate recording seems unnecessary until one remembers the continuing usage in Palestine of older, incomplete recording techniques, such as Petrie's. At Beth-Shean, Fisher did the great majority of the pottery cards himself (as a perusal of the cards demonstrates). Despite this, he did not emphasize sherd material, and his ceramic study was oriented toward whole forms.

Fisher dug by areas, rather than by trenches. This aspect of his method combined lessons learned at Samaria and Egypt with observations gleaned from the study of previous Palestinian excavations. Macalister had attempted to completely clear Gezer by trenching, with disastrous results. On the other hand, by using probes, Reisner had not been able to unravel the problems produced at Samaria by the robbing operations of the Romans. To avoid the fragmentation of strata in different plans, Fisher decided to excavate by a wide exposure of one stratum at a time. He placed an arbitrary grid over the area to be excavated. The grid was labeled by letter and number, clearly designating the location of the area on the overall plan of the site. In this way, it was much easier to achieve tighter recording standards. After an area was dug, the excavator could (it was hoped) put together an entire building and its accompanying materials. To ensure the quality of the excavation, Fisher imported trained Egyptians to function as foremen and technical men. He insisted on their inclusion in the expedition despite the visa problems this caused with the British authorities (UMA/Beisan/Box 1: CSF to Phythian-Adams 3/23/22).

Fisher (1925) claimed to follow the methodology of Reisner (Reisner et al. 1924), and the organized system became known as the Reisner-Fisher method. Later writers, such as G. Ernest Wright (1962a: 73) and Philip J. King (1983a: 41), have accepted Fisher's claim at face value. However, in reality, Fisher did not follow Reisner's theory and method system from Samaria. The excavation of Samaria forced Reisner to conclude that a tell should be excavated with the aim of revealing the human and natural processes that produced it (what modern archaeologists refer to as "formation processes"). To achieve this aim, Reisner concentrated on the disturbances of the debris, employing a tight recording system. Although he does not mention his theoretical aims, Fisher's under-standing of the tell phenomenon can be deduced from this field methodology. He saw a tell as a series of strata formed by the superimposition of architectural remains that could be dated by careful excavation. In an unpublished report to the University Museum, "Report of Work Done to End of July 1921" (UMA/Beisan/Box 1), Fisher refers to "strata of buildings." He made his understand-ing plain in a letter to the district governor: "With the removal of the latest stratum of rooms which are of little historical or architectural interest, we shall get down into strata which promise well for a succession of interesting plans and details" (UMA/Beisan/Box 1: 9/21/21). This architectural understanding is made clear by the boundaries of a locus in the Fisher method (i.e., the walls of a room or building; Albright 1932b; Fisher 1929). Therefore, in his view, a dig should concentrate on exposing architecture and clarifying the various building phases. Nevertheless, Fisher's contemporaries accepted him as the heir to the Samaria tradition, hailing his approach as the "American Method" (Badè 1934: 8).

A number of factors contributed to the changes Fisher made to the Reisner method. World War I delayed the publication of the final Samaria report until after the first three Beth-Shean seasons were concluded. Reisner wrote the Samaria report at Harvard, where he had an academic appointment. As the report shows, the analysis of the material from Samaria solidified Reisner's tentative conclusions regarding tell excavation. Fisher lived and worked in Egypt and so was cut off by the war from an active role in the analysis process. Thus, he was not in a position to be influenced further. The nonstratigraphic nature of the Egyptian sites Fisher visited and worked at (cemeteries and tem-ples) oriented his thinking in a horizontal, architectural way. The University Museum's desire for a sound return in museum display-quality objects further influenced the choices made at Beth-Shean. By digging horizontally with a tight grid, Fisher could meet the Museum's requirements, utilize his own architectural strengths, and still use the Samaria recording system.

The focus on formation processes, and the resulting necessity of careful attention to microstratigraphy, clashes with the often avowed aim in the 1920s of total site excavation. Unless an expedition is considering a very long-term (even multigenerational) commitment to a site, either a different method must be employed or the aims scaled down. For example, the French at Byblos at-tempted to resolve this problem by both a massive financial commitment and a methodology that dealt with the debris question by introducing an artificial stratigraphy. Fisher either overlooked the questions raised by Reisner regarding debris, or he felt confident enough in the ability of his workmen to separate the strata and remove intrusive material as they went along. His Egyptian-trained workmen were nonstratigraphic in orientation, but they were highly skilled in building clearance. Ultimately, the attempt to excavate the tell totally was abandoned, as the University Museum was unable to provide the support needed. A deep sounding was cut to expose the complete stratigraphic record of the site. We do not know if Fisher would have accepted the required change in strategy, because when this occurred, he was no longer associated with the dig.

MEGIDDO: ORGANIZATION AND ADMINISTRATION. In January 1925, the Philadelphia press carried the story of the dismissal of C. S. Fisher from the staff of the University Museum (UMA/Fisher/*Evening Ledger* 13 January 1925). Fisher claimed he was fired because he wished to hire an American assistant and the Museum refused. In his letter of resignation (which the *Evening Ledger* printed), he charged that the University Museum was not doing enough to train young American archaeologists. Gordon stated that Fisher resigned for health reasons and that the dig at Beth-Shean would go on. Gordon later explained his reasons in a private letter to Alan Rowe, a one-time assistant to Fisher who was eventually hired to direct the Beth-Shean work. Rowe had heard Fisher's side of the story, and Gordon felt obliged to inform Rowe of the Institution's view (UMA/Beisan/Box 1: 9/10/25). He wrote that Fisher's "mental and physical health" had deteriorated to the point where it had become "impossible" for him to represent the Museum or conduct work in the field. Gordon said that Fisher had the "false idea that he was persecuted . . . His infirmity began to express itself in malice which I am afraid is one of the ineradicable traits of his character."

Despite his dismissal from Beth-Shean, Fisher's archaeological activity in Palestine was not over. The Oriental Institute of the University of Chicago hired him in 1925 as the field director of the new excavations at the huge site of Megiddo. This was to be the major dig of the Oriental Institute in Palestine. The Institute was founded at the University of Chicago for the study and excavation of the ancient Near East. It was purely secular, having no religious interest or input. This secularism was a reflection of its founder, James Henry Breasted. In the eyes of Albright (1936), Breasted was "the greatest American organizer of humanistic research," and he profoundly influenced work in the Near East. The director of the Oriental Institute from 1925 to 1935, Breasted was a popularizer in the best sense of the term. More than any other American before Albright, he made the study of the ancient Near East acceptable to the academic community. As a token of this acceptance, he was elected to the National Academy of Science in 1919, the first figure from the humanities to be so honored (Albright would also be elected in 1955). The clearest statement of this humanist's position is his study *The Dawn of Conscience* (1933). Albright described this work as "non-religious teleology" (1964a: 214).

The Oriental Institute had been founded with money from John D. Rockefeller, who also made available the astronomical sum of $1 million for the Megiddo excavation (Fisher 1929; Lamon and Shipton 1939). As at Beth-Shean, Fisher planned the excavation of the entire mound. Breasted drew up a careful budget that included a fully professional staff for the first time in American archaeology in Palestine. Included in the budget were the publication expenses, a rarely mentioned element in archaeological expense planning. The expedition was planned for twenty-five years, so full support facilities were needed. Chester C. McCown, a contemporary director of the Jerusalem School, described the preparation of the excavation: "It was equipped with every scientific device and conducted according to every rule that should insure correct historical results . . . no similar expedition could show better equipment or more systematic method, and the work was conducted with necessary thoroughness" (1943: 173). The equipment included a complete darkroom, a captive balloon for photography, and a dig house, which had among its amenities a full-size tennis court!

The first area cleared was on the east slope, to provide a place for the backdirt to be dumped (Fisher 1929; Guy 1931). Tombs were discovered and cleared from this area. After the dump from Schumacher's earlier work was cleared away, Fisher laid out a 25-meter grid. As at Beth-Shean, he assigned locus numbers to entire structures, using different sets of numbers for tombs, buildings on the slope, and structures on the tell itself (Lamon and Shipton 1939: xxiii). Under the original plan, the excavators cleared four entire strata. This did not begin to exhaust the mound, for ultimately twenty strata would be isolated (with varying amounts of exposure). Megiddo is an 18-acre mound, with a preexcavation deposit up to 72 feet in places. Excavating the entire mound was an impossible task, even with the resources at the command of the Oriental Institute. After the Crash in 1929, the goal of complete excavation "had to be abandoned because of prohibitive cost" (McCown 1943: 178).

Again, Fisher did not continue as director for very long. P.L.O. Guy replaced him in 1927 and directed the excavations until 1935. He in turn yielded place to Gordon Loud, who broke off work in 1939. Despite the staff changes, much of the Megiddo material was published. "The recent publication of elaborate and magnificent reports . . . now places Megiddo in advance of all other Palestinian expeditions" (McCown 1943: 175). It is an opinion of the Megiddo publications that few now share, for the publications are almost useless. Wright (1970: 14) accords only one sentence to the Megiddo work in his survey of American efforts in the Near East. In his earlier review of volume 2, Wright

(1950c: 57) had to rework each stratum to gain any information. The key problem was stratigraphic, with intrusive graves often not recognized. This resulted
in mixed material being published as homogeneous. Fisher's methodology
deserves the blame for this; intrusive material is not being accounted for in
his approach. Unless direct attention is paid to the daily pottery coming from
the stratum being excavated, there is no way to check the accuracy of the digging. It is also an instructive example of the problems in the Fisher method.
The reworking of Megiddo has become a recurring pattern in the literature of
Syro-Palestinian archaeology (Kenyon 1958; Wright 1958; Yadin 1970, to name
a few). The current excavations will clarify many of the problems associated
with the pre–World War II effort.

Fisher resigned from Megiddo due to ill health (according to the excavators; Guy 1931). Alan Rowe at Beth-Shean heard reports of Fisher's illness and
transmitted them back to Philadelphia (UMA/Beisan/Box 1: Rowe to McHugh
4/23/27). Fisher's departure from Megiddo did not totally sever his links to
the excavations, and he remained an advisor for a further two years.

FISHER AND ASOR: THE ARCHAEOLOGICAL PROGRAM. The continuing voice
Fisher had in Palestinian archaeology, exemplified by his role at Megiddo, was
in no small measure the result of the actions of W. F. Albright. Albright had
become the director of the American School in 1920, after serving as acting
director for a short period (Silberman 1993). He had visited the excavations at
Beth-Shean many times and had high hopes for the results: "The thoroughly
scientific organization and direction of [Fisher's] excavations here have the
admiration and envy of all archaeologists who have seen them without exception" (Albright 1925a: 18). After Fisher was dismissed from Beth-Shean, Albright arranged for him to join the staff of the American School in Jerusalem
as professor of archaeology. Fisher was no stranger to ASOR, having been
director of the Jerusalem School for a short period before 1914. He was also
encouraged to continue to work with excavations in the field. It was a vote of
confidence and an act of compassion that was typical of Albright.

In his new position, Fisher (1925) drew up a plan for the coordination of
archaeological activity in Palestine and Syria. The aim of this program was the
elucidation of the archaeological history of Syria/Palestine, concentrating on
the recovery of a closely dated ceramic chronology. The excavations in this
program were to be jointly sponsored by the American School and an interested
academic institution. The American School would provide the guidelines for
excavation and the archaeological expertise; the sponsoring institution would
provide funding. The Fisher method would be the guide for all of the excavations in the program. Both Fisher and Albright would function as archaeolog-

ical advisors to various digs in the next decade within the structure of the coordination program.

The inclusion of Syrian archaeology reflects one of Albright's goals: the understanding of Syria/Palestine as a single unit. This was an advantage he had over his European counterparts: They were divided by the Mandate system. On the debit side, the ASOR program enshrined the Fisher method, preventing methodological experimentation. It was not until the 1950s that the domination of the Fisher method was broken, and the impetus for methodological change would come from British circles, not American.

Fisher's connection to ASOR caused problems for Albright and inhibited the acceptance of the developing Albright methodology. Although Breasted gave an institutional stamp of approval to Fisher and ASOR by hiring him after he joined with Albright, the University Museum was antagonistic. Indeed, Gordon extended his opposition of Fisher to include Albright and ASOR. In November 1925, Gordon (UMA/Beisan/Box 1: 11/9/25) wrote to the new director at Beth-Shean, Alan Rowe, to inform him that Albright and ASOR were trying to take credit for the work at the site. He urged Rowe to "make our Expedition and its work entirely independent" of both Albright and ASOR. Albright had corresponded with Fisher about Beth-Shean material on at least two occasions, particularly regarding the inscriptions (UMA/Beisan/Box 1: WFA to CSF 10/14/21; 6/17/22). His name had also been mentioned in many letters of both Fisher and Rowe regarding questions of chronology at Beth-Shean. Rowe responded to Gordon (UMA/Beisan/Box 1: 11/27/25) that, since the fieldwork started, he had not been in communication with Albright.

What particularly incensed Gordon was an article in *BASOR* reporting on the 1925 spring trip by the Jerusalem School, which had included a visit to Beth-Shean. "It is ardently hoped," wrote Albright, "for the future of Palestine archaeology, that it will be possible for him [Fisher] to renew his work here under the most favorable auspices" (1925a: 18). This report appeared in the issue following the publication of Fisher's program and the announcement of his affiliation with the Jerusalem School. Gordon angrily wrote to inform Rowe at Beth-Shean:

> At a more recent date, the Bulletin of the Archaeological Institute of America [Gordon is mistaken; ASOR was by now the publisher] contains a report from Dr. Albright, printed over his own signature, and dated at Jerusalem. In this report, Dr. Albright undertakes to give an account of the work at Beisan without mentioning the Museum. He makes the statement that Dr. Fisher is the person who should continue the excavations. This was written at a time when Dr. Fisher

had resigned according to our wish, and it appears that this published statement of Dr. Albright was an attempt to interfere in the affairs of the Museum at Beisan. He also appears to have regarded Dr. Fisher as somehow in his employ. The whole matter is a mystery to me and until it shall have been made abundantly clear on the part of the Archaeological Institute, I would suggest that you exercise caution in dealing with Dr. Albright whom I do not know and with whom I have never had any communication. (UMA/Beisan/Box 1: 12/3/25)

The accusations in Gordon's letter shocked Rowe, for he had experienced no previous problems with Albright. In his response, Rowe suggested a possible explanation: "I am utterly surprised at the course Albright has taken, and I cannot but help thinking that Fisher is at the back of it all, for Albright and he always were very friendly together. On the other hand, on the surface at least, Albright was extremely nice to me when he called here some time ago. The statements that Fisher should continue the work here are, to say the least of them, insulting both to the Museum and to myself" (UMA/Beisan/12/22/25). In defense of Albright, Rowe later pointed out that the trip reported on in *BASOR* had been made in the spring of 1925, before Rowe had been hired (UMA/Beisan/Box 1: Rowe to Gordon 3/19/26). A few months later, Albright again angered Gordon by apparently taking credit for translating the stelae found at Beth-Shean. Rowe responded by again stressing the "Fisher connection." "He [Albright] is a very close personal friend of Dr. Fisher . . . I think the best thing we can do is ignore his [Albright's] pretensions" (UMA/Beisan/Box 1: 6/5/26). When ASOR offered the use of space at the Jerusalem School, the controversy prevented Rowe from accepting the offer. "Dr. Albright's actions hardly warrant us having anything to do with his school," wrote Rowe in dismissing the offer (UMA/Beisan/Box 1: to Gordon 10/21/26).

Gordon distrusted Albright much more than Rowe did, and the death of Gordon allowed Rowe to rebuild his connections with Albright. Correspondence between the two men became more frequent (e.g., UMA/Beisan/Box 2: WFA to Rowe 12/11/28; 5/20/29). However, the rapprochement did not extend to Fisher. He remained persona non grata to both the University Museum and Alan Rowe. After leaving the active direction of the Megiddo excavations, Fisher wanted to publish a corpus of Palestinian pottery. He wrote to Miss McHugh, the acting director of the Museum, asking for permission to utilize Beth-Shean material in his schema (UMA/Beisan/Box 1: 20/25/27). She wrote to Rowe, assailing Fisher's apparent ambition, exemplified by both the proposed pottery corpus idea and the Fisher-ASOR archaeological program: "I do not know whether to say in the East, or in Palestine alone, or in Palestine and Egypt. I have never been quite sure how large a field he would like to control!" (UMA/Beisan/Box 1: 1/23/28). Miss McHugh was clearly going to follow the views of the deceased Gordon. Rowe agreed wholeheartedly with her about the inadvisability of joining with ASOR as a cosponsor of Beth-Shean. "I do not see," he wrote, "how we can allow the excavation in what is undoubtedly the best site in Palestine, to suffer from the results of this so called cooperation, which after all would be but a thinly disguised control of the work by persons having no connection whatever with the Museum" (UMA/Beisan/Box 1: 2/15/28). In the view of the University Museum, the "Fisher connection" was a grave error on the part of ASOR.

The Albright Method: The Triumph of Realia

William Foxwell Albright developed his archaeological expertise through a combination of surveys, excavations, and publications. When Albright became acting director of the Jerusalem School, and then director, he began a lifelong study of the pottery of Palestine, which was aided by his access to collections gathered by previous excavators for the various national schools. He studied ceramics with the two acknowledged masters of Palestinian pottery, C. S. Fisher at Beisan and Père Vincent of the Ecole Biblique. In the preface to his first volume on Tell Beit Mirsim, Albright wrote the following tribute:

> I wish to acknowledge my personal indebtedness to Pere Vincent, Mr Phythian-Adams, and Dr. Fisher, from whom I learned the elements of ceramic praxis during the years 1920–22. Since then I have not only carried on or assisted in numerous excavations myself, but I have also visited scores of excavations under other auspices and have collected and examined pottery from hundreds of sites in various parts of Palestine and Syria. (1932b: xiv)

Regarding Père Vincent, Albright added a footnote: "To Pere Vincent I am under peculiar obligation; occasional divergence from his views does not affect my profound admiration for his scholarly genius and for his knowledge of pottery" (xiv n. 2). Albright was a close personal friend of Vincent's, naming his son Hugh after the French Dominican (Running and Freedman 1975). After Albright's annual survey trips, he would bring the pottery collected back to the Jerusalem School, where Fisher and Vincent would look at the material. Each would examine it independently, and then they would all compare notes. From his examination of literally thousands of sherds, Albright gained a familiarity with the pottery that surpassed the knowledge of both Fisher and Vincent.

Tell el-Ful

In 1922 Albright (1922a, 1922b, 1922d, 1924b) began excavations at the site of Tell el-Ful, which he identified as the biblical site of Gibeah of Saul. This is the site Edward Robinson wanted to identify as Gibeah (see chapter 1), but he had been stymied by the general lack of knowledge of tell formation. Albright had a minimal budget of $1,000 for his first season at the site. With this limited means, he planned an excavation of four weeks. In keeping with the prevailing archaeological opinion, he intended to totally clear the site. There were "no obstacles to its complete excavation" (1922b: 10), but he encountered problems arranging for the purchase of the site from the local villagers. He ended up being taken to court by a crooked lawyer on trumped up charges! He was acquitted, and the Mandatory government stepped in under the Antiquities Laws and set the price (Albright 1924b). After that experience, which cut short the first season, the excavation proceeded smoothly in 1923. He returned for a final season in 1933.

After surveying the site, Albright had five trenches dug on the small hilltop. They ran radially from the center of the hill to the edge. He isolated five phases at Gibeah: a prefortress phase and four phases of fortification (1924b). The first fortress phase Albright associated with King Saul of Israel. An important collection of datable Iron Age pottery was the major result of the work. One of the forms that drew Albright's attention was the cooking pot, a very common element in the Tell el-Ful repertoire. He commented on the paucity of published examples, a result of the usual fate of the cooking pot in antiquity: breakage during use (10). Because very few examples survived in one piece, sherd material had to be examined to make use of a potentially excellent source of chronological information. Thanks to the limited occupation of the site (rarely exceeding 1.5 m. in depth), Albright was able to gain a clear picture of its history, despite his limited means.

In 1964, King Hussein of Jordan wanted to build a summer palace at the site, King Saul not being the only monarch to see Tell el-Ful as a good locale for a residence. Paul Lapp, then the director of the Jerusalem School, led a salvage operation that had as its goal the redating of Albright's phases (Sinclair 1976). In his work, Lapp discovered that very little correction was necessary and that Albright's reconstruction was essentially correct. The astuteness of Albright's work in this, his first excavation (not only the first he directed but the first he even worked on!), underlines the soundness of his ceramic under-standing even at this early point in his career. It is a measure of the genius of the man.

In 1923, Albright (1923c) was involved in the "excavation" of a tumulus near Jerusalem. After running a trench into the tumulus, he reported the pres-ence of eleventh-century b.c. pottery. It was an excavation out of keeping with the work Albright had already done at Tell el-Ful, much more in line with Wilson's tunneling in nineteenth-century Jerusalem. It is no surprise that Al-bright never published this excavation; undoubtedly, he was not proud of the methodology he used.

Survey Activity

The annual tours that Albright (1921b, 1923b, 1923d, 1924a, 1928a, 1929) made under the auspices of the Jerusalem School formed a prominent role in his training as an archaeologist. On these tours, he developed his knowledge of pottery and topography. The annual trips focused on locating sites and surface surveys. These were not casual tourist trips; they were rugged, physically de-manding excursions that lasted for weeks in the field. Most of the tours were made either on horseback or on foot, which gave the participants a thorough exposure to the areas under study. They were generally multidisciplinary in staffing and approach (Silberman 1993).

Albright's trips were generally concentrated on specific geographical areas, such as the Dead Sea Valley (1924a). The subject areas for the survey trips were chosen because (1) Albright had not thoroughly surveyed the area; (2) there were active field excavations that could be visited; and (3) on certain occasions, a specific research question was to be considered. On his surveys, Albright modeled his efforts on the work of Edward Robinson in the nineteenth century. In Albright's (1949: 25) opinion, Robinson was a revolutionary figure whose method could function as a successful model for twentieth-century endeavors. Albright's bilingual childhood brought his natural linguistic gifts to the fore. He took the fundamentally sound linguistic methodology of Robinson and added his own ceramic expertise, to go beyond Robinson, producing a sound method for not only locating biblical sites but for dating them. This combined methodology was tested and refined on the annual treks.

Tell Beit Mirsim

On a survey trip covering the Shephelah in 1924, Albright (1924c: 4) examined a site, Tell Beit Mirsim, that "proved to be exceptionally interesting." The tell was easily accessible, not covered with a cemetery, and surface remains indicated habitation from the Early Bronze Age through the Iron Age. "What an opportunity for the excavator—and the site is entirely unexcavated!" (5). Once Albright had sufficient support to again mount an excavation for the Jerusalem School, he returned to this promising site and changed the course of Palestinian archaeology.

Melvin Grove Kyle, the president of Xenia Seminary, a Presbyterian school in Pittsburgh (now the Pittsburgh Theological Seminary), had collaborated with Albright (1924a) on the 1924 Dead Sea Valley survey. Kyle wanted Xenia Seminary to work in tandem with ASOR on an excavation. He was interested in Tell Beit Mirsim as a result of Albright's identification of the site as the biblical city of Kirjath-Sepher ("Book-city"). Motivated primarily by a biblical interest, Kyle (1934: 30) hoped the site would yield an ancient library. In contrast to the seminarian's interest, Albright (1938b) had primarily archaeological reasons for excavating Tell Beit Mirsim. He wanted to clarify Petrie's ceramic chronology and demonstrate the value of ceramic typology in archaeological research. As a result of the 1924 survey, Albright believed that Tell Beit Mirsim's habitation covered a sufficient chronological range to enable him to undertake a systematic treatment of the pottery.

The joint expedition to Tell Beit Mirsim followed ASOR's newly presented Fisher plan. Kyle (personally) and Xenia Seminary provided the funding and Albright provided a trained staff. In four seasons of fieldwork, the Tell Beit Mirsim excavation team spent only $16,000. The first two seasons' expenses came out of Kyle's own pocket, an act of generosity that Albright deeply appreciated (1933b: 6). It is worth noting that Albright's expenses for nearly ten months of excavation were slightly more than the budgeted amount for a single four-month season at Beth-Shean. Albright (1938b: 7–8) kept expenses down by eliminating salaries for the professional staff and by not paying transport costs for the staff members. (It remains the pattern on research excavations to pay the cook, but not the archaeologists!) As a result, students and archaeologists already on the ground in Palestine took most of the expedition's positions. The local workforce numbered on average sixty to seventy men and boys, reaching a total of 120 in the third season. Tell Beit Mirsim brought together a diverse group of scholars, both new and established. Albright and Kyle codirected all four seasons, which occurred every other year from 1926 through 1932. James L. Kelso, who would later work with Albright at Bethel, aided Albright for three out of four field seasons, only missing 1928. C. S. Fisher, father of the ASOR plan, worked in the field with Albright only once, at Tell Beit Mirsim in 1928. Nelson Glueck, a young biblical scholar fresh from graduate study in Germany, joined the staff for the last two seasons. He would become one of the leading voices in biblical archaeology. John Bright, a student of Albright's at Johns Hopkins (where Albright had been since 1930) and later an important biblical historian, gained his first experience in the 1932 season. The appeal and excitement of working with Albright overcame the lack of financial reward, and the Tell Beit Mirsim staff never lacked personnel (Long 1997).

The Albright Method

Albright (1938b: 8) claimed to follow the "Reisner-Fisher technique" at Tell Beit Mirsim. However, he adapted Fisher's method to fit the ceramic goals he had set for the excavation. He took the area orientation of Fisher and the recording system of Reisner and added the intensive study of the ceramic material from the tell to produce the field methodology of Tell Beit Mirsim. A 20-meter grid was laid out on the tell, with all finds recorded by day, locus, and square. In especially promising loci (which could be rooms or distinctive features, if, in the excavator's opinion, these warranted a separate label), all of the dirt was sifted. Each day, the pottery was "read" (examined) by Albright and his staff. In keeping with Reisner's approach, record keeping was very important. Certainly, Albright recognized the time-consuming nature of such a system: "The director and his foreign assistants must be ready to go to work with their own hands, or to spend entire days at a single point of interest" (1932a: 67). But this was the only way adequate control could be maintained over the excavation. The telescope of Petrie had no place in the equipment of W. F. Albright! If the information to be recorded became so overwhelming that the director was unable to spend any time at the actual excavation, a full-time organization and professional support staff would have to be brought in, along the lines of that at Megiddo. In that case, "a small expedition ceases to have a scientific reason for existence" (67).

Although top plans were made, the focus of the excavation was on the ceramics. The first publication (Albright 1932b) dealt exclusively with the pottery, demonstrating its importance in Albright's eyes. He wanted to produce a closely dated corpus of pottery that could function as a type collection for south Palestine. This goal was aided by the fortuitous (in archaeological terms) circumstance of the repeated destruction of the ancient city. This left the basic strata relatively easily discernible, even in the broad horizontal approach of the Fisher method. The tell-wide layers of ash and burnt brick provided vertical separations for the pottery of the various phases. Thus, Albright could be sure of the relative chronological relationships of his material.

When Albright (1932b, 1933a, 1938b, 1943) published his Palestinian ceramic calendar based on the pottery of Tell Beit Mirsim. "he took the discipline out of the mists of oral tradition" (Wright 1970: 27). Albright used comparative typology, exhaustively researching all possible parallels for the Tell Beit Mirsim ceramics. The pottery volumes (1932b, 1933a) focus almost exclusively on formal characteristics. Using both photographs and drawings, Albright presents the ceramics according to the sequence principles elucidated by Petrie. By utilizing the wealth of unpublished sherd material gathered on various survey tripsand reexamining previously excavated material, Albright was able to present a well-ordered sequence for the Middle Bronze Age, Late Bronze Age, and Iron Age. Unfortunately, only the end of the Early Bronze Age is represented in the ceramic repertoire at Tell Beit Mirsim, so this period remained less secure in Albright's chronology. To fill this gap, he directed his student, G. Ernest Wright, to study the pottery of Palestine from its beginnings to the end of the Early Bronze Age as a dissertation topic. It was published (Wright 1937) before the Tell Beit Mirsim Bronze Age volume appeared.

By the time he directed the excavations at Tell Beit Mirsim, Albright was the unchallenged master of Palestinian pottery, and the pottery-oriented publications of this dig solidified his dominance of the field. Even after seventy years, Albright's chronology is fundamentally unchanged. From the perspective of the 1980s, these volumes were still "ideal ceramic textbooks for students of Palestinian archaeology" (King 1983a: 80).

Albright's addition of ceramic typology to the Fisher method alleviated some of the interpretational problems connected with this approach. "[Fisher's] method is only sound," wrote Albright, "when applied with adequate knowledge of pottery and ceramic typology; otherwise it may conceal thoroughly unsound execution and interpretation" (1938b: 14). To ensure successful excavation, Albright believed that Palestinian archaeology needed to place ceramic typology in the forefront:

> The systematic archaeologist is thus forced to employ two divergent
> principles at almost every step in his work: stratigraphy, or the study
> of the relations of objects to the layers or deposits in which they are
> found and the relation of these deposits to one another; typology, or
> the classification of objects according to types, following taxonomic
> methods, and the comparison of objects belonging to a type with
> one another, in order to determine chronological and technical rela-
> tionships . . . At an early stage of archaeological research in any
> given country, all the advantage is with the stratigrapher. At a later
> stage the typologist finds more to do and the trained typologist even-
> tually acquires an advantage over the mechanical stratigrapher, ex-
> cept in dealing with undisturbed deposits. (1940: 53–54)

Albright's stratigraphic understanding was limited because of the influence of Fisher. Very few tell deposits rate as "undisturbed," yet the Fisher methodology could not comprehend the disturbed nature of tell material. Fisher's colleague at Samaria, George Reisner, did consider the problems of tell debris, and his report was available to Albright in 1924. Yet, by using the term "Reisner-Fisher technique," Albright (1938b: 8) makes clear that he considered Fisher the true heir of Reisner. Fisher was on the ground in Palestine, connected with ASOR, so any influence Reisner's publication could have had on Albright was minimized.

Albright turned to ceramic typology to deal with the problem of tell debris: "We should have repeatedly found ourselves at a loss and have made wrong analyses and attributions if it had not been for the precision with which we used the pottery criteria" (1938b: 9). In keeping with a ceramic orientation, the published section drawings of Tell Beit Mirsim are schematic and uninformative. They represent a step backward from the Ashkelon sections. Walls float unattached across the page, with no indications of connecting material. This is not surprising because "all problems of the attribution of walls to accompanying strata were attacked by considering the pottery context" (9).

The Albright method, with its reliance on ceramic typology, contained the seeds of disaster. Stratigraphic study took a secondary role, diverting attention from the pioneering work of Reisner (Dever 1993). Albright's success at Tell Beit Mirsim gave the Fisher method viability that it would otherwise not have merited. The Albright method prevented experiments in stratigraphic excavation, leading to methodological stagnation in Palestine. There was no need to develop field techniques that could expose and clarify microstratigraphy, because pottery typology held the promise of pinpointing intrusive material. Unfortunately, the success of the method depended on the excavator's having a vast knowledge of pottery. No one else active in Palestine could approach Albright's grasp of the ceramic corpus, which prevented a repetition of the universally acknowledged success of Tell Beit Mirsim. The Albright method, developed to avoid a methodological dead end, became itself a trap for the unwary.

Moreover, the particular stratigraphic conditions of Tell Beit Mirsim permitted Albright to have greater success with his method than another site might have provided. This was demonstrated at Albright's own excavation in 1934 of the site of Beitin, the biblical city of Bethel (Albright and Kelso 1968). In the first season in 1934 four areas were opened up with an exposure of 200 square meters. No coherent phase plans could be produced from the scattered nature of the soundings. The section drawings are schematic and almost valueless, with walls floating in space (plate 10). Bethel did not have the series of destructions that eased interpretive problems at Tell Beit Mirsim (although it did suffer a catastrophic destruction at the end of the Bronze Age). Albright was forced back on ceramic typology alone to understand the archaeological history of the site. The result is rather superficial, with only gross serialization possible. Albright again focuses on the destructions, rather than the intermediate phases. Due to the poor section drawings, the reader must take on faith the separation of strata. Sir Mortimer Wheeler (1954), in his survey of archaeological methodology, used the Area II section from Bethel as an example of a useless section drawing. This could not have pleased Albright, but his archaeological reputation overshadowed the inadequacies of the Bethel excavations. His demonstrated ability to accurately date the ceramics of Palestine obscured the stratigraphic failures of his methodology. Upon the rock of ceramic typology Albright would build the edifice of biblical archaeology.

Pottery: Albright's True Realia

In the study of pottery, the rational, mathematical mind of Albright found its archaeological niche. The preoccupation with ceramics is an expression of what I believe underlies all of Albright's scholarship, archaeological and otherwise: the search for realia. In this context, realia are data gained by explicitly scientific methods, the results of rigorous experimentation, on which sound and enduring conclusions can be built. In his study of language, Albright found realia in the science of linguistics. He displayed a linguistic orientation in his scholarship from his earliest writings to his last published book (Albright and Mann 1971). Linguistics provided him with the means to analyze rationally the languages and texts of the ancient Near East. Like Edward Robinson, Albright's mathematical training found an outlet in linguistic analysis.

For Albright, pottery was the "linguistic" aspect of field archaeology. In his rigorous comparative analysis, he made pottery a candidate for realia. The Tell Beit Mirsim collection gave him the dated material he needed to systematize the ceramics of Palestine. Through those publications, he provided archaeologists with a ceramic corpus that could be used as an independent check for other sites. Unlike other published pottery collections, such as Petrie's Tell el-'Ajjul material or Duncan's corpus (1930), Albright presented the actual pots in question, not "types." G. Ernest Wright (1940) explained the Albright approach in a review of a French treatment of archaeology and the Bible. According to Wright, the goal of the Albright method was to be able to date a "homogeneous locus" to within a quarter century on ceramic typology alone: "This is, of course, the ideal of almost all archaeologists of the younger school" (401).

The desire to date pottery with the precision demanded by the Albright method caused anomalies to be overlooked. The idea of a "homogeneous locus" is key to the issue. A locus was determined to be homogeneous on typological, not stratigraphic grounds. Albright lacked the necessary stratigraphic understanding, and the accompanying field techniques, to make a stratigraphic determination of a "clean" locus. Fisher's influence prevented Albright from translating Reisner's theoretical ideas about tell formation into a practical field methodology. Therefore, a locus was "clean" if its pottery assemblage contained only forms that on comparative grounds did not conflict chronologically. Such a clean locus could then be used to test other material. This could become a circular trap, simply reinforcing preconceived ideas about pottery groups. Pottery forms are assumed to be chronological, not cultural markers. Albright's was not the best method for a tell site, because it placed stratigraphic study into a secondary position. Not until more stratigraphically oriented field methods were introduced into Palestine were the problems inherent in the Albright method resolved. Despite these limitations, Albright's success made ceramic study the hallmark of American excavations in Palestine into the present day.

The clarification of the ceramic sequence was not an end in itself. Albright needed the ability to accurately date ceramics so that he could ascertain the periods of habitation and date the destruction of Palestinian tells. With that ability, he could answer the questions of biblical history that became increasingly more important to him. Albright hoped to ground biblical studies in the realia of archaeology.

The Dominance of Albright

By the late 1930s, Albright's unchallenged mastery of the pottery of Palestine came together with economic and political factors to ensure his dominance of the field. The man who began the "golden age" as a folklorist (Silberman 1993) and linguist had become its leading archaeologist. Ironically, at the pinnacle of his archaeological influence Albright turned away from fieldwork and preferred to be called an Orientalist.

Economic Factors

The worldwide economic downturn of the 1930s influenced Palestinian archaeology. The major excavations of the 1930s such as Beth-Shean and Megiddo suffered along with the small-scale work. The large digs had to make major changes in methodology as they were unable to find the funding to continue their aim of total excavation. The travails of the Beth-Shean expedition are a good example of the economic impact on archaeology in Palestine. The University Museum's Beisan work first felt the bite in 1930. That year's budget was $6,500, about half of the earlier annual budgets. Jayne, the University Museum's new director, urged Fitzgerald, Rowe's replacement at Beisan, to dig in the cemetery as opposed to the tell: "The cemetery has the advantage also of producing a large quantity of museum objects which for the first year [of Fitzgerald's directorship] it will be well to show since the Board's lack of enthusiasm regarding the work at Beisan is, I am sure, traceable to the lack of tangible results" (UMA/Beisan/Jayne to Fitzgerald 5/19/30). "Tangible results" in the Museum's vocabulary means objects worthy of exhibition. In a period of shrinking resources, the University Museum could not afford to support a dig that did not significantly enhance either its collection or its reputation. In other words, the results had to help raise money if a dig was to continue.

In 1931, Jayne wrote to Fitzgerald reporting a "heavy diminuation [*sic*] of our income" (UMA/Beisan/11/23/31). As a result, a telegram was sent late in December of that year suspending fieldwork for an entire year. In 1933, the museum found $11,500 for Beisan, but with a limited budget and less money likely in the future, Fitzgerald wanted to try a sounding. Jayne approved of the idea, while still hoping for a complete clearance of the tell (UMA/Beisan/Jayne to Fitzgerald 7/5/33). In 1935, after a year of idleness, Jayne wrote to Alan Rowe, who remained connected to the expedition, indicating rather bleak prospects for digging (UMA/Beisan/4/15/35). After another missed season, Rowe favored closing the work, arguing that Garstang was taking all of the workmen in the fall for Jericho, and that he himself was not getting any younger. Most important to Rowe, the limited financial resources available should go for publishing the results already achieved (UMA/Beisan/Rowe to Jayne 4/20/36). The death knell was sounded in December 1938 as a result of the continuing political unrest. "My Board has decided," wrote Jayne to Rowe, "that in view of the political situation in Palestine, the Beisan expedition had best be liquidated" (UMA/Beisan/12/7/38).

The Oriental Institute shared the economic troubles of the University Museum. Even the immense resources of John D. Rockefeller did not permit the Megiddo team to carry on as planned. The total excavation of the massive mound of Megiddo had to be abandoned in 1935 due to the prohibitive cost (McCown 1943: 178). The death of Breasted in November of that year made the decision of the Institute easier. One of the side effects of the economic crunch was the reevaluation of the Fisher method's aim of total excavation. McCown, a successor to Albright in Jerusalem, reflects this rethinking: "Will archaeologists a generation hence pronounce the same blessing on the excavators who have recently been so ruthlessly ravishing the mounds of Palestine and blithely reconstructing its history out of their imaginations? It has been suggested that the antiquities ordinance should require a small but essential part of each tell to be left to future generations" (172–73). G. M. Fitzgerald agreed with this sentiment, labeling the original Beisan aim of total excavation "a ridiculous work to clear the whole area down to virgin soil" (UMA/Beisan/ GMF to Jayne 5/26/34).

Not all "big dig" excavations were forced to change the aim of total excavation. The French excavations at Byblos continued unchanged through the 1930s. The ability of the Byblos team to remain committed to the goal of total excavation reflects a different sense of personal proprietorship in fieldwork than the Americans demonstrated. The French showed a singular lack of personal ego, viewing the dig not as the scholarly property of one individual but as a multigenerational project. With this understanding, there was no pressure for major annual excavation seasons, hence no major budget was needed. This served to insulate Byblos from economic pressure.

Albright avoided the pressure of economics by digging both inexpensively and in joint projects. He never directed an excavation as the representative of Johns Hopkins, but rather as an ASOR expert. As such, he was not personally pressured for excavation funding. Also, his joint digs with Xenia Seminary (Tell Beit Mirsim and Bethel) were run on very small operating budgets, as he and his staff were not salaried (unlike at Megiddo and Beth-Shean). His ceramic methodology could yield usable results from limited exposures, eliminating the need for costly wide exposures. The ASOR connection freed Albright to be associated in an advisory capacity with a number of excavations such as Beth Shemesh and Tell en-Nasbeh. As a result, he remained in control of the data at little economic cost.

Field Knowledge

Albright's ten years in Palestine greatly contributed to his dominant position in archaeology. Combined with his personal gift of ceramic analysis, his continuing presence in the field gave him the clearest view of the emerging archaeological history of Palestine. His fieldwork was free of museum guidelines that encouraged the collection of artifacts over the advancement of understanding. He brought a unifying vision to the archaeological data, although his biblical archaeology had its own biases. The one drawback of Albright's presence in Palestine was the narrow focus it gave to his archaeological methodology (despite the multinational nature of archaeology in Palestine). He was influenced too strongly by Fisher, whereas if he had been based in the United States, say, he might have become aware of methodological experimentation in other branches of archaeology.

Biblical Archaeology: The Great Debate

American theology in the 1920s witnessed a fierce controversy over the nature of the Bible. This was the fundamentalist-modernist controversy. Fundamentalists held to the "fundamentals," beliefs growing out of an acceptance of a verbally inspired Bible. The modernists were willing to accept critical study of the Bible. The vehement controversy split denominations, seminaries, and even individual churches (Furness 1954; Rian 1984; Sandeen 1970). The infamous "Scopes Monkey Trial" was one engagement of this war. "He who is not for me is against me" was too often the scriptural guideline in evaluating the "correctness" of an individual scholar's positions. Under pressure, each side in the debate became hardened, so someone like Albright would be a target for either side.

Apologetical Archaeology

The fundamentalist-modernist debate influenced archaeology in Palestine, where Fundamentalism developed an apologetical school of archaeology that desired to use archaeology to support an inerrant, literal interpretation of the Bible. Most writers using archaeology in this manner were not themselves archaeologists, being either clergymen or biblical scholars. This school made the literal reading of the Bible the interpretative guide for archaeology. Kyle, a Presbyterian clergyman, was one of the few apologists with archaeological experience. Like Robinson before him, Kyle was a mission-minded believer, having served on the Presbyterian Board of Foreign Missions. He contributed to *The Fundamentals*, a series of articles presenting various doctrinal positions normative in fundamentalism. Before gaining direct archaeological field experience, Kyle (1920a, 1920b, 1924) wrote three works on archaeology and the Bible similar in style to the writings of A. H. Sayce. However, unlike Sayce, Kyle did not allow archaeology to be an independent test of biblical accuracy. He used it as an apologetical tool to demonstrate the veracity of the fundamentalist view of biblical history. For Kyle, the only motivation for archaeology in Palestine was its ability to defend the Bible.

Kyle wrote his own report on the joint ASOR-Xenia expedition to the Dead Sea Valley, entitling it *Explorations at Sodom* (1928)! His unscientific account of the expedition is in the pilgrim tradition of pre-Robinson days. He concluded his work with a comment on the value of archaeology: "Archaeological research is progressing rapidly and when the trustworthiness of scripture is finally and completely established, any theory based upon the untrustworthiness of the ancient documents will come down like a house of cards. FACTS ARE FINAL" (78). For Kyle, the Hand of God will support the Word of God, more particularly, Kyle's own fundamentalist understanding of the Word of God. This understanding set his agenda and guided his research.

At Tell Beit Mirsim, Kyle (1934) wrote a glorified daily diary. It is enjoyable reading, providing insight into the trials and triumphs of a normal day on a Palestinian excavation in the late 1920s. The results of the work at the site did not cause him to make any changes in his understanding of archaeology. For him, archaeological results were not subject to interpretation and provided evidence of the trustworthy nature of the Bible. Kyle shared the common fundamentalist view of science as a collection of concrete facts, not subject to theory and interpretation. (This same belief underlies the current resurgence of "scientific creationism.") When Kyle died, Albright (1933b) wrote a moving tribute to his sponsor. He alluded to the theological differences between himself and Kyle, but noted that this never influenced their fast friendship. It is possible that Kyle might have modified his views if he had been able to evaluate the Tell Beit Mirsim dig more fully (he died as the analysis was starting).

Liberal Archaeology

The theological opponents of the fundamentalists also had their archaeological auxiliary. The liberal theologians of the 1920s challenged the historicity of the Bible and the conservative theological message. Particular efforts were focused on the removal of the supernatural from biblical accounts and from individual faith. W. C. Graham and H. G. May (1936) of the University of Chicago were liberal theologians who collaborated in a study of Palestinian religious development based on the Megiddo material.

William Frederic Badè, an ordained Moravian linguist, was a professor of the Old Testament and Semitic languages at the Pacific Theological Seminary (later the Pacific School of Religion). He accepted the documentary hypothesis and was interested in the evolutionary development of the Hebrew religion (Zorn 1988). An archeological novice, he corresponded with Albright and arranged to begin excavations at the site of Tell en-Nasbeh in 1926. In keeping with the times, he sought to excavate the entire site. Although he studied American Southwestern field methodology (Zorn 1988), he turned to Fisher for guidance in Palestine and followed the Reisner-Fisher method religiously. Badè (1934) published a field manual that gave increased visibility to the Fisher

methodology. He died in 1936, before publishing the site material in a systematic way. Chester C. McCown, one of Albright's successors as director of the
Jerusalem School, published the final report.

McCown was a New Testament scholar of liberal persuasion. He presented
the archaeological results of the golden age from the liberal perspective in *The
Ladder of Progress in Palestine* (1943). The title reflects the liberal theological
hope of human improvement. To McCown, the excavator "does not go [into
the field] with preconceived ideas which he wishes to establish . . . The modern
excavator wishes to restore in his mind's eye a complete civilization, an ancient
society in all its details, and to follow it from its meagre beginnings to its
eventual dissolution. His dominant interest is 'social evolution'" (3). This approach was, despite McCown's disclaimers, a theological choice. The theological liberals of the 1920s and 1930s argued for the ability of humanity to bring
about the Kingdom of God by their own efforts (e.g., see Fosdick 1956).
McCown's hope in the nature of man is best illustrated by his closing paragraph:

> One important fact emerges from archaeological and historical stud-
> ies and further excavation will surely only illustrate and confirm it:
> man has made progress, even in this brief space of time. A far
> larger proportion of mankind have a relatively satisfactory standard
> of living than ever before. Even the worst that the wars of the twen-
> tieth century have brought has not been worse than the evils of the
> past, while, what is more significant, the standards of the present
> are incomparably higher and the area of moral obligation incompa-
> rably broader than ever before. Archaeology, which records the ruins
> of past civilization, is equally replete with evidence of the rebirth of
> the better out of the good of the past. (1943: 350)

Like the fundamentalists, McCown believed that archaeology could "illustrate
and confirm" theological beliefs.

After World War II, archaeological liberalism was dead in Palestine. The
theological movement was crumbling before neo-orthodoxy and had little time
or energy to invest in archaeology. The leaders of liberal archaeology did not
return to the field in the first generation after World War II, effectively negating
their influence. Ironically, the liberal emphasis on cultural evolution is at the
heart of the new anthropological approach in Palestinian archaeology. Liberal
archaeology has returned (in a fashion) in the current minimalist movement
in biblical studies, which has used archaeology to support an ultracritical view
of the Old Testament (see chapter 5).

The British

The British geographical (rather than biblical) orientation toward Palestinian archaeology that characterized the Palestine Exploration Fund was strengthened by political control of Palestine. There were British biblical scholars involved in archaeology, such as Duncan, but their biblical interests did not set the agenda. Garstang (1932) reported on the excavations at Jericho with a primary focus on the archaeological sequence. He did incorrectly correlate the Early Bronze walls with the biblical conquest of the city by Joshua, but the correlation was to explain the archaeology, not vice versa. Admittedly, this correlation was picked up and trumpeted as biblical "proof," but Garstang did not stress that aspect. Duncan, a Presbyterian clergyman, did not have a professional position, but he had trained with Petrie and Macalister. He presented a series of lectures entitled *Digging Up Biblical History* (1931), but the focus was illumination, not apologetics. A British volume written for schoolteachers and Bible students, *Bible and Spade* (Caiger 1936), presented the British establishment view of the value of combining the efforts of critical study and archaeology. The bishop of Bradford (who would achieve passing notoriety by unknowingly unleashing the press in the Simpson Affair) deplored the misuse of archaeology "in the interests of an unscholarly prejudice against the work of those vaguely called 'the higher critics'" (xi). Although conservative scholars in Britain continued to reject higher criticism, they were secondary users of archaeology. British archaeology in Palestine remained an archaeological endeavor following an archaeological agenda. The professionalism of the Department of Antiquities ensured an archaeological perspective in research, effectively preventing British archaeology in Palestine from becoming a branch of biblical archaeology.

The French

French archaeologists came from both secular and religious backgrounds. The professionals at Byblos considered *l'archéologie biblique* a small subdiscipline of their field. Andre Parrot mainly excavated in the Mesopotamian cultural world, but he did work at Byblos with Dunand. "Dans l'archéologie orientale," wrote Parrot in a review of the history of the field, "une section a donc été tout naturellement consacrée à l'archéologie biblique" (1952: 121). To Parrot and his colleagues, biblical archaeology was a branch of Oriental archaeology that pulled together the various strands of research relating directly to the Bible. He found no place for apologetical archaeology and placed archaeological interpretation in the forefront. He correctly pointed out that the precision of archaeology frightened exegetes because it challenged them to view differently the process of revelation (129).

One would expect the Dominican fathers of the Ecole Biblique in Jerusalem to be staunch advocates of biblical archaeology. A perusal of the *Revue Biblique*, the journal of the school, indicates the intense interest that archaeology aroused among the French scholars there. However, the Bible did not set the agenda for archaeological investigations. For example, Père Mallon's prehistoric interests were at best only peripheral to the Old Testament, demonstrating the intellectual freedom at the Ecole. Unlike Protestant scholars, the French fathers did not rely solely on the Bible for religious authority. The subtle pressure on Protestant archaeologists to support the historicity of the Bible (often unacknowledged) was not present in the work of the Ecole. Thus, they could approach archaeology in Palestine as an individual endeavor, as well as an aid to biblical study. Roland de Vaux (1961), who would be most active after World War II, combined archaeology and biblical study in his scholarship, but without a theological agenda. He used the methods of critical scholarship as well as the results of archaeology to arrive at his conclusions. The lack of a theological agenda prevented the development of a French endeavor equal to Albrightian biblical archaeology.

The Biblical Archaeology of W. F. Albright

When Albright came to Palestine he understood the Bible from a pan-Babylonianist perspective, the school of thought associated with Hugo Winckler. As a pan-Babylonianist, Albright was following the lead of his teacher Paul Haupt (Sasson 1993). This was a position Albright later characterized as one of "extreme radicalism" (1933b: 8). In the theological context of the 1920s, a "radical," or "modernist," rejected the Bible in terms of its historical trustworthiness, seeing it as a product of primarily human activity. A "conservative" treated the Bible as generally trustworthy in history and, although human in terms of language and culture, primarily a product of divine origin. "Fundamentalists" interpreted the Bible literally and accepted the doctrine of full verbal inspiration; that is, every word in the original text was dictated by God and therefore was entirely trustworthy in its history. As a pan-Babylonianist, Albright accepted Winckler's principle that the Hebrew narratives represented no more than local versions of Babylonian myths. Although opposed to Wellhausen's emphasis on the independence of early Hebrew thought, Albright did share the Wellhausian dismissal of any historical content in the Pentateuch. This understanding of Albright is disputed by Burke Long (1997). He certainly had no inklings of the impact archaeology would have on his well-ordered theological world.

The early excavations of the 1920s had an immediate effect on Albright. In his early reports in the initial issues of *BASOR*, he acknowledged the impact of archaeology on his biblical thinking. In a report on the Ashkelon excavations, Albright (1922c) reported on the recovery of Philistine pottery, which definitely supported the biblical story of Philistine occupation. Looking to the future, he expected more "discoveries to confute the skeptic and delight the scholar's heart" (14). Reporting on Danish excavations at the site of Shiloh, he demonstrated his changing views. "Again," he wrote, "we have archaeological confirmation of the statements of the Bible" (1923a: 11). Amid the other excavations at biblical sites, Albright decided to dig at Tell el-Ful. The discovery of what he interpreted as Saul's palace and the solidity of the ceramic evidence reinforced his growing respect for the value of archaeology in biblical study. His ceramic expertise enabled him to trust his own data over the critical models of his training. The 1924 trip of the Jerusalem School cemented his new respect for the historicity of the Hebrew Bible. He wrote:

> In this connection there is an interesting fact, which came home to me more vividly this trip than ever before: many of the towns in southern Judah and Simeon were not occupied after the Exile. This process was quite as disastrous as it is portrayed in the Old Testament and the views . . . that the drastic sweep made of the population of Judah at this time is a fancy of post-exilic scribes must be rejected. The present writer once subscribed to this view but has been forced to abandon it because of the pressure of archaeological facts. (1924c: 5–6)

The "archaeological facts" that forced Albright to reexamine his biblical thinking were based on his newly found realia of ceramic chronology. As John Miles (1976) has pointed out in an insightful essay on Albright's thought, historical accounts in the Old Testament that in Albright's pan-Babylonianism had been ignored take on new significance due to the potential of archaeology to elucidate them. Genesis 14, the account of a campaign of five kings in the Jordan Valley region, is such an example. In 1924, Albright (1924a, 1926) decided to survey the Valley area with the goal of establishing its occupational history. He hoped that evidence of the "Cities of the Plain" would be uncovered, which would aid in the understanding of the campaign of the five kings.

The 1924 survey was codirected by Albright and Melvin Grove Kyle, who eagerly joined in the hunt for the Cities of the Plain (which include the famous [or infamous] Sodom and Gomorrah). The expedition was multidisciplinary, including a geologist and a specialist in lithic analysis. Neither Sodom nor Gomorrah was discovered by the survey, but evidence of Bronze Age occupation was found. The survey discovered the massive site of Bab-edh-Dhra on the east side of the Dead Sea, below the crusader castle of Al-Kerak (figure 2.3). Albright (1926) dated the site, on the basis of the pottery, to before the Middle Bronze Age, which would fit the traditional date of the Genesis 14 campaign. Thus, having demonstrated occupation in the valley, Albright believed he had legitimate grounds for hypothesizing the disappearance of Sodom and Go-morrah beneath the Dead Sea (57–62). The discovery of a massive cemetery, which dwarfed the actual habitation site at Bab-edh-Dhra, led Albright to won-der if it had been more than just a town. He interpreted a row of stones standing in an isolated locale separate from the site as a series of masseboth, stones having a cultic significance. "There can be little doubt," Albright ob-served, "that Bab ed-Dhra was a place of pilgrimage, where annual feasts were celebrated, and to which people came, living in booths and merry-making for several days of the year" (61). He made a final observation in the *BASOR* article regarding the religious pilgrimage, concluding, "Doubtless it was cursed with licentious cults" (1924a: 6)! There was no doubt in Albright's mind that he had found the remains of the cult site for Sodom and Gomorrah.

In coming to this conclusion, Albright was a victim of his own presup-positions. Intuitively, he recognized the anomaly of the vast cemetery site in the Ghor, but his immediate leap to a cultic, biblically connected explanation

FIGURE 2.3 Early Bronze charnel house at Bab-edh-Dhra in Jordan. Photo by author

is a result of his own prior expectations. He had a ready-made reason for the site and so did not inquire further into its cultural history. Also, his reasoning was based on survey, not on excavation. When Bab-edh-Dhra was excavated in the 1960s (Lapp 1966), the cemeteries were shown to cover a vast time range, from Early Bronze I (EBI) to Early Bronze IV (EBIV), and the habitation site was more extensive than just the fortress postulated by Albright. Without excavation, he had no way of checking on the date of the undisturbed tombs. Like Robinson nearly a century before, Albright had an exaggerated opinion of the value of survey data.

Throughout the 1920s, Albright reassessed the results and procedures of biblical criticism. In a series of lectures in 1931 he presented the initial results of his rethinking. These lectures were published as *The Archaeology of Palestine and the Bible* (1932a), and they reflected the biblical orientation of his research. In the long discussion of fieldwork in Palestine, biblical interests dictated the assessments. Surveying the University Museum's work at Beth-Shean, Albright dismissed the "unimportant discoveries" of the upper strata dating to the Hellenistic period: "The real interest of Beth Shean to the archaeologist begins when he has penetrated down into the strata which antedate the end of the second millennium B.C." (40). Only with a purely biblical agenda could interest "begin" in Beth-Shean when Albright says it does. In his discussion of the 1924 survey of the Dead Sea Valley, the results were important, not because they indicated the geographical extent of Bronze Age culture, but because they established the correctness of the biblical tradition of settlement in the Valley (48). In an addendum covering the work of 1932, Albright highlighted the possibility of discovering the site of the tabernacle at Shiloh and the support the excavations produced for the biblical account of the site's destruction by the Philistines (57). Clearly, Albright the biblical conservative scholar had obscured Albright the archaeologist.

In this study, Albright approached archaeology in Palestine from two differing perspectives: biblical archaeology and Palestinian archaeology. One of his subsections is entitled "Recent Progress in Palestinian Archaeology" (1932a: 13); yet, on the very next page, he writes of "Biblical Archaeology in Palestine" (14). From the context, it is clear that both terms refer to the same thing: archaeological activity in Palestine. Later in the study, Albright uses "Palestinian archaeology" when he refers to fieldwork and "Biblical archaeology" as a broader term encompassing the interaction of the results of fieldwork with the Bible (e.g., 36, 38). Albright brought biblical archaeology out of the armchair and into the field. Under the rubric of biblical archaeology, he presented fieldwork in terms of its biblical importance, treating archaeology in Palestine as dependent on biblical issues. Yet judgments concerning questions in biblical studies were decided on the basis of archaeological criteria. In this first presentation of Albrightian biblical archaeology, the motivation behind purely archaeological research was the refinement of archaeology's ability to aid biblical studies. In this model, biblical archaeology is the process of constructing biblical theory on the realia of archaeology. Palestinian archaeology had become merely a field adjunct of this process.

As a result of his research, Albright (1932a: 129) drew up a research agenda for biblical archaeology. Although the aim of the agenda was not spelled out, the questions to be researched came out of his archaeologically induced change of heart. The agenda was a program of research to contest the school of Wellhausen. The great German Semiticist proposed that the cultural elements of the Genesis narratives reflected the attitudes and life of the time when the accounts were written down, which he dated a thousand years after Abraham (Wellhausen 1885). Accordingly, the Genesis accounts contain no information of historical value. From this position, Wellhausen went on to reconstruct the history of the Hebrews using an evolutionary framework, which denied the role of Moses as lawgiver and looked to the Exilic period as the main formative event in the recording of the history of Israel. "The theory of Wellhausen will not bear the test of archaeological examination," wrote Albright (1932a: 129), flatly stating his views. From that a priori position, Albright proposed three areas of inquiry to demonstrate the failure of the Wellhausen reconstruction. The first topic needing examination was the Patriarchal period, which Albright placed in the archaeological horizon of the early Middle Bronze Age. The second area involved the nature and antiquity of biblical law, a nonexcavation topic. The final area to be examined was the archaeological evidence of the Exile and the Return.

In his zeal to combat Wellhausen, Albright turned to the study of the Middle Bronze Age. He linked this period to the Patriarchs and made this horizon the archaeological period most associated with his name. From the 1920s into the 1960s, he worked and reworked his reconstruction (e.g., 1924a, 1949, 1961, 1966b). This study took him far beyond the archaeology of Palestine, as he dealt with Egypt, Syria, and Mesopotamia. The ultimate model was a product of Albright the Orientalist, not the archaeologist. His aim was a simple one: to demonstrate the basic accuracy of the biblical depiction of the world of Abraham.

The other field issue in Albright's 1932 agenda, the Exile and Return, became a forgotten concern. Not until the 1970s would research begin to focus on the Persian period in Palestine (e.g., Stern 1982). When Albright proposed this agenda, it was already clear that the Babylonian Conquest was as destructive as the Bible portrays it to have been. Major biblical issues of this period, such as the relationship of Ezra and Nehemiah and the Persian influence on Hebrew thought, are not amenable to solution by excavation or survey.

Instead, the issue of the Hebrew Conquest of Palestine became the other major arena of field research for biblical archaeology. G. Ernest Wright, Albright's ceramic student, made this issue his primary concern. Albright considered the Conquest a nonissue because he believed that archaeology "had already brought confirmation of Joshua, Judges, Samuel, and Kings" (1932a: 128). He came to this conclusion as a result of the work in the 1920s at Megiddo, Jericho, Ai, and Tell Beit Mirsim. The results of the excavations at Et-Tell, the suspected site of Ai, confirmed in Albright's eyes the veracity of Joshua's account: "It is interesting to note, that Ai was destroyed by the Hebrews as narrated in the Book of Joshua and never reoccupied in strict agreement with the Biblical tradition" (1928a: 8).

Albright's analysis of the Conquest issue reveals a fault common to archaeologists: the tendency to interpret general archaeological issues in terms of their own particular site. Tell Beit Mirsim presented clear evidence of a massive destruction at the beginning of the Iron Age, the suggested date of the Conquest. As this seemed to agree with the biblical accounts, Albright did not question the supportive evidence from the Jericho defense system, although the dating was founded on very flimsy grounds. Tell Beit Mirsim yielded a destruction date of c. 1200 B.C., and the Bible records the destruction of cities in the area of this tell; therefore, the Israelites destroyed the site, and the Conquest is demonstrated. Albright had no firm proof for his reconstruction, but nor did he have any negative evidence (at that stage). In his mind, the issue was settled. Only when evidence contradicting a direct reading of the Joshua accounts came to light in subsequent excavations at Ai and Jericho did the Conquest become an issue for biblical archaeology.

Syro-Palestinian Archaeology

Contemporary with the formulation of his agenda for biblical archaeology was the beginning of Albright's analysis of the Tell Beit Mirsim material. As a result of his focus on the realia of pottery, Albright's archaeological questions were predominantly physical in nature. When these questions were combined with a rigorous comparative method that looked beyond the biblical heartland of Palestine into Syria, a broadening of his archaeological horizons could have resulted. Whatever the reason, by 1938, Albright had emerged with a clear separation in his mind of biblical archaeology from Palestinian archaeology.

In 1938, Albright (1938c) used a new term for his field: Syro-Palestinian archaeology. This first appeared in a paper entitled "The Present State of Syro-Palestinian Archaeology," one of a series of papers on "Archaeology and the Bible" presented in a symposium at Haverford College. Albright surveyed Syria/Palestine as a single cultural area, a geographic unity. He gave two justifications for the study of this area: (1) a broadly humanistic aim of comparative archaeology and (2) because Syria/Palestine provided the immediate backdrop to biblical history and literature. He began his survey with the Middle Paleolithic, considered climatology to be of vital import, and urged more work in Syria. He made the prescient statement that "Ibla [Ebla] means nothing to us!" (16).

Albright mentioned events in biblical history in the survey. However, such events as the Hebrew Conquest were discussed in relation to the archaeological history of Syria/Palestine. The framework was archaeology, not biblical narrative. Here the Bible functioned only as another source of historical information. In keeping with this approach, the term biblical archaeology was not used.

Albright was speaking here as an archaeologist, not a biblical scholar; therefore, he viewed archaeology in Syria/Palestine as a branch of general archaeology. This is clear from the first justification he gave for excavation. This change in perspective was most likely a result of his work on the Tell Beit Mirsim material. To properly publish those results he had to think first as an archaeologist. This mental shift carried over into the 1938 presentation. Unfortunately, as Albright became more interested in a broad cross-cultural approach, the separation of Syro-Palestinian archaeology from biblical archaeology faded, and his 1938 article had little impact.

Albright's Theology

Albright's anti-Wellhausen stance in his study *Archaeology of Palestine and the Bible* quickly elicited a theological reaction. He complained, "Two American reviewers have alluded to the writer's supposed tendency to fundamentalism" (1934a: 28). He did sound like a fundamentalist when he discussed the impact of archaeological research on the Bible in phrases reminiscent of prewar conservatives: "Discovery after discovery has established the accuracy of innumerable details, and has brought increased recognition of the Bible as a source of history" (1932a: 128). However, he correctly rejected the accusation of fundamentalism. He had concluded in the book under review that archaeology "does not support either the extreme radical school of Biblical Scholars or the ultra-conservative wing" (129). He had attacked fundamentalism's basis: verbal inspiration. "On the other hand, the theory of verbal inspiration—sometimes miscalled a doctrine—has been proved erroneous" (128). He had placed himself solidly in the middle of the theological spectrum.

Albright's biblical archaeology had no overt theological axes to grind. He walked the middle road, avoiding theological controversy as much as possible. He was able to stay above the fray by virtue of his location. He remained in Palestine at the Jerusalem School until 1929, with the exception of a sabbatical year in 1927. Neither side could call on him as a speaker, and he carefully avoided writing on the issue. His distance from the United States undoubtedly lessened the heat of the fundamentalist-modernist arguments when they finally did reach Jerusalem. Because he was not ordained, he was not forced by denominational pressure to take a specific stance. When Albright did return to the United States, he went to a nontheological, academic position that was not in a seminary. Johns Hopkins provided him with a noncontroversial position that enabled him to continue research in a nontheological context. He did not hold to verbal inspiration (Albright 1932a: 128); hence his own personal faith was not under direct attack. He could afford to be a dispassionate observer.

Theology always took a back seat in the writings of Albright. There are no more than a handful of purely theological (Christian) writings catalogued by Freedman (1975) in his comprehensive bibliography of Albright (more than one thousand entries). Albright was always very private about his own beliefs. In an article for a collection entitled *American Spiritual Autobiographies*, the author approached his subject as a historian (Albright 1948). With slight changes, this article was reprinted in 1964 (Albright 1964a: 301–22). Albright opened with a discussion of the problems inherent in biography and wrote the early portions of his life story in the third person. He wrote about his own theology in a section entitled "Credo ut intellegam." In Jerusalem, he began reading neo-orthodox theologians such as Karl Barth. Combined with his own archaeological research and his wife's conversion to Catholicism, the "outcome could scarcely be in doubt; with powerful forces pulling in opposite directions at all times, one's position is likely to become more or less stabilized in the middle" (320). Albright's discussion remained curiously at a distance. He presented the role of the theologian, but gave only glimpses of his own beliefs (322). He wrote as objectively as possible, but as a result, the reconstruction was only a shadow of the man.

Albright strongly supported the basic historicity of the Bible, but he did not draw any theological lessons from this. He clearly opposed Wellhausen's work, but not with the purpose of supporting the Bible as the Word of God. Unlike his student Wright, Albright was more concerned with what archaeology tells us about ourselves than what it tells us about God. In a sense, his purpose in rescuing the Old Testament from Wellhausen was to make Scripture a usable and valid insight into ancient life. His approach to the Bible and its witness was primarily as an archaeologist and Orientalist.

Conversely, Albright allowed biblical studies to set the agenda for archaeology. However, he asked only questions that were in essence historical, such as When was this city destroyed? He dealt only with questions that were answerable with demonstrable data. He did not deal with questions of faith; he was always determined to be the scientist. There was a naïveté about Albright on this issue (Dever 1993). Whether he willed it or not, his attempt to ground biblical studies in science had an immense theological impact. Any scholarly model that affects the way the Bible is viewed will always cause changes in theological thought, and Albright's biblical archaeology was no exception.

Nelson Glueck

The leading archaeological figure associated with a more conservative position on the Bible was Nelson Glueck (figure 2.4). Being Jewish, Glueck was a unique

FIGURE 2.4 Nelson Glueck. Courtesy of American Schools of Oriental Research (ASOR)

figure in the Protestant-dominated endeavor of biblical archaeology. He was an ordained rabbi who held a doctorate from the University of Jena in Germany. He went to Jerusalem in 1926 to study at the American School. Albright was the director at the time, and Glueck soon joined the Tell Beit Mirsim excavation, which provided the raw material for his training. He followed Albright's example and became a pottery expert under the Master's tutelage. "This he accomplished," said Albright, "by working through the pottery of each day recording its features and regularly attending our informal sessions on the stratigraphy and typology of the pottery." The result was impressive: "While he learned the principles of stratigraphy, it was as a typologist that he distinguished himself" (1971: 3). Albright could give no higher praise.

In 1932, Glueck (1934) began a survey of Transjordan, which at the time was largely archaeological terra incognita. Later, he expanded his surveys to include Sinai, the Negev, and the Jordan Valley (1935, 1939, 1940, 1946, 1951, 1959, 1965). Along with his survey interests, he excavated Khirbet-et-Tannur (a Nabatean temple) and Tell el-Kheleifeh, a site he identified as King Solomon's port city of Ezion-Geber (Glueck 1959). This twentieth-century Robinson surveyed over fifteen hundred sites, most never before recorded. He mapped them, sampled their pottery, and determined the local Arabic name. With this data, he would postulate a biblical identification.

Glueck eventually became director of the Jerusalem School for three different periods. He was in Jerusalem during the worst of the civil disorders that preceded World War II. During the war itself, he continued his surveys while scouting for the Office of Strategic Services (OSS), the wartime precursor of the CIA (Albright 1971; Fierman 1986). According to Fierman, Glueck was surveying water sources for a retreat line should the Germans break through at El Alamein (20). He also envisaged a more active role for himself, making plans to "organize a guerilla band of picked Arabs whom I have known for many years" (from a letter quoted in Fierman 1986: 22). Philip King criticized Glueck's OSS role, saying he thereby lost the confidence of the Arabs: "It is an unwritten law in the Mideast that archaeology and politics should never be mixed; when they are, it is always to the detriment of archaeology" (1983a: 103 n. 19). In principle, King is correct, and certainly any archaeologist who gets involved in modern Mideast politics risks great damage to archaeology (Meskell 1998). However, in Glueck's case, he was working for the governing power in Transjordan, which was allied to his own country. Moreover, he undoubtedly shared a reluctance to combine archaeology and espionage, and resigned at the end of the war.

On the basis of his regional surveys, Glueck reconstructed the archaeological history of Transjordan. He postulated a dense occupation in the late Early Bronze Age, which almost disappeared in the following Early Bronze IV phase. The decay of the urban centers he associated (following Albright 1932a) with the events surrounding the fall of Sodom and Gomorrah told in Genesis 18: 18–19: 29. During the rest of the Bronze Ages, Glueck believed Transjordan to have been virtually abandoned, arguing that the population remained nomadic or seminomadic, in marked contrast with Palestine: "The explanation both for the period of intensive settlement and for those of extended abandonment of these countries is to be found rather in strictly human, and particularly in political and economic factors than in climactic change" (1935: 141). In the thirteenth century B.C., urban settlements reappear, the homes of the biblical Ammonites, Moabites, and Edomites. This supported a late dating of the Israelite Conquest. Obviously, if the Israelites encountered the above-enumerated peoples, then the entrance into the Land did not occur until there were people in Transjordan to be encountered. Glueck's evidence would be taken up and used by Albright and Wright in their Conquest model (see below). He postulated a second major gap for the Late Iron II period through the Persian period.

Glueck's reconstruction has been overturned by more recent data. In a major review of Glueck's model, James Sauer (1986) has convincingly demonstrated that the Middle and Late Bronze Ages were urban periods in at least northern and central Transjordan: "It is clearly incorrect that Transjordan was largely semi-nomadic in the Late Bronze Age. Rather, a system of city-states like that found in Palestine can be documented" (8). The Late Iron II/Persian period is also a time of settlement in Transjordan. Despite these necessary revisions, Glueck's work remains "the standard reference work for the past forty years," in the words of another survey director in Jordan (MacDonald 1982: 37).

Glueck's excavations at Tell-el-Kheleifeh were much less successful. He uncovered a major structure that he originally identified as a copper smelter (1959: 163–65): "Each of the walls of its rooms was pierced by two rows of carefully constructed apertures, which could only be flues" (164). He found very little supporting evidence on the site for this interpretation of the building, and his idea has since been nearly universally rejected. Glueck (1977) eventually realized that the holes were from decayed timbers. His investigations of the Nabateans (1965) have survived critical scrutiny much better, again partly because most of the data derive from survey work, not excavation.

Glueck and the Bible

Glueck had a deep love for the Hebrew Bible, and a biblical orientation is never far below the surface in his archaeology. He held a very positive view of the historicity of Scripture. In *Rivers in the Desert*, he addressed the question "Is the Bible true?", opening his response with a disclaimer: "The purpose of the Biblical historian and archaeologist is, however, not to 'prove' the correctness of the Bible. It is primarily a theological document, which can never be 'proved' because it is based on a belief in God, whose Being can be scientifically suggested but never scientifically demonstrated" (1959: 30–31). Unlike some Protestant conservatives, he did not insist on a literal interpretation of Scripture. In keeping with the rabbinic tradition, he accepted the existence of legend and folklore in the Bible, and from that standpoint he issued a famous (or infamous) statement: "It may be categorically stated that no archaeological discovery has ever controverted a Biblical reference" (31).

Glueck wrote after the work of both Kenyon at Jericho and the French at Et-Tell had challenged a straightforward acceptance of the book of Joshua, and he must have been aware of these discoveries and the issues they raised. A possible explanation for his statement may lie in his view of what constituted a "biblical reference." By allowing folklore and legend to enter the picture, Glueck did leave room for a nonliteral approach to a purported historical account. This is not explicitly stated, but it appears to be the only possible way of reconciling his statement with the evidence known at the time he made it. He was a major public figure in biblical archaeology, and his views on the reliability of the Bible helped give the Albright school an aura of fundamentalism.

Summary

After Albright left the Jerusalem School to go to Johns Hopkins, he broadened his interests to include psychology (1942a: 5) and the philosophy of history (1964a: 309). Using the insights gained from the study of these diverse fields, he undertook an examination of the development of Hebrew religious thought in the context of the entire Near East. He did not approach the material as an archaeologist, but the foundation for his research remained the realia of biblical archaeology. The result of this labor was his magnum opus, *From the Stone Age to Christianity* (1940).

In this monumental work, Albright synthesized the results of twenty years of archaeological research revolving around the Bible. Using these data as the base, he constructed a case for the uniqueness of Hebrew revelation, in particular the monotheism of Moses. Throughout this study, subtitled *Monotheism and the Historical Process*, Albright approached his data as a philosopher-historian. He defined himself as "a resolute 'positivist' but—only in so far as positivism is the expression of the modern rational-scientific approach to physical and historical reality" (1964a: 140). Although this self-definition was a product of Albright's later writings, it accurately depicted his thinking in 1940. Here he defined the difference between history and science as "primarily a difference in the degree of variability and not in logical method" (1940: 116). For Albright, archaeology was able to bring the degree of variability in biblical history much closer to that of the sciences. He presented Christianity as the culmination of religious development of the ancient Near East, which transcended cultural boundaries and entered the Greek world at an opportune time: "Jesus Christ appeared on the scene just when occidental civilization had reached a fatal impasse" (403). Christianity should be accepted today not because it is true (which Albright did believe), but because it is the highest form of religious thought, unique in the ancient world, and hence acceptable to the scientist.

Albright wrought a revolution in biblical studies. John Miles (1976), in a particularly creative analysis of Albright, portrayed his thought as a "paradigm shift," a term borrowed from a historian of science, Thomas Kuhn (1970). Kuhn identified two types of change in the paradigms that guide scientific research: (1) shifts that occur as the result of new discoveries and (2) shifts that occur as the result of new theories. The new paradigm enables scientists to see their field differently and to make progress in areas that previously were blocked. According to Kuhn, paradigm shifts are irrevocable, with the old paradigm never again able to dominate the field. Miles analyzed Albright's grounding of biblical studies in archaeology as a change in paradigm due to new discoveries. These new discoveries were the archaeological evidence anomalous to "the assured results of higher criticism," that is, the antiquity of law, the evidence of the Babylonian Conquest, and the recovery of the Patriarchal culture. As evidence of the new paradigm, Albright attracted adherents from competing modes of thought and enabled new research to be carried out (by Wright and others). Rooted in the realia of archaeology, Albright upset the apple cart of biblical criticism by bringing (perceived) objective data to bear on the subjectivity of biblical criticism. By rescuing the historical underpinning of the biblical accounts, he changed the paradigm by preventing biblical scholars from dismissing accounts as "unhistorical" on a priori grounds. A whole new set of questions should accompany a Kuhnian paradigm shift, and as a result of Albright's grounding of the Bible in realia, this is what happened. G.

Ernest Wright took the final step and extended Albright's synthesis to its ultimate theological conclusion. He would ask new questions in theology based on Albright's reconstruction, becoming a major figure in the Biblical Theology Movement.

Mortimer Wheeler, the British master of method, described Palestine as a place "where more sins have probably been committed in the name of archaeology than on any commensurate part of the earth's surface" (1954: 30). Albright must shoulder part of the blame for this. He effectively prevented Palestinian archaeology from taking a place in general archaeology by limiting its research agenda to questions of biblical interest. With his biblical agenda, he made Palestinian archaeology a field adjunct to biblical studies. Through ceramic typology, he perfected a method that brilliantly answered historical questions but ignored economic and social ones. When archaeologists realized that nonbiblical questions are equally valid, Albrightian biblical archaeology came under attack.

Albright spoke with a combined voice that appealed to both constituencies of American Palestinian archaeology. His acknowledged ceramic expertise enabled him to gain a hearing from his archaeological colleagues, and his biblical writings made him acceptable to biblical scholars and the biblical supporters of archaeology. The Albright appeal was unique and fixed him in the mind of the general public as *the* Palestinian archaeologist. The popular press was very interested in archaeology in the 1920s (Davidson 1996), and Albright benefited from this interest. His ability to attract students made biblical archaeology the most viable American model in Palestinian archaeology when World War II ended fieldwork. He attracted students because he was perceived as the best in the business. After World War II, the leaders of American Palestinian archaeology would all be students of Albright. As a result, biblical archaeology became the model for American excavation into the 1960s.

3

Biblical Archaeology
Triumphant

In the Palestinian-dominated field research of biblical archaeology, the mantle of Elijah passed on to a student of Albright's, George Ernest Wright (figure 3.1). Wright produced a crucial change in the paradigm of biblical archaeology. He took the "scientific" construct of the field and gave it a positive rationale for existence. He made biblical archaeology the support structure for a positivist theological understanding known as the Biblical Theology Movement. Wright completed the process begun by Albright of making biblical archaeology a synonym for Palestinian archaeology. The Albright-Wright archaeological reconstruction of the history of Israel is what is commonly known as biblical archaeology.

George Ernest Wright: Theologian and Archaeologist

Wright worked actively in both theology and archaeology. One of his students, William G. Dever (1980a: 1), has labeled Wright's career "schizophrenic" because he appeared to oscillate between the two fields. In reality, Wright's theology and his archaeology interacted throughout his professional life, and results in one field often had an effect in the other. The biblical archaeology of Wright reflects this cross-fertilization.

Born in Zanesville, Ohio, George Ernest Wright was a graduate of the College of Wooster, a Presbyterian school in the same state. He

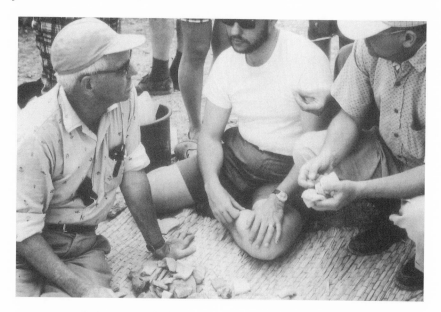

FIGURE 3.1 G. Ernest Wright (left) reading pottery. Courtesy of William G. Dever

felt called to be a minister and so continued his education at McCormick Theological Seminary in Chicago; on graduation, he was ordained into the ministry
of the United Presbyterian Church. In 1934 he visited Israel and joined the
staff of the Bethel excavations directed by Albright. Wright's experiences at
Bethel encouraged him to go to Johns Hopkins to study archaeology. Thanks
to his language training in seminary, he was able to finish quickly, receiving
his M.A. in 1936 and his Ph.D. the following year. He began teaching Old
Testament at McCormick in 1939.

Throughout the war years Wright maintained an interest in archaeology,
reviewing many archaeological publications. He returned to fieldwork in 1956
at Balatah, biblical Shechem. Drew University joined McCormick in sponsoring the excavations. In 1960 Wright moved to Harvard, continuing to excavate
at Shechem. In 1964, while he functioned as visiting archaeological director
at Hebrew Union College in Jerusalem, he began the reexcavation of Gezer.
He functioned as field director for the first year before turning the excavation
over to two students, H. Darrel Lance and William G. Dever. Wright became
president of ASOR in 1966, a post he held until his death in 1974. A strong
president, he oversaw the opening of the American Center of Oriental Research
(ACOR) in Amman and encouraged work in Cyprus. His most important legacy is the substantial influence his students have had on archaeology in Syria/
Palestine.

Theology

Although he never approached Albright's level of competence in biblical studies (particularly in linguistics), the younger man surpassed his teacher as a
theological thinker. During the McCormick years, Wright established himself
in the public eye as a theologian. Wright the theologian overshadowed Wright
the archaeologist until he began to excavate at Shechem.

During World War II, Wright published his first book on theology under
the title *The Challenge of Israel's Faith* (1944), in which he called for a revival
of the Old Testament in the Christian community. He argued that the neglect
of the Hebrew Scripture in the Christian community had led to a distorted
view of the nature of God, resulting from a belief that the Old Testament was
irrelevant for the formulation of Christian doctrine. "This belief," contended
Wright, "misses the really essential point about the biblical revelation: that is,
God has made himself known, not primarily in ideas, but in events" (101). This
was a call for a return to a fully biblical theology, resting on the witness of both
testaments.

Wright became recognized as a spokesman for a theological perspective
known as Biblical Theology, which attempted to rescue the Old Testament for
the Church (Dever 1959). Biblical Theology grew out of a frustration with the
critical/scholarly approach that secularized Scripture (Barr 1976; Childs 1970;
Wright 1944, 1952). The movement can be considered an attempt at a synthesis
of the fundamentalist-modernist controversy. From the conservative side came
the appreciation of the necessity of placing theological aspects in the center of
biblical study. From the liberals came the critical tools to pare away later ac-
cretions from the original events. The historical/critical methodology of biblical
studies was still accepted, but it was used to concentrate on the events recorded
in the Bible, rather than to focus on the literary treatment of these events.
Certainly Albright recognized the importance that his own work had on the
new theological movement: "Archaeological discovery has been largely responsible for the recent revival of interest in biblical theology . . . Neither an academic scholasticism, nor an irresponsible neo-orthodoxy must be allowed to
divert our eyes from the living faith of the Bible" (1952: 550). Biblical Theology
had the ability to absorb the work of new scholars who were not associated
with its main goals (Childs 1970), a trait that contributed a great deal to its
survival.

Wright believed there was a major problem with the way the Bible was
studied and presented in biblical scholarship. The idea of revelation was un-
settling to the intellectual world, but had to be wrestled with when studying
the Bible. He recognized the "fallacy of a completely objective, cultural, or

dispassionate study of Scripture" (1946: 88). "We need to frankly recognize our presuppositions and not blind ourselves by a denial that they exist," removing the "delusion of objectivity" (89).

In keeping with this aim, Wright presented his own presuppositions: (1) to take biblical theism and supernaturalism very seriously; (2) to see the unifying factor as the will and purpose of God; and (3) to have a sympathetic, understanding faith for the best biblical scholarship (1946: 90–93). From this basis, he formulated the aims of biblical study: (1) to attempt to gain a view of the Bible as a whole; (2) to discover the meaning of the Bible against all other systems of faith; and (3) to take a stand pro or contra the essentials of its proclamation. Wright sought to "re-establish Biblical Theology on a sound intellectual footing" (93). In some ways, he wanted to do for theology what Albright had done for biblical studies. As it was for Albright, biblical archaeology would be Wright's method.

Wright and his colleagues sought to return the divine-human encounter to the central point of focus in theology. Wright attempted to do this by concentrating on the acts of God in history (1952; Wright and Fuller 1957). He insisted on the unity of history and the biblical witness. His archaeological orientation kept him searching for the historical realia underlying the biblical record. This theme received its classic treatment in *God Who Acts: Biblical Theology as Recital* (Wright 1952). In the preface, Wright defined biblical theology as a "defensible entity of its own kind, it is a theology of recital or proclamation of the acts of God, together with the inferences drawn from them" (11). The historical aspect of this definition was key, because the "acts of God" occurred in a specific historical context. "Biblical Theology is the confessional result of the redemptive acts of God in a particular history, because history is the chief medium of revelation" (13). Here was the foundation on which Wright would build his view of biblical archaeology.

Wright rejected an evolutionary model for the development of Israel's faith, believing that such a model drew a false boundary between kerygma and didache: "It is impossible on any empirical grounds to understand how the God of Israel could have evolved out of polytheism. He is unique, sui generis, utterly different" (1952: 21). Thus, the problem of life in ancient Israel was to be understood against the backdrop of the will and purpose of God (see also Wright 1950a), expressed in the belief in Israel's election by grace with the reality of that election demonstrated by the saving acts of God. It was no accident that Wright emphasized the doctrine of election, as it is a foundational doctrine of Presbyterianism. "Election is more primary in Israel than covenant" (1952: 36 n. 1), and in election Wright found the key to understanding Israel.

Israel functioned in an atmosphere of hope based on trust. This was founded "on the certainty of the reality of God's working in every event" (Wright 1952: 25). Israel's most obvious difference from the surrounding Near Eastern countries was the intense attention paid to historic traditions. Wright understood the biblical view of history to be of "a meaningful process en route to a goal," which for him was the irreducible datum of biblical theology (40). Albright had supported this understanding in *From the Stone Age to Christianity* (1940). For Wright, the knowledge of God was "an inference from what actually happened in history"; therefore, "history is the revelation of God" (1952: 44, 50). "We today insist that facts should be verifiable but in Biblical history the primary meaning seen in events, and many matters which are considered events, are not verifiable" (117).

For Wright, faith was not verified by archaeology, but its reliability could be enhanced. Accordingly, if God is known through history, then any aid to the further understanding of the history of the community of Israel is actually an aid to the understanding of God. I believe this is the justification for Wright's archaeology: to better understand the "Mighty Acts of God."

As the work at Shechem began, Wright was highly optimistic about the effect of archaeology on the verification of Scripture: "In this perspective, the Biblical scholar no longer bothers to ask whether archaeology proves the Bible. In the sense that the Biblical languages, the life and systems of its people are illuminated in innumerable ways by the archaeological discoveries, he knows that such a question is certainly to be answered in the affirmative" (1962a: 27). He cautiously distanced himself from apologetical archaeology by stressing an objective approach to the data: "Our ultimate aim must not be 'proof' but truth. We must study the history of the Chosen people in exactly the same way as we do any other people, running the risk of destroying the uniqueness of that history. Unless we are willing to run that risk, truth can never be ours" (27).

Archaeological Training

Wright had his first taste of field archaeology while spending a summer in Israel after graduating from seminary. He developed an early interest in the subject, which the encounter with Albright at Bethel intensified, and at the end of the season at Bethel he went to Johns Hopkins University to study under him.

Following the example of his teacher, Wright specialized in pottery. His M.A. thesis provided the subject matter for his first published article, a study of the ceramic chronology of the Early Bronze Age (Wright 1936). He divided the period into four phases, being the first to isolate an "Early Bronze IV" phase (phase "delta" in 1936, but in Wright 1937 referred to as EBIV). This study became part of his dissertation on the pottery of Palestine from the Neolithic through the end of the Early Bronze Age (Wright 1937). The dissertation focused solely on chronological questions, an approach Wright defended in the introduction: "A detailed study of the value of pottery for the history of human culture has yet to appear—its greatest value is undoubtedly chronological. Yet more exact studies in the future will perhaps allow the student of ethnology, commerce, and related subjects, to make far-reaching deductions from ceramic evidence, for which at present there is so little solid ground" (1). Wright was aware of the theoretical possibilities of ceramic study. However, he realized that unless the material could be securely dated, it would not be usable in any way. He hoped that his work would supplement the Tell Beit Mirsim volumes of Albright by clarifying the complex problems of pre-Middle Bronze pottery, which did not occur there.

Wright followed Albright's comparative methodology, arranging the pottery forms typologically and then checking them against known ceramic sequences, such as those from Beth-Shean and Megiddo. He focused solely on formal characteristics, partly because they were the "safest criteria" but also because he had to work at second hand, rarely handling the sherds themselves. He treated Syria/Palestine as a single cultural unit, comparing material from the northern sites when there was a lack in Palestine. Occasionally, he corrected stratigraphic assignments on typological grounds (e.g., at Megiddo [1937: 44]; this is certainly in the Albright tradition of typology over stratigraphy). For each of his four phases, Wright made correlations with contemporary Egyptian material to provide approximate absolute dates. Throughout the study, he showed a clear eye for form and the willingness to challenge established views if he thought the evidence dictated a change. Only when dealing with the question of Albright's Middle Bronze I (MBI) did Wright not take the evidence to its apparent conclusion. This is probably a result of being a student of Albright's, for Wright was well aware that his division between EBIV and MBI was an arbitrary one, and that Albright's MBI material at Tell Beit Mirsim might be more properly considered part of the EB tradition (1937: 3).

Wright's study was the state of the art for 1937. Albright praised his work in a letter to Elihu Grant, the excavator of Beth Shemesh: "My student, Mr G. E. Wright, who is writing an excellent thesis on the chronology of the EB in Palestine, is visiting the Beth-Shemesh Collection at Haverford; the EB pieces there belong to his phase delta of EB between 2300 and 2100" (UMA/Ain Shems/WFA to Grant 5/23/36). Wright was then invited by Grant to help study his material from Beth Shemesh, and he went on to coauthor the volumes of the Beth Shemesh material that concentrated on the pottery (Wright and Grant 1938, 1939), stressing the date of his new EBIV phase.

The Reviews

In 1939, Wright became a professor of the Old Testament at his alma mater, McCormick Theological Seminary. Despite the theological-biblical orientation necessitated in his career by his seminary appointment, his years at McCormick shaped Wright the archaeologist. Unable to excavate because of the war, he maintained his interest in archaeology by writing a series of reviews of the various archaeological publications that were being printed (Wright 1940, 1941a, 1941b, 1941c, 1941d, 1941e, 1942b). Writing these reviews gave him the opportunity to evaluate the competing methodologies of the previous generation against the standard of the usefulness of their results.

Ceramic issues dominate Wright's reviews, reflecting his own interests. He found Barrois's *Manuel d'archéologie biblique* to be a good handbook but lacking in ceramic exactitude (Wright 1940). He considered this to be a fault of the Ecole and their acknowledged expert, Père Vincent, to be contrasted with the Albright approach of stratigraphy-and-typology, which was no longer content with "ceramic guesswork" but sought to date a "homogeneous locus" to within a quarter century (401). Wright (1941e) was very pleased with Lachish II (Tufnell, Inge, and Harding 1940), considering it to be an excellent publication on the grounds not only that the wealth of cultic information unearthed was of clear biblical importance, but also that the ceramic evidence to date the LB temples was clearly presented. He did not confine himself to Palestinian material, but reviewed Syrian publications as well (1941f, 1942b). He praised Ingholt's Hama report for the "wealth of information" it contained, in particular the excellent pottery sequence dating to the Arab period, even though he was more interested in the second millennium B.C. material from strata M, L, K, and J. Elsewhere (Wright 1941f), he noted in passing that in Ehrich's study of the pottery of the Jebeleh region, twenty-one sherds were petrologically analyzed, but he did not appear to be too interested in the process.

Nonceramic issues received some consideration from Wright, but in a secondary capacity. He criticized Alan Rowe's Beth Shan volume because foundation deposits were used to date the temples (Wright 1941c). He argued that there was no evidence to indicate that the "foundation deposits" actually functioned as such, and that they may have been simply debris covered in the building of the temples and therefore useful only as a terminus post quem for their date. Wright (1941d) even strayed beyond the Old Testament period in reviewing the study of the Medeba map by Avi-Yonah. He could find no fault with Nelson Glueck's survey results published as *The Other Side of the Jordan*, considering his work to be of fundamental significance, declaring, "Glueck's explorations are second in importance to none, unless it is those of Edward Robinson" (Wright 1941b: 194).

During these war years, Wright took advantage of his location in Chicago to attend seminars at the Oriental Institute with Robert Braidwood and Henri Frankfort. The seminars focused on prehistoric matters and stressed an anthropological-ecological approach very different from Albright's historical methodology (Stager, Walker, and Wright 1974: xvi). At the end of his career, looking back on this period, Wright (1975: 107) claimed that the seminars were highly valuable. He was not blind to anthropological concerns, having written about the nonchronological value of pottery for the archaeologist in his dissertation (Wright 1937: 1). Robert Braidwood (according to Wright, the first member of the seminar to enter the field) championed a multidisciplinary approach in his postwar researches. These were focused on the beginnings of domestication in the Levant (Braidwood and Howe 1960). Wright claimed to have a similar multidisciplinary goal at his major excavation of Shechem, but says he failed because the natural scientists he approached did not have an interest in historical archaeology (Stager et al. 1974: xvi). The seminars had an impact on him, but he seems to have appreciated them only at the end of his life. When compared with his approach at Shechem (see below), his praise for the Chicago seminars seems to be more reflective of his own changes at the end of his career than a measure of the impact they had on him in the 1940s.

Wright continued to critique archaeology from his armchair after the war ended. He reacted to the publication of the second Megiddo volume in both a short review (1950c) and a more substantial study (1950b), finding that he had to rework each stratum to make the information useful (1950c: 57). Following the lead of Albright, he advocated a major revision of the Iron Age levels at Megiddo based on the typological study of the pottery. The excavators believed that stratum IV was the major Israelite settlement phase. Albright and Wright challenged this, arguing that the earlier stratum V was incorrectly separated from stratum IV: The proper separation should actually be VB, followed by VA-IVB as one unit (dating to the Solomonic period) and then IVA dating to the ninth century B.C. of King Ahab.

Wright's Developing View of Biblical Archaeology

Wright presented his understanding of biblical archaeology in his first major postwar article, "Biblical Archaeology Today" (1947). He defined this endeavor as "a special 'armchair' variety of general archaeology which studies the discoveries of excavators and gleans from them every fact which throws a direct, indirect or even diffused light upon the Bible" (7). This definition was advanced in response to a perceived confusion in the theory of biblical archaeology:

> The term [biblical archaeology] is often used in almost synonymous parallelism with Palestinian archaeology, but it is obvious that much with which the latter deals has little to do with the Bible nor have all Palestinian archaeologists been primarily interested in Biblical matters. In the past, and occasionally even in the present, the term has been used by some to include virtually the whole of pre-Mohammedan archaeology in Biblical lands. Yet here again it is obvious that Biblical archaeology is something definite and more confined, since Near Eastern archaeology has long since thrown off any primary interest in the Bible, while classical archaeology has rarely had such an interest. (7)

This highly illuminating statement of Wright's own views hints that his own mind may not have been settled on this point. He looked back over the previous generation's efforts and lamented the inadequacy of past excavations and their poor publishing record. He then listed what he considered to be the most urgent tasks for biblical archaeology, with an outline of sites to be dug:

> Specifically New Testament sites have rarely been dug in Palestine, and more attention should be paid to them. Further excavations in Syria and Lebanon, particularly in Iron Age sites, are sorely needed. In Palestine the areas of Galilee, Transjordan, and Samaria have scarcely been more than touched. Such an important site as Hazor should certainly be dug, and renewed studies of such old sites as Gezer, Eglon (Tell-el-Hesi) and Gerar with new excavations should make the older reports more usable. (24)

This paragraph was the only reference Wright made to excavation among the tasks he saw facing biblical archaeology—and the only locale for that excavation was the cultural sphere of Syria/Palestine! By setting such practical parameters to biblical archaeology's fieldwork, Wright treated biblical archaeology and Syro-Palestinian archaeology as synonymous. Despite his de jure view that Palestinian archaeology "has little to do with the Bible," his de facto treatment denied this. Biblical archaeology's field component was the archaeology of Syria/Palestine.

The tension between de jure and de facto definitions underlies the designation of the handicaps Wright saw obstructing the progress of biblical archaeology. The first of these handicaps was the lack of trained biblical archaeologists. In the United States there was only one figure: Albright. Wright noted that the "Oriental Institute, the outstanding center of Near Eastern archaeology in this country, to my knowledge has never had a Biblical archaeologist on its staff" (1947: 7). He did not include the Megiddo staff, which shows recognition of the distinction of Palestinian archaeology from biblical archaeology: the de jure definition at work.

Wright listed the lack of broad humanistic interest and training among archaeology students as another major handicap. "Archaeology is a branch of the humanities," he wrote. "Its aim is the interpretation of life and culture of ancient civilizations in the perspective of the whole history of man" (1947: 8). This was a cultural-historical approach reflective of the de jure view of biblical archaeology. The tension between the de jure separation and the de facto assimilation of biblical archaeology and Syro-Palestinian archaeology resurfaced in Wright's later writings.

Wright returned to the subject in a major way in his popular treatise *Biblical Archaeology* (1962a, revised edition). In this book, first published as he was beginning excavation at Shechem, Wright added an element to his "armchair" definition of ten years before. Describing the role of a biblical archaeologist, he stated that the so-named individual may or may not be an excavator (17). Someone who excavates in the field is not an "armchair" researcher; yet, in Wright's view, an excavator was still a biblical archaeologist, not a Palestinian archaeologist—a return to the de facto equivalency. Wright saw himself as a biblical archaeologist; therefore, what he did was biblical archaeology.

The Wheeler-Kenyon Method

By the time Wright was ready to return to archaeological fieldwork in the Shechem excavations, a revolution was occurring in field methodology in Palestine. The new prophet in field archaeology was Kathleen Kenyon, a British archaeologist who had first worked in Palestine before the war at Samaria (figure 3.2). In 1952 she began a reexamination of Tell es-Sultan, the biblical site of Jericho.

Kenyon had gained her initial archaeological experience with Sir Mortimer Wheeler (1954) in the late 1920s at Verulamium (St. Albans) in England. Wheeler had obtained excellent results through a stratigraphically oriented method that made extensive use of vertical sections. Kenyon wrote, "Excavating on a Romano-British site is possibly the best training a beginner can get. The structural remains are usually substantial and the levels well defined, while the problems involved require careful working out. A student well-grounded in

FIGURE 3.2 Kathleen Kenyon. Courtesy of William G. Dever

such work can easily adapt himself to the more elusive structures of other periods, or the more complex problems of eastern archaeology" (1953: 35).

Kenyon took the Wheeler methodology and applied it to a tell site at Jericho. "The method of excavation," she wrote, "is therefore to combine the complete clearance of a selected area with the recording of stratification" (1953: 94). This was achieved by the use of a grid system; however, unlike Fisher's grid system, the Wheeler-Kenyon grid was used for the actual excavation, not just as a recording tool. In this system, "the site is excavated in a series of squares, separated by baulks which are left standing and which thus provide keys to the stratification" (95). The baulk grid is the visual distinguishing mark of the new techniques, providing the archaeologist with a clear stratigraphic record. Kenyon stressed the necessity of obtaining a large exposure on a tell, arguing that a sondage should be used only for the purpose of determining the range of occupation (102–7). The goal was to gain a stratigraphic understanding of the site, not just the recovery of floor plans. Thus, the excavator of a square did not simply mechanically remove all of the material within the baulks but, when encountering walls, sank probes at right angles to them in order that the layers within the square could be correlated with the wall, which was in turn linked up with the baulk to provide a complete stratigraphic sequence. This was especially necessary on a tell site owing to the common problem of later pitting and robbing. This stratigraphic methodology was much better equipped to handle a tell than the Fisher method or its modifications, and wrought a revolution in the area, ultimately becoming the dominant excavation mode. Wright (1962b: 39) christened the resulting method Wheeler-Kenyon in honor of its principal sponsors.

Albright (1958: 21–22) made a passing reference to the Kenyon methodology in a review of Samaria-Sebaste III. He considered her work valuable but felt that the new methodology should only "supplement rather than displace" what he referred to as "the Reisner-Fisher methods" (22 n. 2).

Wright at Shechem

In 1956, Wright (1965) left the armchair and returned to fieldwork in Palestine, forming the Drew-McCormick Archaeological Expedition. He represented McCormick Seminary as the archaeological director, with Bernhard W. Anderson of Drew University acting as administrative director. Because the American School in Jerusalem was now in Jordanian territory, a site had to be chosen on the Jordanian side of the armistice borderline. Balatah, the site of biblical Shechem, seemed to Wright to be the most promising. In accordance with the "urgent tasks" that he had formulated just after World War II (Wright 1947), it was a site that needed reexcavation for the earlier results to be comprehensible. German excavation teams under the Austrian biblical scholar Sellin and the classical archaeologist Welter had previously worked at Balatah both before World War I and from 1926 to 1934 (Stekeweh was field archaeologist in 1934; results summarized in Wright 1965: 23–34). However, due to the destruction of Sellin's records during the firebombing of Berlin, the publication of the work was in a very preliminary form.

The Shechem Methods

Wright (1969a: 132) excavated Shechem with the stated intention of combining Kathleen Kenyon's new methodology with the ceramic expertise of the Albright school. Furthermore, the complicated nature of the archaeological remains at Shechem would make a perfect training excavation for desperately needed new archaeologists. "It was mandatory, therefore, that some young biblical scholars be trained to carry on the standards set between the wars by W. F. Albright and Nelson Glueck" (Wright 1965: 36). Wright was referring to the ceramic expertise of the aforementioned scholars, the distinctive American specialty that he intended the new students to carry on. Notice that Wright considered "biblical scholars" to be the pool of available talent.

Despite the biblical orientation of his expected team, Wright led a professional archaeological enterprise: "Palestinian and Biblical archaeologists" (notice the linkage of the two) "are no less rigorous in their use of archaeological and historical method than their colleagues in other fields" (1965: xvi). Wright was willing to borrow Kenyon's method simply because it worked. Dever (1980a) has pointed out the "Yankee pragmatism" that lay at the basis of Wright's field archaeology. Wright must be saluted for his willingness to try the new Kenyon method, for it was a radical break with what he had first learned more than twenty years before at Bethel.

At the same time, Wright did not abandon the ceramic orientation he learned from Albright. At Shechem, the locus was the basis for recording. A locus was defined as a consistent and clearly defined small plot that is producing artifacts (Wright 1965: 52). For each locus, the pottery basket number recorded the finds. Wright (1962b: 39) adapted this aspect of the Shechem pottery system from the system of the Israeli archaeologist Yigael Yadin, which was devised for the Hazor excavations in the 1950s. This system allowed the pottery from each locus to act as an independent check on the stratigraphic quality of the dig. In the volume of the Shechem project that deals with the Middle Bronze II pottery, Cole reported on the importance assigned at Shechem to the thorough study of sherd material:

> All pottery was saved from each digging locus until it had been
> washed and examined. Usually several basket separations were
> made within a single digging locus, in order to ensure maximum
> control over the separation of materials from adjacent soil layers. Af-
> ter the washed sherds from each basket were examined to deter-
> mine the periods represented by the analytical pieces (pieces show-
> ing rim, handle, base or distinctive decoration or ware features) a
> record was made of this information and the bulk of the pottery was
> then discarded. From most baskets from potentially significant loci,
> however, a selection of analytical sherds were retained and given in-
> dividual registry numbers. (1984: 3)

Careful attention to the ceramic evidence enabled Wright to reassess the principles governing the interpretation of fill debris. He showed his originality in cautioning against the blanket following of any general rule regarding tell debris: "In the Shechem excavation we have decided on only one definite rule regarding fills: that each one is a special case and requires a special inquiry as to is origin and function" (1962b: 39). Wright's inquiries into the formation of fills were directed to one end: the use of fills in dating structures and layers. The material in a fill can at best provide only a terminus post quem from the latest material it contains. Edward F. Campbell (2002: 5) describes the Shechem methodology as a "conversation between stratigraphy and pottery analysis." The realia of the Shechem excavations completed Wright's break with the Fisher system. Wright's method at Shechem recalled the pioneering work of Reisner, although Wright was not interested in tell formation per se. He did not laud Reisner until a post-Shechem article he wrote on field methodology (1969a). If he had realized the implications of Reisner's work during the Shechem excavations, the escape from the limitations of historically oriented research in Palestinian archaeology might have occurred earlier, and with less pain.

Results from Shechem

Wright (1965) excavated Shechem to uncover a complete plan of the city and its history through reexcavation at carefully chosen locations. He was especially interested in the sacred area uncovered by Sellin, as a clear possibility of biblical correlation existed. Wright wanted to determine the nature of the large structure called a temple by Sellin, and to date it accurately. In Genesis 12: 6–7, Shechem is the site of a Patriarchal place of worship, and a temple at Shechem is mentioned in the biblical accounts of the city in Judges (9: 4 and 9: 46). Wright (1963) had these passages in mind as he dug. He was intrigued by the possibilities of sacred continuity in the temple area and concentrated a great deal of effort on clarifying the stratigraphy of the sacred precinct. Finally, Judges 9: 42–49 relates the story of Shechem's destruction, and Wright also wished to check this (1965; figure 3.3).

Thanks to his careful analysis of the fill material underlying Sellin's temple, Wright postulated an MBIIC date for the first major phase of the structure, which he equated with the biblical style of temple called a migdol, or "fortress-temple," mentioned in Judges 9. He determined the function of the building from its floorplan (which matched what was clearly a temple at Megiddo) and the provision for "standing stones" (masseboth) at the entrance. After the Egyptians destroyed the city at the end of the Middle Bronze Age, the temple was rebuilt on the same locale with a slightly altered orientation. In front of the rebuilt temple Sellin had found a stone socket in situ, which Wright (1965: 86) interpreted as the resting place for a large masseboth found lying across

FIGURE 3.3 The Gate at Shechem. Photo by author

the socket. Wright believed this to be the stone "erected in the sanctuary of the Lord" according to Joshua 24: 26 (figure 3.4). The temple he equated with the temple of Baal-berith mentioned in Judges 9: 4. Wright emphasized the cultic continuity of the site in an article on Shechem for the *Encyclopedia of Archaeological Excavations in the Holy Land*:

> A continuation of this cultic tradition seems to be present in three
> very different types of biblical literature: the patriarchal narratives,
> Joshua 24 and Judges 9, which refer to a sacred place, tree, and cov-
> enant. The name of the deity mentioned there, El-Berith, may well
> go back to patriarchal and Amorite times. At any rate it can no
> longer be simply assumed to be "Canaanite" of the Late Bronze Age
> type. The central cultic object was apparently a sacred stone, which
> in the second millennium appears to have been used, not only as a
> memorial for important ancestors, but also as a witness to an experi-
> ence of theophany or covenant. (1978: 1092)

Wright must be criticized for his reasoning here. The connection of the biblical migdol-style temple to the Field V temple may be an acceptable correlation, considering the physical characteristics of the Shechem structure; that it is a temple is beyond reasonable doubt, especially in light of the recent evidence from Ebla. What is not a certain equation is that the Late Bronze

FIGURE 3.4 The "Standing Stone" at Shechem. Photo by author

standing stone equates with the Patriarchal memorial of a theophany. Wright used the archaeological evidence of sacred continuity to support the historicity not only of the Judges account, but of the Patriarchal account as well. There is no evidence at all for the tree mentioned in Genesis, and essentially it is a leap of faith to equate the MBIIC shrine with activity of the Patriarchs.

Classic Biblical Archaeology

The Shechem expedition came at the high-water mark of biblical archaeology. Albright and Wright had together created an archaeologically based reconstruction of the history of ancient Israel that appeared unassailable. Albright viewed the biblical data as an Orientalist, particularly when dealing with the Patriarchal narratives. He used them as an unconscious model to understand the early second millennium in its entire cultural sphere. Wright came to the Bible as a theologian, seeking to elucidate the historical events that Hebrew tradition interpreted as actions of God. They shared a high regard for the basic historicity of the biblical narratives, based on the conviction that archaeology had provided innumerable examples of support for them. The two men shared the belief in archaeology as realia—realia on which they built biblical archaeology.

The Definition of Biblical Archaeology

Near the end of his active career, Albright (1964a: 307) defined himself not as a biblical archaeologist, or even as a Palestinian archaeologist, but as an Orientalist. His increasing interest in the Orientalist perspective led him to a broad definition of the arena of biblical archaeology. His first major postwar work on Palestinian archaeology was simply entitled *The Archaeology of Palestine* (1949). In this study, he followed the archaeological sequence in Palestine, not a biblical framework. The key use for archaeology in dealing with the Bible was as an aid in the location of sites and in providing illumination—giving a cultural background to the biblical accounts. There are no indications in this study of the anti-Wellhausen agenda. However, it was not the result of a change in Albright's thinking, but rather of his belief that the battle had been won and the Bible set on relatively firm historical footing.

In the 1960s, Albright (1966a, 1966c, 1969) presented his penultimate definition of biblical archaeology. The chronological spread was from 10,000 B.C. to the present day; the geographical milieu stretched from the Atlantic to the Indus, and from southern Russia to south Arabia. "Anything that illustrates the Bible" was a legitimate interest of biblical archaeology (1966a: 13). Albright explicitly stated what Wright (1947) had denied twenty years before: that biblical archaeology was equal to the study of the entire ancient Near East. "Biblical archaeology covers all the lands mentioned in the Bible, and is thus co-extensive with the cradle of civilization" (Albright 1966c: 1). Albright had returned to the overarching views of the nineteenth century. More than this, the Albrightian definition of biblical archaeology reflected Albright himself. Although the chronological framework was somewhat modified in the later article (from 9000 B.C.E. to approximately 700 C.E.: "All other periods are of diminishing returns"; 1969: 1), the definition is presumptuous from anyone but him. Of all the scholars active in studying the ancient Near East, only Albright had the knowledge and ability to talk on equal terms with archaeologists, biblical scholars, and linguistic specialists. By calling himself an Orientalist, he defined what a biblical archaeologist was supposed to be. If we accept his definition, there has been only one full member of the field: Albright himself.

Wright also dealt with Palestinian archaeology without primarily focusing on the biblical connection. In 1961 he wrote an article on Palestinian archaeology for a Festschrift for Albright. Wright was in the middle of his own excavations at Shechem, and this article reflects his archaeological orientation at that time. It was a survey of the archaeological history of Palestine, starting with the Natufian and running through the end of Iron II (i.e., from approximately 10,000 B.C. to A.D. 600). Biblical events were mentioned only when they had an impact on the discussion of various strata; for example, David was mentioned in the discussion of Megiddo (1961: 96), but Abraham was not talked about during the review of the Middle Bronze Age (88). Clearly, in this treatment Palestinian archaeology was its own separate discipline, following Wright's de jure view of biblical archaeology.

After his excavations at Shechem, Wright (1969b) wrote a piece in 1966 entitled "Biblical Archaeology Today" in the collection *New Directions in Biblical Archaeology*. In his view, the aim of biblical archaeology was "to read the Bible in the setting of its time, its people, and its land, to reconstruct its history and to study its literature and religion comparatively" (151). This aim followed the de jure separation, but the remainder of the article treated Palestinian archaeology as the field auxiliary of biblical archaeology.

In the Glueck Festschrift, Wright (1970) looked at the history of American archaeology in the Near East. Understandably, the major focus was on Palestine, although Mesopotamia was discussed. He credited Albright with making a discipline of "Palestinian archaeology" in the Tell Beit Mirsim volumes (notice the terminology; 27). He warned of the beginning of political closure of certain areas of the Near East to American archaeologists. On the positive side, he pointed to the possibilities that were just then opening up in Iran and Lebanon:

> Also, at the present time Jerusalem and Beirut provide two foci for
> different kinds of scholarly interest. The archaeological investigation
> of the ancient Phoenicians has barely begun, though they played
> such an important role as bearers of ancient culture into the Medi-
> terranean lands. Phoenicia, like modern Lebanon, was commercially
> and culturally oriented in two directions at once. Thus from Beirut a
> scholar would have a wide horizon before him. If he is prevented
> from moving eastward into Asia, he can certainly move westward,
> following Phoenician trade routes and exploring their trading colo-
> nies. Thus a major gap in ancient history might be filled. At the
> same time biblical archaeology, so closely tied to Canaanite culture
> both by acceptance and rejection, could not be more enriched by
> needed knowledge. (35)

This is the only appearance of "biblical archaeology" in the entire treatment, but it is revealing. The above statement begins with the "two foci," Beirut and Jerusalem. Beirut is the focus of Phoenician/Canaanite culture; by extension, Jerusalem must be the focus for the other interest mentioned, biblical archaeology. In this passage, the only assumption possible is that the archaeology of Palestine is biblical archaeology. The de facto definition has triumphed.

The Albright-Wright Model: The Patriarchs

From his earliest archaeological investigations through his postfieldwork career, Albright focused on the question of the historicity of the Patriarchs, attacking the core of the Wellhausian reconstruction. His later studies of the Patriarchs dealt with much more than just Palestinian evidence, covering the entire ancient Near East in the second millennium B.C. Albright pulled all of his data together in a *BASOR* article entitled "Abram the Hebrew: A New Archaeological Interpretation" (1961). In this tour de force he used excavation results, Mesopotamian and Egyptian texts, and the biblical record to present a portrait of Abraham as a long-distance donkey caravaneer.

MBI AND ABRAHAM. Basic to the Albright model was his placement of Abraham in the Middle Bronze I (MBI) period in Palestine. Today, this period is recognized as part of the Early Bronze tradition and is called EBIV; I follow Albright's designation during this discussion and refer to MBI and the following period as MBIIA. The Dead Sea survey gave him his first hard dates with the indication that settlement in the Valley ended in MBI (Albright 1924a). However, Genesis records urban centers in this area, the Five Cities of the Plain, leading Albright to conclude, "The date of Abraham cannot be placed earlier than the nineteenth century B.C." (1932a: 137). Further corroboration came from the 1929 discovery of a line of tells running along the eastern Jordan Valley, which he equated with the centers of the five kings mentioned in Genesis 14 (142). Nelson Glueck's surveys (1934, 1935, 1940) in the Jordan Valley confirmed for Albright the linkage of these mounds and the campaign in Genesis: Most of the sites were deserted by the end of MBI, and many were never again inhabited. Albright and Glueck equated the end of these sites with the biblical campaign of Genesis 14.

Albright (1935) interpreted the biblical record as indicating nomadic or seminomadic conditions for Abraham. Once armed with an MBI date for Abraham, he began to bolster this with data turned up by later excavations. Albright's own excavations at Tell Beit Mirsim (I-H) gave evidence of the nonurban character of MBI: "Nelson Glueck's explorations in Transjordan yield the same picture, that of a rapidly declining density of settlement, followed before the end of the twentieth century B.C. by virtually complete abandonment of the country to nomads" (1949: 82). Of particular importance to Albright's schema were the results of Glueck's (1959) survey of the Negev, the scene of a great deal of Patriarchal activity, which located scores of MBI settlements. Albright interpreted these settlements as caravan stops on the way to Egypt.

A series of Egyptian texts provided further evidence for Albright's (1941) picture of the MBI as nonurban. Known as the Execration texts, these texts are curses written on bowls and figurines, which were then ritually smashed. They name adversaries, both cities and groups, of the Middle Kingdom pharaohs, and date from two different periods. The earlier set names more groups but fewer cities. This is understood to indicate the unsettled conditions of MBI Palestine (Albright 1949: 82–83). The later Execration texts list more cities, except in Transjordan, fitting Albright's view of the rise of urbanism in MBIIA Palestine, contrasting with the continuance of nonsedentary groups across the river.

Albright (1961) also found archaeological support for an MBI date for Abraham in the excavations of some of the cities mentioned by name in the Patriarchal accounts. Renewed excavations at Bethel (Albright and Kelso 1968) yielded evidence of its being "extensively peopled" (Albright 1961: 47) in the MBI period. Albright concluded that Shechem was established in MBI, although the evidence was not conclusive. He equated Gerar, the city of Abimelech, with Tell Abu Hureirah in the Wadi Gaza. There are MBI sites in the vicinity, but Albright's confident identification of Gerar and of "its importance as a caravan center" (48) cannot be proved. At points, Albright was willing to amend the biblical text to avoid a confrontation with archaeological evidence. For example, Jerusalem had long been equated with the Salem mentioned in Genesis 14: 18, although it yielded no evidence of MBI habitation. Albright proposed a textual amendment of *selom* to *selom(oh)*; from Salem, a place, to "allied with him" (52). This avoided the issue of Jerusalem's nonsettlement in MBI.

THE AMORITE HYPOTHESIS. Albright and other scholars, including Kathleen Kenyon (1966), linked the Patriarchal migrations into Canaan with larger folk movements at the end of the third millennium B.C. At the end of EBIII, the major urban Palestinian sites were disrupted, and either destroyed or simply abandoned. The succeeding phase was largely nonurban. Based on the evidence at Jericho, Kenyon (1966: 9–33) presented a picture of a new group of invaders who destroyed the EB cities, and after a period of nomadism, settled down in flimsy houses on the major sites. From these developed the urban centers of the Middle Bronze Age.

Albright (1928b, 1935) connected the end of the Early Bronze Palestinian civilization with the Amorites, the biblical equivalent to the Akkadian *amurru*

(Sumerian MAR.TU). According to late third millennium texts from Ur and elsewhere (for references, see Bottéro 1971: 562–66), the amurru were western Semitic peoples who disrupted the urban centers in Mesopotamia. In the Amorite hypothesis, it was these were responsible for the destruction of urban life in Palestine. The movement of Terah and Abraham (Genesis 11: 31) from Ur to Haran and then to Palestine was placed in this context. The new Syrian influences in weaponry, the distinctive caliciform pottery, and the new tomb types that characterize the early Middle Bronze Age were seen as evidence of this folk movement (Albright 1949; Kenyon 1966).

TEXTUAL EVIDENCE. Albright (1932a, 1935, 1961, 1963) employed a variety of textual sources in his Patriarchal reconstruction. The excavations of the Mesopotamian site of Nuzi produced a number of legal texts that on first reading shed light on daily life in Genesis. Albright (1932a: 138; 1961: 47) placed particular emphasis on the Nuzi tablets in explaining the relations of Abraham and Eliezer of Damascus. John Bright, a student of Albright's and a leading biblical historian, presented a good example of the Albright position on customary parallels:

> For example, Abraham's fear (Gen. 15: 1–4) that his slave Eliezer
> would be his heir becomes understandable in the light of slave
> adoption as practiced at Nuzi. Childless couples would adopt a son
> who would serve them as long as they lived and inherit on their
> death. But, should a natural son be born, the adopted son would
> have to yield the right of inheritance. Again, as Sarah gave her slave
> Hagar to Abraham as a concubine (Gen.16: 1–4), so at Nuzi a mar-
> riage contract obliged the wife, if childless, to provide her husband
> with a substitute. (1981: 79)

Although Bright (and Albright) admitted that the parallels from Nuzi did not prove the antiquity of the Patriarchs, they increased respect for the value of the tradition: "One's conviction that the patriarchal narratives authentically reflect social customs at home in the second millennium is strengthened" (80).

Albright saw the adoption of Eliezer by Abraham as an economic transaction, not a provision for a childless situation: "Since—at least in theory—a man could not alienate property, which belonged to his family, he simply adopted the money-lender in order to provide collateral for a loan in time of need . . . It stands to reason that an organizer of and head of caravans would need ample credit in order to purchase donkeys and buy supplies of all kinds before starting out on a trading expedition" (1961: 47).

ABRAHAM THE CARAVANEER. This economic interpretation better supported the model of Abraham as a donkey caravaneer. Albright (1961, 1966a) gathered support for his caravaneer hypothesis from Mari, Ur, Cappadocia, and Egypt. The high-water mark for donkey trade was the nineteenth century B.C. Glueck's work in the Negev turned out to be crucial for Albright in his reconstruction. Why was the MBI period the time of most settlement in an inhospitable region, and why there at all? "The answer to our problem should be obvious" wrote Albright:

> We are dealing with a period of intensive donkey caravan activity . . .
> These and the other data which we have presented are meaningless
> unless we take them at their face value and recognize in the hoary
> figure of "Abram the Hebrew" a caravaneer of high repute in his
> time, the chief traditional representative of the original donkey cara-
> vaneers of the 19th century B.C., when this profession reached the
> climax of its history. (38, 52)

Albright's Orientalist perspective leads him to excesses in his reconstruction. To maintain the crucial connection of the MBI sites in the Negev and the textual evidence of donkey trade, he had to lower the date for MBI by about a century. He justified this on the evidence of two fragmentary inscriptions from the MBII Royal Tombs at Byblos, and on the basis of his restorations made connections to Mari and Egypt. He brought the date of MBIIA down to 1700 B.C. and MBI down to 1800, thus allowing the linkage of the texts and the MBI Negev sites. Albright (1963, 1964b, 1965, 1966b) grew progressively more certain of his lower dating, but this grandiose reconstruction was based on very flimsy evidence.

Although he wrote extensively on other aspects of Israel's history, Albright had made himself the dominant champion of the historicity of the Patriarchs. Biblical archaeology's other great figure, G. E. Wright, did not fully endorse Albright's reconstruction, but he did place them in a Middle Bronze milieu: "We shall probably never be able to prove that Abram really existed, that he did this or that, said thus and so, but what we can prove is that his life and times, as reflected in the stories about him, fit perfectly within the early second millennium, but imperfectly within any later period" (1962a: 40).

After forty years of work, the Albright model was completed. The biblical stories of the Patriarchs had been fully compared to the accepted understanding of the Middle Bronze Age, and with a few modifications had found an acceptable niche. Albrightian biblical archaeology had triumphed over Wellhausen and the critics.

The Albright-Wright Model: The Hebrew Conquest

The second pillar of biblical archaeology's reconstruction of the history of Israel was the Hebrew Conquest and Settlement, recorded primarily in Joshua and Judges. Joshua gives the picture of a swift, centralized campaign that obliterated the Canaanite power centers, allowing Israel free access to the highlands. Judges gives a somewhat different picture of the event, emphasizing the local nature of the military fighting, over a much longer period of time.

ALBRIGHT'S MODEL. From the perspective of the early 1930s, the issue of the Conquest appeared settled (Albright 1932a), a nonissue for biblical archaeology, with the biblical record of Conquest fully supported by archaeology. Albright dated the Exodus and Conquest to the fifteenth century B.C. Thus, when Garstang dated the destruction of Jericho to 1400 B.C., it was clear that the realia of archaeology had underpinned a conservative view of the Conquest and Settlement traditions.

However, the discoveries of the French at Et-Tell and Albright's own excavations at Tell Beit Mirsim and Bethel forced a renewed study of the Conquest. By 1935 Albright had lowered his dating of the conquest to the thirteenth century B.C., primarily due to the Bethel excavations. He had found a massive destruction layer dating to the thirteenth century, which he felt "compelled" to credit to Israelite invaders, and thus adopted "the low date for the Israelite conquest of central Palestine" (1934b: 10). The excavations at Et-Tell, the site Robinson had identified as the biblical city of Ai, challenged Albright's positivist portrayal of the Conquest. The excavator Judith Marquet-Krause (1935) found no indication of a Middle or Late Bronze settlement on the site. The destruction of Ai figures prominently in the Joshua account of the Conquest. If there was no city at the time postulated for the capture of Ai, then clearly, rethinking was needed. Albright (1939) responded to what he considered a "nihilistic" assessment of the issue by the German scholar Martin Noth (1938: 7–22). Noth challenged the historicity of the Conquest, contending that most of the stories relating to the Conquest served an etiological purpose; that is, they were made up to explain a name or a natural feature. Noth directed his energies to an analysis of the oral and literary forms of the Conquest accounts in an effort to recover the original etiological story. Albright vehemently disagreed with this approach, declaring that Noth "goes too far" (1939: 13). He clearly based his challenge on his belief in archaeology as realia: "The ultimate historicity of a given datum is never conclusively proved or disproved by the literary framework in which it is embedded: there must always be external evidence" (12), that external evidence being the province of archaeology.

Noth considered the Ai story to be an etiological explanation of the ruined Early Bronze City, arguing that, given that the name of the city means "the ruin," the later Israelites connected the site with the legendary figure of Joshua. Albright took his own evidence from Bethel and created a counterargument to explain the gap in occupation at Et-Tell. In his eyes, Et-Tell was "unquestionably biblical Ai" (1939: 15), but the story of its destruction should actually be attached to Bethel. The Bible mentions the conquest of Bethel in a separate account in Judges (1: 22–25). According to the book of Joshua, Ai was totally burned by the Israelites. The biblical description of the ferocity of the destruction fit the archaeological evidence from Bethel; therefore, reasoned Albright, it was actually Bethel that Joshua destroyed. Only after the abandonment of the small Iron Age village on Et-Tell did the story get shifted in the telling. A Conquest that dated to the second half of the thirteenth century (around 1230 B.C.) would also fit the destruction of Tell Beit Mirsim C and Lachish. The stele of Merneptah (c. 1220; Albright's date), containing the first extrabiblical mention of Israel, would be the terminus ante quem of the argument. Albright concluded that Noth's argument was "contradicted by the archaeological evidence" (23).

In keeping with his lifelong approach, Albright turned to the ceramic realia for further evidence of the Israelite settlement in the beginning of the Iron Age. He isolated a particular pithos form, the "collared rim" store jar, as a chronological marker of Israelite settlements (1949: 118). These were found at the small Iron I village on Et-Tell, at Tell-en-Nasbeh, Shechem, and the pre-fortress phase at Gibeah. They were also found at Megiddo, which rules it out as a purely Israelite pottery form, as Megiddo is explicitly listed as unconquered in Judges 1: 27. Albright did not openly equate the collared rim pithos with Israelite settlement, but implied it in his presentation. It is quite likely that he was looking for a ceramic marker of the settlement that would be equivalent to the Philistine bichrome ware. However, at best, the collared rim store jar is a marker of early Iron I sites and does not carry any ethnic information (still debated; see Dever 1995b; I. Finkelstein 1996b).

WRIGHT'S MODEL. The construction of the Conquest model is more equally shared between Albright and Wright. During the early McCormick years (he remained there until 1959), Wright kept in close contact with his mentor Albright (Running and Freedman 1975). For Wright (1941a), crucial evidence for the Conquest lay in the differences between the material culture of the Late Bronze Age and the Iron Age. He emphasized the shift from the lowlands to the hill country and the poor construction of the hill villages as opposed to the settlements of the plains dwellers.

Wright examined the work of Garstang at Jericho and was not satisfied with it. If Garstang was right, then Jericho fell at least 150 years before the date Albright was advancing for the Conquest. However, the evidence for the date of the wall was not clear, and Wright felt that he could not come to a conclusion: "Thus the problem of Jericho is more of a problem than ever. Absolutely all we can now say about it with certainty is that the city fell to the Hebrews sometime between cir. 1475 and 1300 B.C." (1942a: 35). Notice that Wright accepted a priori the accuracy of the Joshua account, the only evidence for the destruction by the Hebrews.

The fullest account of the Conquest model is in the revised edition of Wright's *Biblical Archaeology*: "That a violent wave of destruction occurred in southern Palestine during the course of the 13th century B.C. is clear from the excavations. That this was caused by the Israelite invasion is a reasonable historical inference" (1962a: 18). Wright accepted a combined view of the biblical accounts, arguing that the archaeological evidence supported both a swift (but incomplete) campaign and a longer process of localized battles:

> When we put the historical and archaeological data together, we arrive at a view somewhat as follows: There was an Israelite campaign of great violence and success during the 13th century. Its purpose was to destroy the existing Canaanite city-state system, weakening local power to such an extent that new settlement, especially in the hill country, might be possible. In the centuries that followed, however, there was not only the necessity of reducing unconquered city-states but also of continuous struggle with many of the inhabitants who, though their major centers of power had been reduced, still were able to offer resistance to Israelite clans encroaching on their territory. (70)

However, Jericho continued to provide a stumbling block for the Albright-Wright model. Kenyon's (1970) work at Jericho in the 1950s challenged Garstang's conclusions about the destruction of the city. Her excavations demonstrated that Garstang's City D dated to the Early Bronze Age, not to the time of Joshua. The only Late Bronze material was from a few tombs and a small section of the tell. Wright believed the evidence to be too scanty to confirm or deny the Joshua account, concluding, "We must confess a complete inability to explain the origin of the Joshua tradition" (1962a: 80). Nonetheless, he was willing to follow Albright's proposition that the story of the actual destruction of Bethel was transferred to Ai (81). "The break between the two" (i.e., between the well-built Late Bronze city and the succeeding level of "poor straggly houses" at Bethel) "is so complete that there can be no doubt but that this was the Israelite destruction" (81).

Shechem played an understandably prominent role in Wright's treatment of the Conquest (1962a: 76–78). He emphasized the peaceful nature of its stratigraphic record during the thirteenth century, citing it in support of the covenant tradition of Joshua 24. At this point, Wright did not have a solid understanding of the temple sequence in Field V, so the full discussion of the Judges incidents at Shechem waited until his popular book on the site published three years later (1965). Lachish, excavated by Starkey in the 1930s, also yielded evidence of a massive destruction of the Bronze Age city (Tufnell 1958; Tufnell et al. 1940). Wright (1962a: 83) and Albright supported a date for the destruction around 1220 B.C., although Tufnell (36–37) argued for a date in the twelfth century. Wright considered Joshua to be the destroyer of this city, in keeping with Joshua 10: 31–33. "But in any case," he added, "Lachish must have fallen to Israel some time between about 1220 and 1200 B.C." (83). Tell Beit Mirsim was equated by Albright with the biblical city of Debir, which was destroyed by Joshua in the same campaign as Lachish. Albright's excavations indicated destruction in the same general period. The new town, founded on the very thick destruction layer, "was so different from the preceding [town] that we must think of a new people having built it, a people who must have been Israelites, or closely related to them" (Wright 1962a: 83).

At the time Wright was refining his model, the best correlation of archaeology and a Conquest account was found at Hazor. Yadin's (1972) excavations in the late 1950s offered more supporting evidence for a thirteenth-century Conquest; Hazor was violently destroyed, in keeping with the biblical evidence. The excavations also revealed the vast size of the city, supporting the biblical identification of it as the "head of all those kingdoms" (Joshua 11: 10). Wright (1962a: 83) made use of Hazor to further bolster his defense of the basic historicity of Joshua.

Interestingly, Wright rejected the internal biblical chronology for the Conquest. According to I Kings 6:1, the Exodus was 480 years before the building of Solomon's Temple. This would place the Exodus and subsequent Conquest in the fifteenth century B.C. (which was Garstang's date). Wright offered his own calculations to arrive at a late date for the Exodus: "Then twelve generations (between Solomon and the Exodus) of twenty-five years per generation would give us a figure which would place the Exodus during about the third quarter of the thirteenth century, approximately where it should be according to the weight of archaeological evidence" (1962a: 84).

Summary

Both the Patriarchal model and the Conquest model were the result of archaeological data taking precedence over the biblical text. In each case, Albright and Wright used the perceived realia of the field data to modify the biblical record. This is clearest in the treatment of the "Ai problem" and the internal biblical chronology in both reconstructions. The archaeology was used to correct the biblical record, which was used in turn to interpret the archaeology: a circular trap. Wright alternately accepted the witness of the text and rejected it. In this way, he supported the fundamental message of the text—the fact of a conquest—with the realia of archaeology.

4

The Collapse of the Paradigm

The dominance of the Albright-Wright paradigm did not go unopposed: Challenges to the theoretical outlook of biblical archaeology came from within its own ranks as well as from without. When Wright went to Harvard in 1959, Albright was on the point of retirement and, as a result, Wright's program came to be the most popular choice for prospective students. The fact that he was also actively excavating provided an additional incentive to study at Harvard. Ironically, some of the most vigorous challenges to biblical archaeology came from among Wright's own students.

External Attacks

The publication of Wright's *Biblical Archaeology* (1962a) provoked a storm of criticism in Germany directed against the entire methodology of biblical archaeology (Elliger 1959; Noth 1960). Albright (1939) had previously attacked Martin Noth's negative assessment of biblical historicity in the late 1930s, and as Dever (1980a: 3) has rightly observed, the virulent response to Wright may be seen as a belated reaction to Albright as much as opposition to Wright himself.

Karl Elliger (1959), a biblical scholar, reviewed the German edition of Wright's book. The review attacked both his methodology and his results and reproved him for his ignorance of critical issues (95). The heart of Elliger's critique was an attack on the treatment of archaeology by the "Albright Schule" (96–98), and he was clearly bothered by the positivist nature of Wright's treatment. He challenged Wright's acceptance of archaeology as external objective evidence, which the "Alt Schule" had rejected. Elliger reacted more against Wright's conservative biblical understanding than against his treatment of the archaeological data. It was a negative assessment of Wright the theologian, not Wright the archaeologist.

Wright added to the debate in an article entitled "Archaeology and Old Testament Studies" (1958), contending that archaeology's main interests in Palestine were secular, an effort to answer historical and cultural questions. He reiterated biblical archaeology's theoretical understanding of archaeology as objective and biblical criticism as subjective. He attacked the "Alt school" as "nihilistic" and "refusing completely to use archaeological data" (46, 47). He believed that Noth and his colleagues did not truly understand the revolution Albright had wrought in the usefulness of archaeology. A generation before, Albright (1939) had contended that the Germans were still locked into the pre–World War I rejection of archaeology on the grounds of its lack of precision. Wright concluded by stressing that even if one decides that a biblical account is in the form of a tradition, that is not equivalent to a negative assessment of its historical value.

Noth's (1960) response to Wright was more substantial than Elliger's. He strongly disagreed with the Albright-Wright assessment of Alt's work (and, by extention, his own) as "nihilistic" (263 n. 1). He contended that the method of the German scholars was scientific, so it could not be labelled "nihilistic," which is a description of attitude. Nihilism carried strong political overtones in Germany, particularly for a scholar who had lived through the Third Reich. Albright's (1939) naming of the German approach as nihilistic was as loaded with meaning as the labeling of Albright as a fundamentalist. Albright reacted quite harshly to his own "supposed tendency to fundamentalism" (1934a), and Noth's strong dismissal of the charge of nihilism carried the same air of defensiveness. Elliger's implied accusation of fundamentalism against Wright was part of the German reaction against this charge. It is likely that Albright's original contention reflected the political climate of the late 1930s as well as the nature of German methodology in biblical studies.

Noth (1960: 272 n. 2) complained about Wright's accusation that the Germans refused to use archaeology in their studies. He asserted that they had, but without a facile acceptance of the Bible to be found in biblical archaeology. He specifically attacked the equation of Abraham with the MBI period and the use of Nuzi parallels in the Patriarchal reconstruction, noting that Glueck and Albright had put Abraham into MBI because of the Negev settlements, yet they used texts that were centuries later to point out parallels that then functioned as added "proof" of the historicity of the Patriarchs. Noth dismissed Albright's evidence as too divergent, and concluded that in spite of the efforts of Albright and Wright, archaeology shed little light on the issue of the Patriarchs (265–70).

The most damaging question Noth (1960: 271 n. 1) raised dealt with the nature of archaeological evidence: Is it truly external and objective? The fundamental datum of biblical archaeology, the belief in archaeology as realia, was under attack. Noth wondered if the interpretations of the data that the Albright school accepted were based on a particular biblical understanding, which would make them internal, not external to biblical study.

Proving the Bible?

Nelson Glueck's *Rivers in the Desert* (1959) provoked an enlightening exchange on the purpose of biblical archaeology between J. J. Finkelstein (1959) and Wright. Glueck's bald statement regarding the reliability of the Bible and archaeology—"It may be stated categorically that no archaeological discovery has ever controverted a biblical reference" (31)—provided the base from which Finkelstein attacked biblical archaeology in general. He accused Glueck of championing a new thesis that allegedly demonstrated the historicity of the Bible and countered Glueck's statement with a presentation of the Jericho evidence. In the process of discussing this site, he went on to attack Wright's treatment in *Biblical Archaeology* of the Jericho evidence as well (344), arguing that when Wright used the phrase "virtually nothing" in discussing the evidence for Late Bronze occupation at Jericho, he meant "nothing," and the "virtually" was only a "scholarly hedge." Finkelstein added that Wright's use of "discouraging" in reference to the Jericho evidence "speaks volumes on the subject of scholarly detachment in the area of Biblical Studies" (344).

Wright (1959) responded by saying that the "historicity" school may have overstated its case, but that this thrust was only a small part of the growth of the discipline of archaeology in Palestine. Mentioning the work of Harvard, Yale, Penn, and the Oriental Institute, Wright maintained that "fundamentalist" money was never a major support of archaeological research (103). Clearly sensitive to the charge of fundamentalist domination of the field, he had written against such an understanding elsewhere (Wright 1958). He did not admit that the biblical connection began archaeology in Palestine, that ASOR had been supported in part by religious institutions, or that Tell Beit Mirsim was almost fully funded by a fundamentalist, Melvin Grove Kyle. But he was indulging in something of an overreaction; moreover, he ignored his own theological agenda, which he carried with him to Shechem.

Regarding the statement of Glueck's that touched off the furor, Wright admitted it was extreme, but pointed out the qualifications that Glueck used, such as the existence of legend in the Bible, concluding that "the total context is not as extreme" (1959: 106). He stressed that *Rivers in the Desert* was not a scholarly work, but was meant for a popular audience. Moreover, Glueck believed deeply in his faith and was an emotional man; the implication was that he allowed himself to get carried away. Wright did not agree with the straightforward apologetical overtones of Glueck's statement, although his own views at this time were almost as positivistic.

It should be noted that Finkelstein seemed to equate scholarly detachment with a lack of any a priori framework for interpretation, and while accusing Wright of operating within a preexisting framework, he himself interpreted his data to fit his own preconceived ideas. A preconceived notion is not in itself a bad position to start from; the key lies in recognizing it for what it is and being willing to allow it to be challenged. Certainly Wright was willing to test his ideas about the historicity of the Bible; it is why he dug at Shechem. He was very forthright about his own a priori assumptions as early as the 1940s (Wright 1946). Nonetheless, Finkelstein implied that anyone accepting the theology of the Bible was incapable of "scholarly detachment." For him, such a presupposition was unacceptable; by implication, the theological rejection of the Bible was the only valid position for a detached study of it. Clearly, this too must be rejected: Both positions are presuppositions. If they are admitted to be such and their potential bias recognized, then a holder of either position can be "detached." Theological beliefs do influence archaeological interpretation, and a negative theological position has just as much potential for bias as a positive one.

Postwar Fundamentalist Archaeology

Wright was much more liberal theologically than the very conservative scholars who continued to be involved in archaeology in Palestine after World War II. Joseph P. Free became a leading spokesman for the Christian fundamentalist position in archaeology, who did set out to "prove" the Bible (figure 4.1). Free had a Ph.D. in French, but became enamored with archaeology. Unlike many conservative writers using archaeology in their studies, he actually worked in the field. He was influential in conservative circles, because he produced students with some knowledge of archaeology, not just the Bible. He ran a program in Biblical Archaeology at Wheaton College (Illinois), founding it in 1940. Free wrote his major textbook, *Archaeology and Bible History*, to answer "the

FIGURE 4.I Joseph P. Free at Dothan. Courtesy of Wheaton College

need for a book true to the Scriptures and at the same time sufficiently documented" (1950: vii). He made no attempt to hide his bias, flatly stating, "The
writer holds a very conservative position" (ix). Free had two uses for archaeology in his schema: to illuminate the world of the Bible, and as "a valuable
part of . . . apologetics" (1). He called himself a fundamentalist and a "Bible
Believer" (350). He accepted the idea of verbal inspiration, believing the Bible
to be accurate in all respects (3). From that position, Free totally rejected higher
critical thinking. He claimed that the confirmation of the Bible was not his
primary aim, but the thrust of the study is totally apologetical.

Free (1953, 1954, 1955, 1956, 1958, 1959, 1960) directed the excavation of
the biblical site of Dothan in the 1950s. He chose Dothan because it was connected with the Patriarchal cycle of stories. Methodologically, he followed the
classic Fisher method, but with some influence from the work of Kenyon at
Jericho. Squares were laid out using baulks, but apparently they did not function as sections. Free died in the 1960s before any report could be drawn
together, and no thorough summary has as yet appeared, so it is impossible to
assess how thorough his recording was. The most important discovery is Tomb
I, a huge tomb dating to c. 1300 B.C. (Free 1960). The tomb has yielded more

than a thousand vessels. John Monson, a Ph.D. archaeologist from Harvard, now leads the program at Wheaton College, and he intends to publish the Dothan material as extensively as possible (personal communication, 2002).

The Challenge from Within

Students of Albright and Wright, and biblically focused archaeology colleagues, also challenged the Albright-Wright synthesis. The new generation of students trained by Wright at Shechem was nearly all clergymen, but many left the pulpit to focus on archaeology. William Dever has described this career change as "not 'defrocked,' but unsuited" (personal communication 1983). These students, like all students, felt the need to distance themselves from their mentors. The result was cataclysmic for biblical archaeology.

Paul Lapp

One of the first to directly challenge Wright was Paul Lapp. Lapp fit the mold of biblical archaeology, being an ordained clergyman and a pottery expert. He studied under both Albright and Wright, doing his dissertation on the pottery of the Hellenistic and early Roman periods in Palestine (Lapp 1961), a study that remains normative for this ceramic horizon. He directed the Jerusalem School from 1961 to 1965 and remained as professor there until 1968. He began in the field at Shechem, where, under Wright's tutelage, he developed his ceramic expertise. He went on to direct the excavation of 'Araq el-Emir, the site of an apparent Jewish temple during the Hellenistic period (Lapp 1962). He also reexcavated Ta'anach and Tell-el-Ful for the American School. His career was cut short in Palestine by the Arab-Israeli war of 1967. Lapp was strongly pro-Arab, and decided to dig on Cyprus rather than remain in Jerusalem. Tragically, as he was preparing for the excavation at Idalion in 1970, he drowned while swimming off the coast of Kyrenia. He was only 39 years old.

In a series of lectures given in 1966, Lapp (1969) attacked both the presuppositions of biblical archaeology and Wright's own field methods. He first looked at the process of historical research, emphasizing the presuppositions of any historian, and concluded, "History is ultimately a personal construction" (28). That being said, he directly challenged Wright, contending that only a secular historian could produce an "objective" history of the Bible, for such a scholar would not be concerned with "God's Great Acts" (64) and would not suffer from the same bias as theologians. Thus Lapp, like Finkelstein before him, evidently thought that a secular historian's bias would not affect his history in any negative way. For Lapp, "objective" appeared to equal "nontheological"; yet, that choice is in itself a theological one.

Lapp believed that biblical archaeology should be subject to the same archaeological standards as any other branch of archaeology; he would get no argument from Wright on that point. Similarly, he saw biblical archaeology as primarily an archaeological endeavor, in keeping with Wright's de facto definition. Lapp and Wright diverged over the accuracy of the Bible. Lapp considered it the "height of sacrilege" to think archaeology could answer the question "Is Christianity true? The person who does that *undermines* faith by making it less than a gift" (91). Here is the heart of Lapp's challenge: scholarship based on faith versus scholarship based on empirical fact.

Lapp became enamored with the field methodology employed at Tell Deir 'Alla, an excavation in Jordan under the direction of H. Franken of Leiden (figure 4.2). In a long review of Franken's work, he again attacked the methodology of Wright and biblical archaeology (Lapp 1970). Franken aimed to clarify the chronology of the Late Bronze–Iron Age transition by a stratigraphic,

FIGURE 4.2 H. Franken at Tell Deir 'Alla in Jordan. Photo by author

not a typological, study of the pottery. Lapp considered American methodology as developed by Albright and Wright to be too rigidly locked into a typological analysis of the pottery that would be collected under the Wheeler-Kenyon method. This rigidity prevented the objectives of the excavation from being the determinant of the methodology employed (1970: 244).

Certainly Lapp put his finger on a weakness of biblical archaeology. However, by attacking the field methodology, he was only chasing the tail, not the dog that wagged it. As long as biblical archaeology focused only on questions of Kulturgeschichte, its practitioners would use a method best designed to answer those questions: the modified Wheeler-Kenyon method. To break free from such a trap, a new theory was needed that would permit a broader range of questions. Lapp's review was more of a polemic against Wright than a positive statement of what archaeology in Palestine should be. Wright had dismissed Lapp from his position as director of the Jerusalem School, which added a personal element to the debate. There is no way of knowing what direction Lapp would have taken, due to his tragic death off the coast of Cyprus.

Roland de Vaux

In the Festschrift for Nelson Glueck, Roland de Vaux (1970), one of the deans of Palestinian archaeology, wrote a quiet paper that was devastating in its insight into biblical archaeology. De Vaux was a French Dominican, director of the Ecole Biblique in Jerusalem (figure 4.3). Although he did not consider himself a biblical archaeologist, in many ways he exemplified what a biblical archaeologist should have been. Throughout his career, he used the social sciences, the techniques of biblical criticism, and archaeological data to explain the history of Israel. The Bible may have been a central part of his research, but it was not to the exclusion of other questions.

De Vaux was very active in field research in Palestine. He directed nine seasons of excavation at Tell el-Far'ah (north), the site of Tirzah, one of the capitals of the northern kingdom of Israel (de Vaux 1951, 1952, 1962). The archaeological history of Tell el-Far'ah matched well with its political history as recounted in the Bible. De Vaux (1973) was also involved in research on the Dead Sea Scrolls, directing the excavations of Khirbet Qumran, the remains of the community that buried the scrolls. Methodologically, he was not at the forefront in Palestine, content to use a modified Fisher method in his work. Ceramically, he was not in the same class as Wright and Albright, but was consequently less dogmatic in his classifications. Others were better in the dirt, but de Vaux had few peers at synthetic interpretation. His general studies (de Vaux 1961, 1967), with their broad database, walk a middle ground between

FIGURE 4.3 Roland de Vaux (left) and William Dever (right). Courtesy of William G. Dever

the positivist approach of Albright and the more negative views of Noth. Adding to the quality of de Vaux's work is his elegant style, which comes through even in translation. In de Vaux, the Ecole reached its pinnacle.

De Vaux condemned as an abuse attempts to "confirm" the Bible through archaeology (1970: 67). He accepted Wright's belief that the faith of Israel was founded on the interventions of God in history, but pointed out that archaeology can only validate the event on which the biblical writer has placed his interpretation, and part of that interpretation is seeing an event as the act of God. De Vaux had developed this position earlier in *Bible et Orient* (1967), particularly in the section entitled "Peut-on écrire une théologie de l'Ancien Testament?" (59–71).

As a monk, de Vaux was at heart a man of faith, and began each day on excavation with a mass. He was willing to assume the veracity of a biblical account: "Lack of archaeological evidence would not be sufficient in itself to cast doubt on the affirmations of the written witnesses" (1970: 70); even if the footprints of the Divine were harder to find, they were no less valid. Placing himself in the middle between biblical archaeology and biblical criticism, he believed that compromise was possible: "There should be no conflict between a well established archaeological fact and a critically examined text" (70). The key was his definitions of "well established" and "critically examined," which allowed him to escape current or potential areas of conflict. Following de Vaux's dictum, the problem of Jericho that so vexed the Conquest model could be neatly evaded by declaring either the archaeology not "well established" or the text not correctly understood from the critical perspective. In general, de Vaux believed that biblical archaeology had done very well in establishing the first part of the equation; it was the lack of a critical examination of the biblical text that he discerned in Wright and biblical archaeology.

A major problem in biblical archaeology that de Vaux dwelt on was the confusion of correlation between cause and effect. He used the example of the Conquest. Clearly, many sites in Palestine were destroyed at the end of the Bronze Age, the time at which the Albright-Wright reconstruction placed the Conquest. De Vaux pointed out the weakness in the reconstruction: that we have no clue archaeologically as to the perpetrators of the destructions claimed to be the work of the Hebrews (1970: 75). He compared this to the problem in classical archaeology of the Fall of Troy. The destruction of Troy VIIA is often attributed to the Greeks of the *Iliad*. However, a direct causal relationship cannot be demonstrated, although a correlation of the two sets of data, literary and archaeological, can be reasonably put forward. Finally, de Vaux reiterated his criticism of the lack of critical study in biblical archaeology—a direct challenge to Wright.

William G. Dever

A student of Wright's, William G. Dever, followed the lead of de Vaux to its ultimate end and totally rejected the validity of biblical archaeology. Dever began his career as a theology student, writing a thesis on the "Present Status of Old Testament Theology" (1959), and was ordained into the Protestant clergy. His interest in theology took him to Harvard to study under "one of the most vigorous exponents of theology today": G. E. Wright (Dever 1959: 157). However, by that point, Wright had lost his primary interest in theology and was deeply involved in archaeology, particularly with the Shechem project. In 1962, Dever accompanied Wright to Shechem and became enamored with archaeology. Like Wright, Dever (1974) felt the attraction of realia and became a pottery expert; his dissertation concentrated on the clarification of the EBIV period through the study of its ceramics. In 1965 he became director of the Gezer excavation, and later served as head of the Jerusalem School. Because of his "in-house" credentials, Dever's challenge of biblical archaeology was particularly influential. After leaving Jerusalem, he went to the University of Arizona, directing a program in Syro-Palestinian archaeology, which combined anthropological with traditional Near Eastern archaeology.

Dever (1974) fired a broadside against biblical archaeology in the 1971 Winslow lectures, challenging the whole idea of a discipline called biblical archaeology. His main target was Wright's de facto equivalency of biblical archaeology and Palestinian archaeology. Like Wright before him (see below), Dever found at Gezer that archaeological data speak only in response to a question, and that biblical archaeology was unacceptable as the dominant mode in Palestinian archaeology because it asked only very limited questions.

According to Dever, the new staff needed for excavation in Palestine would not ask the questions posed by biblical archaeology, but those raised by anthropological archaeology as practiced in North America. No longer would archaeology in Palestine be a subfield of biblical studies, relying on the Bible for its agenda. Syro-Palestinian archaeology (as Dever christened it, borrowing the term from Albright) would be treated as a field of general archaeology, subject to the same concerns and using the same methods. This would benefit both archaeology and biblical studies: (1974: 31):

> The separation I have advocated will allow Palestinian archaeology to develop the kind of professionalism which I think is healthy, for it would mean at the very least the raising of standards and the development of new cross-disciplinary programs with our scientific and anthropological colleagues which will multiply many times the value of our excavation and research—not the least for biblical history. But the irony is that as long as our concern is primarily biblical history, Palestinian archaeology will not be able to develop its full potential, and it will remain an amateurish affair not able to command the respect of scholars in other fields, rendering more of a disservice than a service to the cause of biblical studies. (1974: 31)

Essentially, Dever called for the recognition of what Wright (1947) had first advocated in his earliest definition of biblical archaeology: that Palestinian and biblical archaeology have differing interests. Dever rejected "biblical archaeology" as the name for the discipline, because the new questions being asked in the field would demand it: "The term 'Biblical Archaeology' imposes a limitation upon our discipline in both scope and time . . . It assumes nothing of importance happened in the Land of the Bible except in the brief period of the second and first millennia B.C." (1974: 33). In his new enthusiasm, Dever, like any other evangelist, overlooked some of the problems of the new Syro-Palestinian archaeology. In the Winslow lectures, he made it clear that, like Lapp, he thought objectivity was a problem only for theologians, not archaeologists. Dever (1980a) has since admitted that all scholars have this problem, and that Wright was not overly biased in his archaeology.

The Final Straw: The Loss of Realia

Wright's rediscovery of the actual conditions of archaeology in the field at Shechem and later at Gezer added to the pressures directed against biblical archaeology. The raison d'être for biblical archaeology was the belief in the objectivity of the archaeological record. The true subjective nature of the archaeological process questioned this basic tenet. Wright was forced to reexamine his own position, and as a result, he reacted passively to the mounting attacks on biblical archaeology.

The Lessons from the Field

The Shechem field method started a process of profound change in Wright. He decided to use the methodology of Kathleen Kenyon, and this decision forced him to pay close attention to stratigraphy. He soon came to realize that the complex record of a tell site allows for many interpretations (Wright 1962b: 39). Stratigraphic questions could not be answered with a blanket principle, for each case had to be examined on its own merits and decided from its individual context. Without a guiding principle, individual interpretation came to the forefront. Through this analytical process, Wright began to think that data and interpretation were more closely linked than he had previously been willing to accept. If this were true, then archaeological data were not the objective realia called for by biblical archaeology.

As the Shechem excavations ended, Wright turned in 1964 to Gezer, a site in the state of Israel. Like Shechem, Gezer had been excavated before (by Macalister and Rowe; see above), using older, less sophisticated methodology. Wright was archaeological director at the Hebrew Union College Biblical and Archaeological School that year, and the school sponsored the excavations. He functioned as the director for the first season, after which he removed himself from active fieldwork to allow his student, William Dever, to take over (Dever et al. 1970, 1974). Wright and Glueck (the president of the sponsoring institution) formed an executive committee to free Dever and his assistant, Darrell Lance, to concentrate on the actual excavation and analysis.

The Gezer excavations employed volunteer labor and ran a field school, both firsts for American excavations in Palestine. The initial excavation staff reflected the Shechem approach, being composed largely of ceramic specialists. These men were mostly former students of Wright, and many were ordained clergy (Dever 1974: 12). The staff quickly changed, however, being joined by specialists from other disciplines. Gezer fulfilled Wright's hopes for such an approach, which had been frustrated at Shechem (Stager et al. 1974: xvi).

Dever actively pressed for the multidisciplinary approach, which by 1970 was a permanent fixture (Dever et al. 1970). He presented this in an article on methodology for *Eretz-Israel* (Dever 1973), calling for the application of the refined Gezer method to one-period sites. Due to the intensity of recording, this methodology does not allow for more than a moderate exposure of any area under study, and thus, following Wright, Dever called for more problem-solving archaeology. Most important, Dever posed questions: What is the basic conception of the excavator? What can we realistically hope to accomplish? "Classical" biblical archaeology no longer had an answer.

During Wright's presidency, ASOR sponsored renewed excavations at Tel el-Hesi, the birthplace of systematic excavation in Palestine. From its inception in 1970, work at the site was multifaceted, using specialists from many scientific disciplines as well as traditional archaeologists. In 1968, the Hesban project, sponsored by Andrews University and affiliated with ASOR, brought a multidisciplinary approach to Jordan. Like Gezer and Hesi, Hesban trained numerous students who went on to lead projects of their own. These excavations brought the multidisciplinary approach pioneered in the Near East by Robert Braidwood to biblical historic sites.

I think Wright's support of these changes also reflected his questioning of the objective nature of the archaeological record. If, as Wright was beginning to suspect, data speak only in response to a question, then more information might be gathered by more questions. A multidisciplinary staff would naturally ask more questions of the data than would a Kulturgeschichte-oriented staff.

Archaeological Reaction

Wright (1971) made clear his awareness of the loss of realia when he rejected his old confidence in the objectivity of archaeological data in an article for the *Biblical Archaeologist* entitled "What Archaeology Can and Cannot Do," a direct reference to Roland de Vaux's earlier paper (1970). He quite openly stated, "Archaeological data can only speak in response to a question" (1971: 73). Wright now accepted the use of models and hypothesis testing in archaeology, first making this clear in the 1968 Sprunt lectures at Union Seminary (Wright 1969c). In these theological studies, Wright stated that models impose a necessary form on material—necessary, he reasoned, because we do not receive our data raw and unfiltered. In other words, the interpretation of a fact is an integral part of that fact.

Overt model building and hypothesis testing were new for Palestinian archaeology, although they were a recognized element of anthropological archaeology as practiced in the United States and Europe (Willey and Sabloff 1980). Wright, as we have seen, encouraged the cooperation of anthropological archaeologists and natural scientists on ASOR-sponsored excavations. Despite this apparent support for anthropology, however, he remained adamantly opposed to compartmentalization and specialization, two elements that he particularly associated with anthropological archaeology (1971: 73–75). Wright believed that anthropologists had "short-changed the humanistic aspects of archaeology" in an overzealous attempt to remain " 'non-historical' and 'scientific' " (73). Finally, he returned to the vexing question of the objectivity of archaeology in an extremely atypical declaration: "Ambiguity is a central component of history" (75). Realia could no longer be found in the dirt.

Paul Lapp's sudden death in 1970 forced Wright to become directly involved in Lapp's field project at Idalion in Cyprus (Stager et al. 1974). Wright was needed to help secure a permit from the Cypriote Department of Antiquities. During the Idalion project, Wright stayed at the Ledra Palace Hotel in Nicosia. Each morning he would send instructions via Sophocles Hadjisavvas, a young Cypriote archaeologist who was commuting from Nicosia to Idalion (personal communication 2003). Dr. Hadjisavvas continued in archaeology and served as director of the Cyprus Department of Antiquities from 1999 to 2004.

Idalion was yet another example of the multidisciplinary approach that had gained such a fervent disciple in Wright. He placed Ruben Bullard, a geologist who had worked with Wright at Shechem and Gezer, in charge of coordinating the scientific specialists. Bullard discovered one of the clay sources of the famous Cypriot White Slip ware of the Late Bronze Age (Stager et al. 1974: xvii). Bullard later worked on Cyprus at Kourion in 1984 with the University of Arizona excavations in the city site. Frank Koucky, Bullard's teacher, also joined the Idalion team and became the main geologist on the project.

Wright (1974) presented a paper at a 1972 colloquium at MIT on complex societies, addressing the issue of the tell as a basic unit in the Near East. His presentation was still essentially historical, dealing with the tell as an independent unit rather than an element of a regional study. Gordon Willey (1974: 146), the moderator of the colloquium, criticized Wright's " 'traditional' archaeological perspective." Still, the mere fact of his presence at a prestigious anthropological colloquium demonstrated the changes in Wright.

In a posthumously published "fireside chat," Wright (1975) continued his new-found approach, praising the "new archaeology" of American anthropology and urging his students to explore new options in theory and method.

However, he insisted on a humanistic orientation: "I remain unabashedly a humanist!" (115). In an earlier work, he had defined his humanism as follows: "I am an individual with a history not entirely predetermined by gene or environment. I am a creature of choices, a bundle of biases in my past and present relationships with others, with my environment. In other words, what is important to say is that I am a historical being always making choices . . . I too possess a power structure with the ability to create what no tradition, no depth psychologist, no environmentalist—no combination of them—can entirely predict" (1969a: 63–64). Wright (1975: 115) warned the "pure scientists" that archaeology deals with human beings and thus must remain a humanistic discipline.

Theological Reaction

Biblical Theology came under general attack during the same time that Wright was rethinking his views on realia. Wright's idea of history as the sole medium of revelation was challenged on the grounds that it left out the possibility of revelation in word (Barr 1961, 1976; Childs 1970). Israel's belief in revelation in history—considered part of the uniqueness of Israel by Wright—was shown to be a commonly held belief in the ancient Near East (Albrektson 1967). The relevance of Wright's theology (a concept important in the 1960s) was called into question (Childs 1970: 82–87): Even if God did act in Israel's history, does that have any meaning for today? Under these attacks, the consensus that had formed around Biblical Theology broke apart. By 1970, Brevard Childs (1970; Dever 1985) declared the "death" of the movement.

A Foundation of Sand

In the 1968 Sprunt lectures at Union Theological Seminary, Wright (1969c) worked out the theological implications of the loss of realia in archaeology, which should also be seen against a backdrop of the theological challenges to Biblical Theology. He remained convinced that archaeology should be a tool for the theologian: "If the Bible is the revelation of a new reality in a Near East time and place, why should not the historian's tools be my ally?" (67). However, he had lost faith in the role of archaeology. I think his encounter with the actual state of the archaeological record had changed his views on the directness of the Hand of God in history. "God works in this world by mediate means," said Wright. "Our problem is to know and do what we are called to do" (130). The verification of the Acts of God, which Wright was so confident of before the

Shechem excavations, was now unachievable, and he concluded that "the problem of the Scripture's truth and validity cannot be solved" (184), abandoning
his previous positivist stance. "In the end we can never measure this Biblical
reality with reality itself, whether we attempt this measurement in the field of
value or in the field of fact . . . God has not committed his truth to respond
adequately to our tests" (185). Despite decades of research, the goal of biblical
archaeology, to ground the Scripture in realia, was no longer possible. Wright
had come full circle. His theology had originally provided the impetus for his
archaeological research. Now, that same research forced him to abandon his
theological stance.

The Joshua Commentary: A New Direction

Wright died while working on a commentary on the book of Joshua in the
Anchor Bible Series. However, he did complete an important introduction,
which presents a fascinating example of the profound changes in his thinking
wrought by his archaeological loss of faith (Wright and Boling 1982). The
subject under study was one of the key subjects of biblical archaeology: the
Conquest. "The conquest has received little theological study," wrote Wright,
"though, of course, it has been of great importance for Palestinian and biblical
archaeologists because of the apparent opportunity for an external check on
both biblical and archaeological chronology" (34). For Wright, archaeology's
role as an external, objective check on the excesses of biblical criticism had
become only apparent, not true reality.

  Wright employed all the resources at his command in setting the stage for
the theological analysis of Joshua. He discussed the history of modern critical
study of the text (Wright and Boling 1982: 37–72), demonstrating his mastery
of all the critical apparatus. He thought the final form of Joshua was the work
of a Deuteronomic editor who used several preexisting sources. He found the
character of Joshua the individual to be central to the tradition, which he preferred to see as the product of traditions of a Holy War (72, 27–37).

  Wright also discussed the "historical problems" of the book of Joshua
(Wright and Boling 1982: 72–88). He praised the recently deceased Albright
as "the dominant creative figure in the attempt to place the Bible in a perspective of the whole of ancient history" (73). Downplaying his own important
contributions, he credited Albright with establishing the basic chronology that
linked the events of Joshua to the thirteenth century B.C. He then recognized
a major weakness of the biblical archaeology reconstruction: "Yet a carefully
defined statement of what archaeology is and is not, does and does not do, has
been hard to articulate. Such a statement must follow the experiments of re-

construction, and first attempts may need future modification when the polemical period which is always created when general assumptions are badly shaken is past" (74). Wright considered de Vaux's (1970) article in the Glueck Festschrift to be one of the "outstanding attempts" at such a statement. He then presented his own position on "What Archaeology Can and Cannot Do" (74–80), which owes much to his earlier article of the same title (Wright 1971).

After a quick sketch of the development of the field, Wright predicted that the new multidisciplinary staffs on American excavations would generate a much greater amount of controlled information in the 1970s and 1980s. This is one prophecy that has proved to be 100 percent accurate. He then presented his postexcavation assessment of the relationship of biblical events and archaeology:

> With regard to biblical events, however, it cannot be overstressed that archaeological data are ambiguous. Fragmentary ruins, preserving only a tiny fraction of the full picture of ancient life, cannot speak without someone asking questions of them. And the kind of questions asked are part and parcel of the answers "heard" because of predispositions on the part of the questioner . . . It is small wonder, then, that disagreement and debate arise. A destruction layer in the ruins does not tell us the identity of the people involved. Indeed, we know that certain black soot and charcoal layers do not necessarily mean destruction. An accidental fire in one part of the town or city, certain industrial pursuits, or even an earthquake may be the answer. (Wright and Boling 1982: 76)

Wright has learned the lessons of the dirt.

Wright still believed archaeology could contribute to biblical study: "Yet the nature of the remains does not mean that archaeology is useless" (Wright and Boling 1982: 76). However, for archaeology to contribute it must be understood as a source of

> historical reconstructions [that] have varying degrees of probability. In studying antiquity it is important to recall that models and hypotheses are the primary means by which reconstruction is possible after the basic critical work is done. And, furthermore, it takes a great deal of humility to say frankly what the physical sciences have had also to say; predisposition of minds at any one period frame the type of questions asked of the material and become a part of the "answers" we suppose we have obtained from our investigations. (77)

The old positivism is gone. The parameters of realia in biblical archaeology are circumscribed and finite:

> Final *proof* of anything ancient must be confined to such questions
> as how pottery was made, what rock was used, what food and fauna
> were present, etc. Certainly this proof does not extend to the validity
> of the religious claims that the Bible would place upon us, and we
> must remember that the Bible is not a mine for scientifically
> grounded certainties about anything. It is instead a literature that
> places before us one of history's major religious options.(Wright and
> Boling 1982: 77)

Wright turned to Roland de Vaux to find a guiding principle: "The dictum of de Vaux is axiomatic: 'Archaeology does not confirm the text, which is what it is; it can only confirm the interpretation which we give it'" (Wright and Boling 1982:79). In summary, Wright expanded on his earlier (1971: 75) observation regarding the ambiguity of history: "We are historical organisms by intrinsic nature, and ambiguity is always a central component of history, whether of the humanities, of social science, or of natural science" (Wright and Boling 1982: 80).

The Destruction of the Model

Wright had been forced by his own field experience to come to terms with the actual subjective process of archaeology. In so doing, he had to disregard the view of archaeology as the realia of biblical studies, going against two generations of work by biblical archaeology. His repudiation of the field's theoretical base amounted to the destruction of the movement. After biblical archaeology lost its theoretical foundation, the twin pillars of the Albright-Wright reconstruction, the Patriarchs and the Conquest, soon collapsed.

The Collapse of the Patriarchal Model

Major studies by Thomas Thompson (1974, 1978) John Van Seters (1975), and William Dever (1970, 1977, 1980b) challenged Albright's Patriarchal model. These studies attacked from both biblical and archaeological positions, for if the Patriarchal narratives could be cut loose from their Middle Bronze moorings, then biblical criticism could regain its once dominant role in the discussion of Genesis and the Albright revolution would be overturned. Thompson, Van Seters, and Dever disagreed over aspects of the EBIV (MBI) period (see

Dever 1977, 1980b) but were united in their view that Albright's Patriarchal model was a distortion of the archaeological record. Van Seters was more concerned with questions of biblical criticism, and it was primarily Thompson and Dever who critiqued Albright's archaeological data.

Following the work of Dever (1970) on the EBIV period it became clear that Albright's dates for the beginning of MBIIA had to be raised to c. 2,000 B.C. (Dever 1985), pushing his MBI back into the third millennium. Albright depended heavily on the Royal Tombs at Byblos for his dating, but the full publication of the tomb material by Olga Tufnell (1969) allowed Thompson (1974) and Dever (1977) to demonstrate conclusively that his dating of the tombs to the eighteenth century B.C. was wrong. Thus, the connection of the caravan texts from the nineteenth and eighteenth centuries B.C. to the MBI (EBIV) sites that Glueck had surveyed in the Negev could no longer be maintained. These sites are now placed in the last quarter of the third millenium B.C. The urban data included in Albright's reconstruction have also been challenged. Dever (1977: 99) dismissed Albright's characterization of the EBIV settlement at Bethel as extensive, contending that only a few sherds represent that early phase of the town, and the same date for Shechem was also rejected (Dever 1970: 142–44).

Thompson and Van Seters argued that the Patriarchal accounts contain no historical value, and any attempt to place them in the early second millennium, as biblical chronology requires, is doomed to failure. Dever approached the problem as an archaeologist, dismissing the Patriarchs as a biblical problem, not an archaeological one: "It should be noted that few archaeologists who specialize in MBI have even alluded to Albright's view, and none has accepted it" (1977: 102).

Thompson (1974: 62–88) discussed the evidence for the Amorite connection, pointing out that the picture of Amorites migrating into Syria/Palestine ultimately depends on the biblical stories of the Patriarchs. Only in Genesis, he contended, does a picture emerge of migration from the Euphrates valley to Palestine (Thompson 1978). In rejecting the Amorite hypothesis, Thompson also argued for continuity between EBIV and MBIIA, downplaying any evidence of nomadism in Palestine. Dever initially accepted the Amorite hypothesis (1970), but has since rejected this as an explanation for the new features in MB Palestine (1980b). However, he strongly differed with Thompson's idea of continuity between EBIV and MBIIA and dismissed his notions of nomadism as naïve (1980b: 53–55): "Finally, the 'Amorite' question may be resolved. The considerable linguistic evidence for an 'Amorite' population in Syria-Palestine is now credible—not on the supposition that an 'Amorite' invasion from Upper Syria and Mesopotamia had taken place, but by the recognition

that the indigenous Middle Bronze Age population had *always* been West Semitic or 'Amorite'" (58).

The destruction of the Patriarchal model has not gone unchallenged and
attempts to reconnect the Patriarchs and the EBIV period have been made.
John Bimson (1983) has argued that the key to placing the Patriarchal accounts
in the archaeological sequence is to recognize that a long period of time is
involved. He contended that Abraham dates to the EBIV predominantly, but
that later Patriarchal activity dates to the MBIIA period. Bimson rejected the
Amorite hypothesis (61) but pointed out that this rejection did not negate the
journeys of Abraham, only their connection to a hypothetical "Amorite" invasion. After all, the biblical accounts center on only one family, not an entire
national group. Interestingly, despite supporting the historicity of the patriarchs, Bimson did not accept archaeological evidence as completely external
and objective, realizing the "limitations of archaeological evidence, and the
uncertainties surrounding its interpretation" (88–89). Even in the approach of
a scholar sympathetic to the endeavor of biblical archaeology, the old certainty
was gone.

Conservative scholarship retained the linkage of the Patriarchs and Middle Bronze Age Palestine, although not to the EBIV period. Alfred Hoerth, a
University of Chicago–trained archaeologist who worked extensively in Egypt
and Nubia, directed the archaeology program at Wheaton College after the
death of Free. Hoerth was a student of Braidwood and brought a multidisciplinary perspective to the conservative religious school. His recent overview,
Archaeology and the Old Testament (1998), retains the linkage of the Patriarchs
and the Middle Bronze Age. Hoerth places Abraham mostly in the MB, seeing
his world as more urban than the EBIV would permit (75–123). He is not a
fundamentalist and denies the ability of archaeology to "prove" the Bible (18–
22).

Against the Conquest

The Albright-Wright Conquest model has also been severely strained in recent
years. As far back as the 1960s, George Mendenhall (1962) postulated a non-
invasion model for the rise of Israel, believing that peasant revolt and social
revolution better explained the conditions of the Late Bronze Age–Iron Age
transition. This hypothesis was expanded in a massive treatment of the social
context of early Israel by Norman Gottwald: "On closer examination, it turns
out that there is as much—and maybe more—to be said against using the
archaeological results to support the conquest model as there is in its favor"

(1979: 198). Gottwald followed the lead of de Vaux in emphasizing the lack of certainty in assigning a destruction layer to the Hebrews. Many destructions of Palestinian tells both before and after the thirteenth century have been essentially ignored, "but much can happen in twenty-five years that need not be attributed to a single historical agent" (202). The lack of evidence at Jericho and Ai, two central stories in the Joshua cycle, also led Gottwald to discount the traditional picture. He concluded:

> As a self-sufficient explanation of the Israelite occupation of the
> land, the conquest model is a failure. On the literary-historical side,
> the biblical traditions are too fragmentary and contradictory to bear
> the interpretation put upon them by the centralized cult and by the
> editorial framework of Joshua. On the archaeological side, the data
> are too fragmentary and ambiguous, even contradictory, to permit
> the extravagant claims made by some archaeologists and historians
> using archaeological data . . . What must be avoided is a facile circle
> of presumed confirmation of the conquest, built up from selective
> piecing together of biblical and archaeological features which seem
> to correspond, but in disregard of contradictory features and without
> respect for the tenuous nature both of the literary and of the archae-
> ological data. (203)

Gottwald explained the rise of Israel as a sociological reaction by oppressed peasants to the harsh rule of Late Bronze urban power structures. As a result, Israel rejected the urbanized lifestyle and the political order of kings and city-states. It must be pointed out that Gottwald's blanket rejection of the biblical account of a conquest supported a theological rejection of traditional biblical religion. He hoped that his study would "close the door firmly and irrevocably on the idealist and supernaturalist illusions still permeating and bedeviling our religious outlook. Yahweh and 'his' people Israel must be demystified, dero-manticized, dedogmatized and deidolized" (1979: 708). This is a position poles apart from Wright's "Mighty Acts."

A recent survey of the history of Israel and Judah rejected any attempt to reconstruct "the age of conquest" (Miller and Hayes 1986: 90). Although still arguing for a Conquest, John Bimson (1978) also rejected the Albright-Wright thirteenth-century reconstruction, preferring to date it back into the fifteenth century B.C. Amihai Mazar, in *Archaeology of the Land of the Bible* (1992), sum-marized the tension between text and archaeology: "In some cases (southern Transjordan, Arad, 'Ai, Yarmouth, and Hebron) there is an outright conflict between the archaeological findings and the conquest narratives, while in others (Lachish, Hazor, Bethel) archaeology does not contradict these stories" (334). As *Harper's Bible Dictionary* puts it, "Scholars continue to debate the nature and date of the Israelite occupation" (Mattingly 1985: 178).

Summary

The decade of the 1960s witnessed the collapse of the paradigm of biblical archaeology. Wright had begun those crucial ten years supremely confident in the ability of archaeology to provide an objective answer to the Kulturgeschichte questions of biblical archaeology. Yet, at the end of that decade he had rejected such a view by declaring, "Ambiguity is a central component of history" (1971: 75). Death added to the problems of the field, claiming Albright, Glueck, de Vaux, and Wright himself in the space of five years. In an ironic twist, the students Wright had trained pioneered the new paradigm of Syro-Palestinian archaeology.

5

The Legacy of Biblical Archaeology

In the 1970s, the fate of biblical archaeology was hotly debated (Cross 1973; Dever 1974), and even the term "biblical archaeology" was called into question (Dever 1974, 1976, 1985). Although not all American archaeologists in Syria/Palestine rejected the earlier terminology (Lance 1982), most now prefer "Syro-Palestinian archaeology," or a specific political/geographic term (Dever 2003). Unfortunately, the analysis of the obvious faults of classic biblical archaeology tended to shroud the positive aspects of its legacy. With the death of both of the main architects of the field, the remaining supporters of the Albright-Wright reconstruction have become removed from the mainstream of archaeology in Palestine. Today, the new paradigm of Syro-Palestinian archaeology dominates U.S. field research in Palestine, and classic biblical archaeology is being dismissed as an outdated paradigm of no particular importance. However, the recognition of its positive contributions would restore a much needed balance to the current understanding of the growth and development of the field.

No Room at the Inn

Contemporary with the various attacks on biblical archaeology's reconstruction of the early history of Israel was a debate on the value and nature of biblical archaeology itself. The entire paradigm has been rejected as a workable approach to archaeology in Palestine. In the Winslow lectures, William Dever (1974) established the credentials for a nonbiblical endeavor called Syro-Palestinian archaeology and has continued to refine the theoretical approach for this discipline (1981, 1985, 2001).

Dever was not content with the establishment of Syro-Palestinian archaeology, but attacked the validity of any entity calling itself biblical archaeology: "In the first place, we ought to stop talking about 'Biblical archaeology.' There probably is no such thing, and I would say by definition there cannot be" (1974: 33). Dever saw the definition of biblical archaeology as implying a special kind of archaeology that deals with the Bible, somehow different from regular archaeology. At best, such a term was misleading; at worst, simply wrong. Dever realized that the biblical scholar whose interest was limited to the archaeology of the time period of the Bible had a legitimate narrow focus; for that, he advocated "archaeology of the Bible" or "archaeology of the biblical period" instead of biblical archaeology. For Dever, the term biblical archaeology was too loaded with potential misunderstanding, whatever its de jure definition.

Dever (1981) turned to anthropology for a theoretical base, finding it in the "new archaeology" (or processual archaeology) of Binford. Ironically, processual archaeology is very positivist in its approach to the archaeological record. Dever embraced the new paradigm not because it included a more nuanced appreciation for the archaeological record, but because it was *abiblical*. As he became more versed in the argumentation, Dever (2001) did see some of the flaws associated with processual archaeology.

The validity of the independence of Syro-Palestinian archaeology has been universally recognized. Even scholars who continue to advocate a role for biblical archaeology accept the existence of a branch of general archaeology going by the name of Palestinian or Syro-Palestinian archaeology (e.g., see Lance 1982). What still continues to cause passionate disagreement is Dever's elimination of biblical archaeology as it was classically defined.

The Problem of Perspective

Frank Moore Cross (1973), a linguistic specialist who studied under Albright and taught Dever, took issue with Dever's rejection of biblical archaeology in a memorial tribute to Albright. Cross contended that Dever did not correctly understand Albright's views on biblical archaeology: "William Foxwell Albright regarded Palestinian archaeology or Syro-Palestinian archaeology as a small, if important, section of biblical archaeology. One finds it ironical that recent students suppose them interchangeable terms" (4–5). Dever responded to this implied criticism: "That misses my point: they are not interchangeable terms. 'Syro-Palestinian archaeology' is not the same as, not a small part of 'biblical archaeology.' I regret to say that all who would defend Albright and 'biblical archaeology' on this ground are sadly out of touch with reality in the field of archaeology" (1982: 104). Dever's attacks were directed against the de facto view of biblical archaeology and from an archaeological perspective. Cross viewed biblical archaeology from a biblical perspective; the distinction is crucial. Neither Cross nor Dever has fully understood Albright on this point. Dever contended that Albright "never conceived of Palestinian archaeology as a separate discipline or branch of general archaeology" (1981: 24 n. 22), whereas in reality, Albright did see Palestinian archaeology as a separate discipline. He presented such an understanding in the Haverford symposium, discussing Syro-Palestinian archaeology as a branch of general archaeology (Albright 1938c). He had just finished excavation at Tell Beit Mirsim and was approaching Palestine from an archaeological perspective, not a biblical one. The understanding that Cross presented—Palestinian archaeology as a section of biblical archaeology—was Albright's, but only from a biblical perspective. The crux of the matter is that Albright used both perspectives at various points in his career: that of a biblical scholar who saw all the ancient Near East as a backdrop for the Bible, and that of an archaeologist working in a geographically distinctive branch of general archaeology.

The confusion of perspective led to differing reactions. Darrell Lance (1982), Dever's colleague at Gezer, still accepted Albright's classic definition for the chronological and geographical spread of biblical archaeology as the only viable definition for biblical archaeology. "When 'biblical archaeology' is conceived of in this way," responded Dever, "it is no discipline at all but is equivalent to the whole of ancient Near Eastern studies as they bear on the Bible. In short the definition is so broad that it is meaningless" (1982: 104). The key word for Dever is "discipline" (see also Dever 1985); the definition of biblical archaeology must force it to be interdisciplinary. This is recognized by Lance:

> Biblical archaeology is the sub-specialty of biblical studies which
> seeks to bring to bear on the interpretation of the Bible all the infor-
> mation gained through archaeological research and discovery . . .
> When the biblical archaeologist steps into technical matters of Pales-
> tinian archaeology, he or she becomes a Palestinian archaeologist
> whose work of excavation, analysis, and publication must go on with
> the same kind of critical rigor that would be expected in any other
> aspect of critical biblical or historical study. (1982: 100)

In other words, a biblical archaeologist does not excavate in Palestine; he or she only assimilates information. Whatever Lance's de jure definition, the above statement implies that biblical archaeology is de facto an armchair, interdisciplinary endeavor. Lance fears the denial of professional status to an archaeologist working in Palestine who has as a goal "the elucidation of the biblical text" (100). Dever (1982: 104) considers Lance to be "professional," but the potential for discrimination is present.

Biblical Archaeology after the Divorce

Biblical archaeology still has validity as a name for the interaction sphere of archaeology and the Bible. Throughout his writings, Dever (1974, 1976, 1981, 1982, 1985, 1993, 1995a, 2001, 2003) has advocated a continued relationship between biblical studies and archaeology in Palestine. Each discipline has its own methodologies and research interests, although archaeology is the only source of new data for biblical studies. This new biblical archaeology should use the results of both disciplines (biblical studies and archaeology) to aid each other (Dever 2001).

The Maximalists versus the Minimalists

Unfortunately, the new biblical archaeology is an endeavor racked by fierce polemics. The wide-ranging discussion is conveniently referred to as the maximalist-minimalist controversy (the literature is extensive; see *What Did the Biblical Writers Know and When Did They Know It?* by Dever 2001, and *The Bible Unearthed* by I. Finkelstein and Silberman 2001 for the latest treatments of the debate). This shorthand refers to the different approaches taken by the protagonists to the text of the historic books in the Hebrew Bible. Like the fundamentalist-modernist controversy of the 1920s, sometimes the arguments have degenerated into personal polemics, poisoning the atmosphere for rational debate. Although the debate is fundamentally a biblical-theological-ideological argument, each side has used archaeological data to bolster its position. Ironically, archaeology is once again being used as a weapon to further particular biblical-theological perspectives. The new biblical archaeology is not in that way very different from the old.

The main archeological issues being debated revolve around different models interpreting the Iron I and Iron II archaeological record. These periods witnessed the formation, flowering, and destruction of the Hebrew kingdoms. Although the existence of the states of Israel and Judah are attested in extrabiblical sources, the Hebrew Bible contains extensive records that the maximalists use as a major source for interpreting the beginnings of Israel and the nature of the kingdoms. The minimalists deny the relevance of the Hebrew Bible to the historical kingdoms, considering the texts to be hopelessly flawed documents of the post-Exilic era.

The collapse of the Albright-Wright Conquest model and the pioneering survey work of Israel Finkelstein in the central hill country sparked a reassessment of state formation in ancient Israel and Judah. Finkelstein's study, *The Archaeology of the Israelite Settlement* (1988), identified nearly three hundred settlements of the LB–Iron I transition across the country. Most of these are newly founded sites, yet show strong continuity with Late Bronze material culture: "All archaeologists and virtually all biblical scholars have abandoned the older conquest model, or even 'peaceful infiltration' and peasants revolt models for 'indigenous origins' and/or 'symbiosis' models in attempting to explain the emergence of early Israel in Canaan" (Dever 2001: 41). Despite this blanket statement, conservative scholars have continued to argue for the presence of some external influences in the establishment of early Israel (Hoffmeier 1996). Since the publication of the survey data, Finkelstein and Dever have engaged in a long debate on the ethnicity of the settlements and the development of the Israelite state (for some of the debate, see Dever 1991, 1993, 1995a, 1995b, 2001; I. Finkelstein 1996b, 1999; I. Finkelstein and Silberman 2001). As Dever (2001: 43) points out, the debate has been an archeological one, without reference in a major way to the biblical text.

The tenth century B.C. of the United Monarchy is the nexus point in the maximalist-minimalist debate. Here, both the biblical text and the archeological data are contested. The archeological-historical reconstruction of the United Monarchy in the tenth century was one of the apparent triumphs of the biblical archaeology of Albright and Wright. This reconstruction dominates the contemporary general overview texts (Ben-Tor 1992; Hoerth 1998; Mazar 1992; Shanks 1999). The minimalist interpretation is that the United Monarchy is a creation of a later period, a mythical Golden Age that was necessary to restore national pride after the Exile. The archaeological corollary of this has been to bring down the dates of the tenth-century materials into the ninth and eighth centuries B.C. (I. Finkelstein 1996a, I. Finkelstein and Silberman 2001). The Mention of the "House of David" on the stele from Tell Dan has caused consternation among the radical minimalists, leading Lemache and Thompson (1994) to say it is a forgery. This charge has been solidly refuted (Rainey 2001).

Although Finkelstein and Silberman concur that the evidence of the stele validates a historical David, they contend that the architectural remains traditionally associated with the United Monarchy should be attributed to later mon-

FIGURE 5.1 Tenth-century B.C. gate at Gezer. Photo by author

archs. Megiddo has been recently reexcavated by Finkelstein and others, and the carbon dates from the site are one of the linchpins of the argument for lowering the ceramic chronology. Archaeologists use many attributes of the true sciences, but there is a danger in this: It can give a veneer of accuracy that belies reality. The use of radiocarbon dating is an example. A date given as 880 B.C. ±60 means an equally valid date range of 940 B.C. to 820 B.C. The dates from Megiddo need to be seen in this light. An average means nothing, but an overlap range does have meaning. The maximalist view has maintained a strong defense of the original tenth-century dating for the defensive systems at Hazor, Gezer, and Megiddo (Dever 2001; figure 5.1).

Toward the Future

When all the rhetoric is stripped away, both sides in the maximalist-minimalist debate essentially share the same theoretical and methodological approach to the archaeological record, that is, a somewhat modified processsualist/semi-positivist approach. I believe this uniform archaeological methodology is part of the problem. The minimalist archaeological argumentation on the United Monarchy follows an almost Wrightian vision of archaeology as realia. On the maximalist side, only Dever is beginning to expand his view of archaeology. He mentions postprocessualism approvingly and even calls for a reading of archaeological data as text (following Ian Hodder; see Hodder 1992 for a more developed statement), although he still views it from the outside (Dever 2001: 65–95). Where the combatants disagree is on the value placed on the biblical record. Dever is willing to see the Hebrew Bible as a source of information that can provide data on ancient life in Palestine. He presents a strongly argued case for consistency between the biblical and the archaeological texts for the Iron II period (97–244).

The archaeological record can be highly fluid in its meaning and interpretation. Perhaps we can modify de Vaux to say "There should be no conflict between a critically examined archaeological text and a critically examined biblical text." Some have taken Ian Hodder to mean that there is no correct or incorrect interpretation of such a work of literature. This takes the analogy too far. What Hodder means is that material remains are ordered according to a logic held by past peoples. Too often, the biblical narrative has been forced to conform to an archaeological model. A glaring historical example is the Albright-Wright Conquest model, an archaeological construct, being equated with the biblical record.

We need to avoid the trap of "temprocentrism." We do not know what meanings a specific object or even a site carried in its own lifetime. What we may see as primary in an artifact's importance may have been unknown to the original users. When I was a graduate student, the question came up in a seminar regarding the contents of a specific structure discussed in an excavation report. When I questioned the interpretation placed on it by the report, one of my fellow students said, "We are anthropologists; we ignore the idiosyncratic!" Too often this is the case in interpretation. We seek patterns, a legacy of our processual approach to archaeology, even when they are not there. Sometimes we even create them ourselves, then trumpet the "discovery" of them in the record. We must remember that we do not dig the "type" site. We excavate the remains of individuals. In fact, the idiosyncratic artifact or site may be more insightful than the patterned one. Wright (1975) was correct when he warned the "pure scientists" that archaeology deals with human beings and thus must remain a humanistic discipline.

An excavation should be a dialogue, not a monologue. One of the basic aspects of any archaeological endeavor is a research design. No excavation will enter the field without one. We all agree that data speak only in response to a question and that the question we seek to answer shapes our field methods. However, remember the military stricture that no plan of battle survives contact with the enemy unchanged. An archaeologist must approach a site with a question, but should not seek a specific answer. The danger comes when we try to dictate what the answer should be. We need to remain flexible and respond to the site formation processes and to the material recovered from the site. We must be especially wary when we apparently find what we seek.

The Positive Legacy of Classic Biblical Archaeology

Biblical archaeology as defined in the field by Wright and Albright is gone. Even the visible remains of the once dominating edifice—the Patriarchal model and the Conquest model—have been removed. Biblical archaeology has been dismissed as parochial, lacking in theory and method, and reactionary (Dever 1985, 2001). This characterization has obscured the positive legacy that biblical archaeology has passed on to Syro-Palestinian archaeology.

Cultural Unity

Albright (1938c) strongly emphasized the union of Syria and Palestine as a single cultural unit. Due to the political situation at the time, the British and the French tended to view the northern and southern portions of the Levant in isolation from each other. As an American, Albright could see the fundamental cultural unity of the area without the clouding of political boundaries. This is vitally important today, when modern politics continues to divide the region into antagonistic spheres. Israeli, Jordanian, Lebanese, Syrian, and Palestinian archaeologists labor under the handicap of perceived political implications of their research (Meskell 1998; Silberman 1989). Unfortunately, the annual meeting of ASOR is often the only opportunity for the Arab and Israeli scholars to share information face-to-face. The more such information is shared, the clearer it becomes that ancient Syria and Palestine were basically one culture. Thanks to biblical archaeology, American Syro-Palestinian archaeologists are oriented to think in terms of one culture. This gives American scholars an advantage that will only increase as politics continues to polarize the Near East. Dever's proposal (2003) to drop the term "Syro-Palestinian" may lead to the loss of a regional perspective. A broad geographic term such as the Archaeology of the Eastern Mediterranean Levant may suffice.

Intensive Investigation

The Holy Land is one of the most intensively studied archaeological regions in the world, providing a wealth of raw data for archaeologists. In many areas, scholars still must work at clarifying the basic ceramic and cultural sequence, but in Palestine, the basic building blocks for an archaeological history are in place. To a great degree, this is the result of biblical archaeology's obsession with questions of Kulturgeschichte. Albright, Wright, and Glueck concentrated much of their research on the clarification of the ceramic sequence and the resulting chronology of Syria/Palestine. Their heirs in Syro-Palestinian archaeology have the freedom to ask wide-ranging questions because of the labor of the previous generation. However, it must be admitted that Syro-Palestinian archaeology displays a legacy of the Kulturgeschichte orientation of biblical archaeology: a tendency to ask chronological questions of ceramics. It is not the sole feature of the ceramic program on new projects, but it still dominates more research energy than it should.

Professionalism

Albright and Wright worked at establishing high standards and often employed more advanced methods than contemporary "professional" archaeologists in Palestine. This was particularly true of Albright. Wright quickly saw the advantages in the methodology of Kenyon and popularized her work among American archaeologists and continued to demonstrate methodological flexibility at the end of his career, when he advocated the new multidisciplinary methodology.

A current example of the professional legacy of biblical archaeology is the East Frontier Archeological Project. James K. Hoffmeier, one of the spokesmen for a maximalist position, is an Egyptologist. Trained in biblical archaeology at Wheaton College, Hoffmeier went to Toronto to study Egyptology. He currently teaches at Trinity International University and is leading a field project in the northern Sinai. The main goal of the project is the elucidation of the New Kingdom frontier. Although Hoffmeier (1996) has a personal interest in examining possible routes of the Exodus, it is a secondary goal. The project is operating with an Egyptological agenda, but carefully investigating where biblical data may intersect. Recognizing his own limited field experience, Hoffmeier has gathered an international, fully professional, multidisciplinary team (of which I am a member), many of whom have no interest in the biblical record. The excavations at Tell el Borg have produced evidence of an Amarna-era temple, a Ramesside temple with carved friezes, and a series of large mudbrick fortresses. The geologists have identified a previously unknown branch of the Nile and mapped the New Kingdom topography (figure 5.2). This information has clarified the location of the beginning route of the Way of Horus, the New Kingdom military road to Palestine.

FIGURE 5.2 Stephen Moshier conducting magnetometry survey at Tell Borg for the East Frontier Archeological Project in the North Sinai, Egypt. Photo by author

The project sponsored a symposium in 2001, which invited critical examination of the project and its methodology. The symposium included archaeologists, biblical scholars, and geologists and welcomed self-defined maximalists as well as those with more moderate views. Although many of the papers (to be published in a forthcoming volume) dealt with issues of the current maximalist-minimalist debate, the North Sinai project was thoroughly critiqued in both formal papers and informal conversation. Hoffmeier's openness to criticism is rare in archaeology and exemplifies the biblical archaeology legacy of professionalism.

Summary

Biblical archaeology rested on two fundamental a priori assumptions: that the Bible was historical, and that archaeology provided an external, objective source of realia. These in turn were dependent on a belief in the Bible as the Word of God and on a nineteenth-century understanding of science as an endeavor that was immutable and unaffected by the presuppositions of the scholar. Archaeology was properly one of the humanities, and as such it was the handmaiden of history. Thus, the endeavor of archaeology in a historical era should be the elucidation of this history and should be geared to answer the questions of Kulturgeschichte. The Bible was the historical document of Palestine; therefore, it was the source of the agenda for biblical archaeology. This agenda was historical, biblical, and, in its ultimate extent, apologetical.

The avowed aim of biblical archaeology from Robinson to Wright was the grounding of the Bible in the realm of realia. Albright specifically wished to make biblical studies a science through the twin tools of linguistic analysis and archaeology. Archaeology was to establish objective criteria for judging the historical validity of the biblical record. General cultural evolution was of no interest to the theoreticians of biblical archaeology. In essence, only a small segment of cultural evolution was of interest: the evolution of Spiritual Man. Albright aimed to write a meaningful, objective history of the development of biblical religion in *From the Stone Age to Christianity* (1940). Wright took this attempt one stage further by emphasizing the theological implications of a historically verifiable Bible.

Biblical archaeology understood cultural change to be the result of historical and ideological (even divine) factors. Hence it developed, in the ceramic methodology of Albright, a field methodology geared to elucidate questions of chronology and political history. Dever cited biblical archaeology for its failure to create a coherent theory and method for the field: "The lack of methodology meant that the fundamental historical-theological issues were never resolved, neither the general questions of faith and history, nor the specific questions" (1985: 60). Here I must disagree with Dever. The "fundamental issues" were never resolved because of an unsound method, not the lack of method. The demonstration of the historical validity of the Bible depended on archaeology being realia. Historical questions were addressed through an appropriate methodology. For a generation, it appeared that these questions were resolved. Only when the results in the field proved that archaeology is not purely objective did biblical archaeology collapse. The only flaw lay in the understanding of the sought answers as objective data untouched by the questions.

The history of biblical archaeology should function as a warning to the danger of letting our presuppositions overcome the nature of the data. In a sense, it is an example of ideological archaeology. The practitioners of biblical archaeology had a well-developed ideological framework in which to pursue their research, and they proved to be remarkably flexible in absorbing questionable data and modifying these to fit their system. The current debate between the maximalists and the minimalists illustrates that no Syro-Palestinian archaeologist can honestly deny that this can be a trap for any archaeologist.

Dostoevsky in *Notes from Underground* wrote, "Man has such a predilection for systems and abstract deductions that he is ready to distort the truth intentionally, he is ready to deny the evidence of his senses in order to justify his logic." We must look inside ourselves, approach archaeology with humility and not with arrogance, and be constantly alert to our own subjectivity. This is perhaps the most valuable legacy of classic biblical archaeology.

Bibliography

ABBREVIATIONS

AASOR   *Annual of the American Schools of Oriental Research*
AJA   *American Journal of Archaeology*
BA   *The Biblical Archaeologist*
BAR   *Biblical Archaeology Review*
BASOR   *Bulletin of the American Schools of Oriental Research*
JBL   *Journal of Biblical Literature*
JPOS   *Journal of the Palestine Oriental Society*
JSOT   *Journal for the Study of the Old Testament*
NEA   *Near Eastern Archaeology*
PEQ   *Palestine Exploration Fund Quarterly*
RB   *Revue Biblique*

Abel, F.-M. 1939. "Edward Robinson and the Identification of Biblical Sites."
    JBL 58: 365–372.
Adkins, Lesley, and Roy Adkins. 2000. *The Keys of Egypt: The Obsession to
    Decipher Egyptian Hieroglyphs*. New York: HarperCollins.
Albrektson, B. 1967. *History and the Gods*. Lund, Sweden: Glerup.
Albright, W. F. 1921a. "Recent Observations of Our Acting Director." *BA-
    SOR* 4: 2–7.
———. 1921b. "A Tour on Foot through Samaria and Galilee." *BASOR* 4: 7–
    13.
———. 1922a. "Preliminary Reports on Tel el-Ful." *BASOR* 6: 7–8.
———. 1922b. "Gibeah of Saul and Benjamin." *BASOR* 6: 8–11.
———. 1922c. "The Excavations at Ascalon." *BASOR* 6: 11–18.
———. 1922d. "The Excavations at Tell el-Ful." *BASOR* 7: 7.

———. 1923a. "The Danish Excavations at Shiloh." *BASOR* 9: 10–11.

———. 1923b. *Contributions to the Historical Geography of Palestine. AASOR* 1–2: 1–46.

———. 1923c. "Interesting Finds in Tumuli Near Jerusalem." *BASOR* 10: 2–3.

———. 1923d. "Some Archaeological and Topographical Results of a Trip through Palestine." *BASOR* 14: 2–12.

———. 1924a. "The Archaeological Results of an Expedition to Moab and the Dead Sea." *BASOR* 14: 2–14.

———. 1924b. *Excavations and Results at Tell el-Ful (Gibeah of Saul). AASOR* 4.

———. 1924c. "Researches of the School in Western Judea." *BASOR* 15: 3–11.

———. 1925a. "Bronze Age Mounds of Northern Palestine and the Hauran: The Spring Trip of the School in Jerusalem." *BASOR* 19: 5–19.

———. 1925b. "Report of the Director of the School in Jerusalem." *BASOR* 20: 9–16.

———. 1926. "The Jordan Valley in the Bronze Age." *AASOR* 6: 13–74.

———. 1928a. "Among the Canaanite Mounds of Eastern Galilee." *BASOR* 29: 1–8.

———. 1928b. "The Egyptian Empire in Asia in the Twenty-First Century B.C." *JPOS* 8: 223–56.

———. 1929. "Progress in Palestinian Archaeology During the Year 1928." *BASOR* 33: 1–29.

———. 1932a. *Archaeology of Palestine and the Bible.* New York: Fleming H. Revell.

———. 1932b. "The Excavations of Tell Beit Mirsim, I: The Pottery of the First Three Campaigns. *AASOR* 12.

———. 1933a. "The Excavation of Tell Beit Mirsim, IA: The Bronze Age Pottery of the Fourth Campaign." *AASOR* 13: 55–127.

———. 1933b. "In Memoriam: Melvin Grove Kyle." *BASOR* 51: 6–7.

———. 1934a. "Book Reviews." *BASOR* 54: 28.

———. 1934b. "The Kyle Memorial Excavation at Bethel." *BASOR* 56: 1–15.

———. 1935. "Palestine in the Earliest Historical Period." *JPOS* 15: 193–234.

———. 1936. "James Henry Breasted." *American Scholar* 5, no. 3: 287–99.

———. 1937. "Edward Robinson." *Dictionary of American Biography* 16: 39–40. New York: American Council of Learned Societies, Charles Scribner's Sons, 1937.

———. 1938a. "The Chronology of a South Palestinian City, Tell El-Ajjul." *American Journal of Semitic Languages and Literatures* 55: 337–59.

———. 1938b. "The Excavation of Tell Beit Mirsim, III: The Iron Age." *AASOR* 17.

———. 1938c. "The Present State of Syro-Palestinian Archaeology." In *The Haverford Symposium on Archaeology and the Bible,* ed. Elihu Grant. New Haven: American Schools of Oriental Research, 1–46.

———. 1939. "The Israelite Conquest of Canaan in the Light of Archaeology." *BASOR* 74: 11–23.

———. 1940. *From the Stone Age to Christianity: Monotheism and the Historical Process.* Baltimore: Johns Hopkins University Press.

———. 1941. "New Egyptian Data on Palestine in the Patriarchal Age." *BASOR* 81: 16–20.

———. 1942a. *Archaeology and the Religion of Israel.* Baltimore: Johns Hopkins University Press.

————. 1942b. "Sir W. M. Flinders Petrie." *BASOR* 87: 7–8.

————. 1943. "The Excavation of Tell Beit Mirsim, I.: The Iron Age." *AASOR* 21–23.

————. 1948. "William Foxwell Albright." *American Spiritual Autobiographies.* New York: Harper and Brothers, 156–81.

————. 1949. *The Archaeology of Palestine.* Harmondsworth, UK: Penguin.

————. 1952. "The Bible after Twenty Years of Archaeology." *Religion in Life* 21: 537–50.

————. 1958. "Recent Progress in Palestinian Archaelogy: Samaria-Sebaste III and Hazor I." *BASOR* 150: 21–25.

————. 1961. "Abram the Hebrew: A New Archaeological Interpretation." *BASOR* 163: 36–54.

————. 1963. *The Biblical Period from Abraham to Ezra.* New York: Harper and Row.

————. 1964a. *History, Archaeology, and Christian Humanism.* New York: McGraw-Hill.

————. 1964b. "The Eighteenth Century Princes of Byblos and the Chronology of Middle Bronze." *BASOR* 176: 38–46.

————. 1965. "Further Light on the Chronology of Middle Bronze Byblos." *BASOR* 179: 38–43.

————. 1966a. *Archaeology, Historical Analogy, and Early Biblical Tradition.* Baton Rouge: Louisiana State University Press.

————. 1966b. "Further Light on the Chronology of the Early Bronze IV–Middle Bronze IIA in Phonecia and Syria-Palestine." *BASOR* 184: 26–34.

————. 1966c. *New Horizons in Biblical Research.* London: Oxford University Press.

————. 1969. "The Impact of Archaeology on Biblical Research." In *New Directions in Biblical Archaeology* ed. D. N. Freedman and Jonas C. Greenfield. Garden City, NY: Doubleday, 1–4.

————. 1971. "Nelson Glueck in Memorium." *BASOR* 202: 2–6.

Albright, W. F., and J. Kelso. 1968. "The Excavation of Bethel." *AASOR* 39.

Albright, W. F., and C. S. Mann. 1971. *The Anchor Bible Matthew.* Garden City, NY: Doubleday.

Alt, Albrecht. 1939. "Edward Robinson and the Historical Geography of Palestine." *JBL* 58: 373–77.

Badè, W. F. 1934. *A Manual of Excavation in the Near East.* Berkeley: University of California Press.

Baikie, J. 1923. *A Century of Excavation in the Land of the Pharaohs.* London: Religious Tract Society.

Ball, C. J. 1918. "The Relation of Tibetan to Sumerian." *Proceedings of the Society of Biblical Archaeology* 40: 95–100.

Barkay, Gabriel. 1986. "The Garden Tomb: Was Jesus Buried Here?" *BAR* 12: 40–53.

Barr, J. 1961. *The Semantics of Biblical Language.* New York: Oxford University Press.

————. 1976. "Biblical Theology." In *Interpreters Dictionary of the Bible, Supplement.* Nashville: Abingdon, 104–11.

Ben-Tor, Amon, ed. 1992. *The Archaeology of Ancient Israel.* Jerusalem: Open Press.

Biddle, Martin. 1999. *The Tomb of Christ.* Phoenix Mill, UK: Sutton.

Bimson, John. 1978. *Redating the Exodus and Conquest. JSOT,* Supplement Series 5. 2d ed. Sheffield, UK: Almond Press.

———. 1983. "Archaeological Data and the Dating of the Patriarchs. In *Essays on the Patriarchal Narratives,* ed. A. R. Millard and D. J. Wiseman. Winona Lake, Indiana: Eisenbrauns, 53–89.

Birch, S. 1872a. "Introduction." *Transactions of the Society of Biblical Archaeology* 1: i–iii.

———. 1872b. "The Progress of Biblical Archaeology." *Transactions of the Society of Biblical Archaeology* 1: 1–12.

Blakely, Jeffrey A. 1993. "Frederic Jones Bliss: Father of Palestinian Archaeology." *BA* 56.3: 110–15.

Bliss, F. J. 1894. *Tell el Hesy (Lachish.)* London: Palestine Exploration Fund.

———. 1907. *The Development of Palestine Exploration.* New York: Scribner.

Bliss, F. J., and R.A.S. Macalister. 1902. *Excavations in Palestine During the Years 1898– 1900.* London: Palestine Exploration Fund.Bottéro, J. 1971. "Syria During the Third Dynasty at Ur." In *The Cambridge Ancient History.* Cambridge, UK: Cambridge University Press, I: 2, pp. 559–66.

Braidwood, R., and B. Howe. 1960. *Prehistoric Investigations in Iraqi Kurdistan.* The Oriental Institute of the University of Chicago Studies in Ancient Civilization No. 31. Chicago: University of Chicago Press.

Breasted, J. H. 1933. *The Dawn of Conscience.* Chicago: University of Chicago Press.

Brewer, J. 1939. "Edward A. Robinson as Biblical Scholar." *JBL* 58: 355–63.

Bright, John. 1981. *A History of Israel.* 3d ed. Philadelphia: Westminster.

Bruneau, P., and J. Ducat. 1965. *Guide de Delos.* Paris: E. de Boccard.

Caiger, S. L. 1936. *Bible and Spade.* London: Oxford University Press.

Callaway, J. A. 1980. "Sir Flinders Petrie: Father of Palestinian Archaeology." *BAR* 6.6: 44–55.

Campbell, E. F. 1983. "Judges 9 and Biblical Archaeology." In *The Word of the Lord Shall Go Forth: Essays in Honor of David Noel Freedman,* ed. C. Meyers and M. O'Conner. Winona Lake, Indiana: Eisenbrauns, 263–71.

———. 2003. *Shechem III: The Stratigraphy and Architecture of Shechem/Tell Balatah.* Boston, MA: American Schools of Oriental Research.

Chadwick, Owen. 1970. *The Victorian Church.* New York: Oxford University Press.

Childs, Brevard S. 1970. *Biblical Theology in Crisis.* Philadelphia: Westminster.

Churchill, Winston S. 1949. *Their Finest Hour.* Boston: Houghton Mifflin.

Cleator, P. E. 1976. *Archaeology in the Making.* London: Robert Hale.

Coburn, C. n.d. *Recent Explorations in Palestine.* Meadville, PA: World's Bible Conference.

Cole, D. P. 1984. *Shechem I: The Middle Bronze IIB Pottery.* Winona Lake, Indiana: American Schools of Oriental Research.

Cross, Frank M. 1973. "W. F. Albright's View of Biblical Archaeology." *BA* 36: 2–4.

Crowfoot, J. 1929. "Excavations on the Ophel 1928." *PEQ:* 150–66.

Curtius, E., and F. Adler. 1897. *Olympia, die Ergebnisse der von dem deutschen Reich veranstalteten Ausgrabung.* Berlin: A. Asher.

Davidson, Lawrence. 1996. "Biblical Archaeology and the Press: Shaping American Perceptions of Palestine in the First Decade of the Mandate." *BA* 59.2: 104–114.

de Vaux, Roland. 1951. "La troisieme campagnes de fouilles a Tell el-Far'ah pres Naplouse." *RB* 58: 566–90.

———. 1952. "La quatrieme campagnes de fouilles a Tell el-Far'ah pres Naplouse."
RB 59: 551–83.

———. 1961. *Ancient Israel*. New York: McGraw-Hill.

———. 1962. "Les fouilles de Tell el-Far'ah." *RB* 69: 212–53.

———. 1967. *Bible et Orient*. Paris: Les editions du Cerf.

———. 1970. "On the Right and Wrong Uses of Archaeology." In *Near Eastern Archaeology in the Twentieth Century*, ed. James A. Sanders. Garden City, NY: Doubleday, 64–80.

———. 1973. *Archaeology and the Dead Sea Scrolls*. London: Oxford University Press.

Dever, William G. 1959. "Present Status of Old Testament Theology." Master's thesis,
Butler University.

———. 1967. "The Excavations at Gezer." *BA* 30: 47–62.

———. 1970. "The 'Middle Bronze I' Period in Syria and Palestine." In *Near Eastern
Archaeology in the Twentieth Century*, ed. J. A. Sanders. Garden City, NY: Doubleday, 132–63.

———. 1973. "Two Approaches to Archaeological Method: The Architectural and the
Stratigraphic." *Eretz Israel* 11: 1–8.

———. 1974. *Archaeology and Biblical Studies: Prospects and Retrospects. The Winslow
Lectures*. Evanston, IL: Seabury-Western Theological Seminary.

———. 1976. "Archaeology." *Interpreter's Dictionary of the Bible, Supplement*. Nashville:
Abingdon, 44–52.

———. 1977. "Palestine in the Second Millennium B.C.E.: The Archaeological Picture." In *Israelite and Judean History*, ed. J. H. Hayes and Maxwell Miller. London:
SCM Press, 70–120.

———. 1978. "Gezer." In *Encyclopedia of Archaeological Excavations in the Holy Land*,
vol 2, ed. M. Avi-Yonah. Englewood Cliffs, NJ: Prentice-Hall, 428–39.

———. 1980a. "Biblical Theology and Biblical Archaeology: An Appreciation of G.
Ernest Wright." *Harvard Theological Review* 73: 1–15.

———. 1980b. "New Vistas on the EB IV ('MB I') Horizon in Syria-Palestine." *BA-
SOR* 237: 35–64.

———. 1981. "The Impact of the 'New Archaeology' on Syro-Palestinian Archaeology." *BASOR* 242: 15–30.

———. 1982. "Retrospects and Prospects in Biblical Archaeology." *BA* 45: 103–8.

———. 1985. "Syro-Palestinian and Biblical Archaeology." In *The Hebrew Bible and Its
Modern Interpreters*, ed. D. Knight and G. M. Tucker. Philadelphia: Fortress Press,
31–74.

———. 1991. "Archaeological Data on the Israelite Settlement: A Review of Two Recent Works." *BASOR* 284: 77–90.

———. 1993. "What Remains of the House That Albright Built?" *BA* 56.1: 25–35.

———. 1995a. "Will the Real Israel Please Stand Up? Archaeology and Israelite His-
toriography: Part I." *BASOR* 279: 61–80.

———. 1995b. "Ceramics, Ethnicity, and the Question of Israel's Origins." *BA* 58.4:
200–213.

———. 1998. "Archaeology, Ideology, and the Quest for an 'Ancient' or 'Biblical' Israel." *NEA* 61: 139–52.

———. 2001. *What Did the Biblical Writers Know and When Did They Know It?* Grand Rapids, MI: Eerdmans.

———. 2003. "Whatchamacallit: Why It's So Hard to Name Our Field." BAR 29.4: 57–61.

Dever, W. G., H. D. Lance, R. G. Bullard, D. P. Cole, and J. D. Seger. 1974. *Gezer II: Report of the 1967–70 Seasons in Fields I and II.* Jerusalem: Hebrew Union College Jewish Institute of Religion.

Dever, W. G., H. D. Lance, and G. E. Wright. 1970. *Gezer I: Preliminary Report of the 1964–66 Seasons.* Jerusalem: Hebrew Union College Jewish Institute of Religion.

Driver, S. 1891. *Introduction to the Old Testament.* Edinburgh: T and T Clark.

Dunand, M. 1939. *Fouilles de Byblos I: Fouilles 1925–1932. Text and Plates.* Paris: Paul Gauthier.

———. 1954. *Fouilles de Byblos II: Fouilles 1933–1938. Part I. Text.* Paris: Paul Gauthier.

———. 1958. *Fouilles de Byblos II: Fouilles 1933–1938. Part II. Text.* Paris: Paul Gauthier.

———. 1973. *Fouilles de Byblos V: L'architecture, les tombes, le materiel domestique, des origines neolithiques a l'avenement urbain.* Paris: Paul Gauthier.

Duncan, J. G. 1930. *Corpus of Dated Palestinian Pottery.* London: British School of Archaeology in Egypt.

———. 1931. *Digging Up Biblical History.* London: Society for Promoting Christian Knowledge.

Dyson, S. J. 1981. "A Classical Archaeologist's Response to the 'New Archaeology.'" *BASOR* 242: 7–14.

Egypt Exploration Fund. 1883. *Eqypt Exploration Fund*: 86.

Elliger, K. 1959. Review of G. E. Wright's *Biblische Archaologie, Theologische Literaturzeitung.* 84: 94–98.

Fargo, V. 1984. "BA Portrait: Sir Flinders Petrie." *BA* 47: 220–23.

Fierman, F. S. 1986. "Rabbi Nelson Glueck: An Archaeologist's Secret Life in the Service of the OSS." *BAR* 12.5: 18–23.

Finkelstein, Israel. 1988. *The Archaeology of the Israelite Settlement.* Jerusalem: Exploration Society.

———. 1996a. "The Archaeology of the United Monarchy: An Alternative View." *Levant* 28: 177–87.

———. 1996b. "Ethnicity and Origin of the Iron I Settlers in the Highlands of Canaan: Can the Real Israel Stand Up?" *BA* 59.4: 198–212.

———. 1999. "State Formation in Israel and Judah: A Contrast in Context, a Contrast in Trajectory." *NEA* 62.1: 35–52.

Finkelstein, Israel, and Neil A. Silberman. 2001. *The Bible Unearthed: Archaeology's New Vision of Ancient Israel and the Origin of Its Sacred Texts.* New York: Simon and Schuster.

Finkelstein, J. J. 1959. "The Bible, Archaeology, and History: Have Excavations Corroborated Scripture?" *Commentary* 27: 341–50.

Fisher, C. S. 1925. "A Plea for the Systematic Coordination of Archaeological Research in Palestine and Syria." *BASOR* 18: 15–27.

———. 1929. *The Excavation of Armageddon*. Oriental Institute Publications 4. Chicago: University of Chicago Press.

Fosdick, Harry Emerson. 1956. *The Living of These Days*. New York: Harper and Brothers.

Free, Joseph P. 1950. *Archaeology and Bible History*. Wheaton, IL: Van Kampen Press.

———. 1953. "The First Season of Excavation at Dothan." *BASOR* 131: 16–20.

———. 1954. "The Second Season of Excavation at Dothan." *BASOR* 135: 14–20.

———. 1955. "The Third Season of Excavation at Dothan." *BASOR* 139: 3–10.

———. 1956. "The Fourth Season of Excavation at Dothan." *BASOR* 143: 11–17.

———. 1958. "The Fifth Season at Dothan." *BASOR* 152: 10–16.

———. 1959. "The Sixth Season at Dothan." *BASOR* 156: 22–27.

———. 1960. "The Seventh Season at Dothan." *BASOR* 160: 6–13.

Freedman, David N. 1975. *William Foxwell Albright: A Comprehensive Bibliography*. Cambridge, MA: American Schools of Oriental Research.

Furness, N. 1954. *The Fundamentalist Controversy*. New Haven: Yale University Press.

Gardiner, E. N. 1925. *Olympia, Its History and Remains*. Oxford: Clarendon.

Garstang, John. July 1920–Dec. 1921. "Work of the Department of Antiquities of Palestine." *PEQ*: 57–63.

———. 1932. "Jericho: City and Necropolis." *Annals of Archaeology and Anthropology* 19: 3–22.

Glueck, Nelson. 1934. "Explorations in Eastern Palestine." *AASOR* 14.

———. 1935. "Explorations in Eastern Palestine, II." *AASOR* 15.

———. 1939. "Explorations in Eastern Palestine, III." *AASOR* 19–21.

———. 1940. *The Other Side of the Jordan*. New Haven: American Schools of Oriental Research.

———. 1942. "In Memoriam: Sir W. M. Flinders Petrie." *BASOR* 87: 6.

———. 1946. *The River Jordan*. New Haven: American Schools of Oriental Research.

———. 1951. "Explorations in Eastern Palestine, IV." *AASOR* 25–28.

———. 1959. *Rivers in the Desert: A History of the Negeb*. New York: Farrar, Cudahly, and Strauss.

———. 1965. *Deities and Dolphins*. New York: Farrar and Strauss.

———. 1977. "Tell el-Kheleifeh." In *Encyclopedia of Archaeological Excavations in the Holy Land*, ed. M. Avi-Yonah and E. Stern. Englewood Cliffs, NJ: Prentice-Hall, 713–21.

Gordon, Charles. 1885. "Eden and Golgotha." *PEF*: 78–81.

Gottwald, Norman K. 1979. *The Tribes of Yahweh: A Sociology of the Religion of Liberated Israel, 1250–1050 B.C.E.* Maryknoll, NY: Orbis.

Graham, W. C., and H. G. May. 1936. *Culture and Conscience: An Archaeological Story of the New Religious Past in Palestine*. Publications in Religious Education, Handbook of Ethics and Religion. Chicago: University of Chicago Press.

Grove, C. 1869a. "From the Original Prospectus." *PEQ* 1: 1–2.

———. 1869b. "Quarterly Statement of Progress." *PEQ* 1: 6–10.

———. 1869c. "Brief Narrative of the Proceedings of the Fund." *PEQ* 1: 10.

———. 1869d. "Statement of Progress." *PEQ* 2: 63–65.

———. 1870a. "Annual General Meeting." *PEQ* 3: 142.

———. 1870b. "The New Survey." *PEQ* 4: 157–61.

Guy, P.L.O. 1931. *New Light from Armageddon: Second Provisional Report (1927–29) on the Excavations of Megiddo in Palestine.* Chicago: University of Chicago Press.

———. 1938. *The Megiddo Tombs.* Oriental Institute Publications 38. Chicago: University of Chicago Press.

Hardwick, S. E. 1965. "Change and Constancy in William Foxwell Albright's Treatment of Early Old Testament History and Religion, 1918–1958." Ph.D. diss., New York University.

Hitchcock, R., and W. B. Smith. 1863. *The Life, Writings and Character of Edward Robinson, D.D., LL.D.* New York: Anson D. F. Randolph.

Hodder, Ian. 1992. *Theory and Practice in Archaeology.* London: Routledge.

Hoerth, Alfred. 1998. *Archaeology and the Old Testament.* Grand Rapids, MI: Baker Books.

Hoffmeier, James K. 1996. *Israel in Egypt: The Evidence for the Authenticity of the Exodus Tradition.* New York: Oxford University Press.

Jahn, J. 1839. *Biblical Archaeology.* Andover, MA: Gould, Newman, and Saxton.

Keller, Werner. 1956. *The Bible As History.* London: Hodder and Stoughton. Originally published as *Und die Bibel hat doch Recht: Forscher beweisen die Historische Wahrheit.*

Kenyon, Kathleen. 1953. *Beginning in Archaeology.* 2d ed. London: Phoenix House.

———. 1958. "Some Notes on the Early and Middle Bronze Age Strata of Megiddo." *Eretz Israel* 5: 51–60.

———. 1966. *Amorites and Canaanites.* London: Oxford University Press.

———. 1970. *Archaeology in the Holy Land.* 3d ed. New York: Praeger.

———. 1974. *Digging up Jerusalem.* New York: Praeger.

King, Philip J. 1983a. *American Archaeology in the Mideast: A History of the American Schools of Oriental Research.* Winona Lake, Indiana: American Schools of Oriental Research.

———. 1983b. "Edward Robinson: Biblical Scholar." *BA* 46: 230–34.

Kuhn, Thomas. 1970. *The Structure of Scientific Revolutions.* 2d ed. Chicago: University of Chicago Press.

Kyle, Melvin Grove. 1920a. *Moses and the Monuments.* Oberlin, OH: Biblioteca Sacra.

———. 1920b. *The Problem of the Pentateuch: A New Solution by Archaeological Methods.* Oberlin, OH: Biblioteca Sacra.

———. 1924. *The Deciding Voice of the Monuments in Biblical Criticism.* Oberlin, OH: Biblioteca Sacra.

———. 1928. *Explorations at Sodom.* London: Religious Tract Society.

———. 1934. *Excavating Kirjath-Sepher's Ten Cities.* Grand Rapids, MI: Eerdmans.

Lamon, R., and G. Shipton. 1939. *Megiddo I, Seasons of 1925–1934 Strata I–V.* Oriental Institute Publications 42. Chicago: University of Chicago Press.

Lance, H. Darrel. 1982. "American Biblical Archaeology in Perspective." *BA* 45: 97–102.

Lapp, Paul W. 1961. *Palestinian Ceramic Chronology 200 B.C.–A.D. 70.* New Haven: American Schools of Oriental Research.

———. 1962. "Soundings at 'Araq el-Emir (Jordan)." *BASOR* 165: 16–34.

———. 1966. "The Cemetery at Bab-edh-Dhra, Jordan." *Archaeology* 19: 104–11.

———. 1969. *Biblical Archaeology and History.* New York: World Publishing.

———. 1970. "The Tell Deir 'Alla Challenge to Palestinian Archaeology." *Vetus Testamentum* 20: 245–56.

Layard, A. Henry. 1891. *Nineveh and Its Remains.* London: John Murray.

Lemache, Niels Peter, and Thomas Thompson. 1994. "Did Biran Kill David? The Bible in the Light of Archaeology." *JSOT* 64: 3–22.

Lewis, Jack P. 1988. "James Turner Barclay: Explorer of Nineteenth-Century Jerusalem." *BA* 51.3: 163–71.

Long, Burke O. 1997. *Planting and Reaping Albright.* University Park: Pennsylvania State University Press.

Lynch, Edward. 1849. *Expedition to the River Jordan and the Dead Sea.* Philadelphia: Lea and Blanchard.

Macalister, R.A.S. 1906. *Bible Sidelights from the Mound of Gezer.* New York: Scribner.

———. 1912. *The Excavations of Gezer, 1902–1905 and 1907–1909.* 3 vols. London: Palestine Exploration Fund.

———. 1925. *A Century of Excavation in Palestine.* London: Religious Tract Society.

———. 1926. "Excavations on the Hill of Ophel Jerusalem 1923–1925." In *Palestine Exploration Fund Annual,* vol. 4. London: Palestine Exploration Fund.

MacDonald, B. 1982. "The Wadi el-Hasa Survey 1979 and Previous Archaeological Work in Southern Jordan." *BASOR* 245: 35–52.

Mandatory Government of Palestine. 1920. *Official Gazette of the Government of Palestine,* no. 29.

Marquet-Krause, Judith. 1935. "La deuxiéme campagne de fouilles à Ay (1934): Rapport sommaire." *Syria* 16: 325–45.

Mattingly, G. L. 1985. "Conquest of Canaan." In *Harper's Bible Dictionary.* San Francisco: Harper and Row, 270–71.

Mazar, Amihai. 1992. *Archaeology of the Land of the Bible.* The Anchor Bible Reference Library. New York: Doubleday.

McCown, C. C. 1943. *The Ladder of Progress in Palestine.* New York: Harper and Brothers.

McRay, John. 1991. *Archaeology and the New Testament.* Grand Rapids, MI: Baker Book House.

Mendenhall, George. 1962. "The Hebrew Conquest of Palestine." *BA* 25: 66–87.

Meskell, Lynn. 1998. *Archaeology Under Fire: Nationalism, Politics and Heritage in the Eastern Mediterranean World.* London: Routledge.

Miles, J. A. 1976. "Understanding Albright: A Revolutionary Etude." *Harvard Theological Review* 69: 151–75.

Miller, J. M. 1977. "The Israelite Occupation of Canaan." In *Israelite and Judean History,* ed. J. H. Hayes and Maxwell Miller. London: SCM Press, 213–84.

Miller, J. M., and J. H. Hayes. 1986. *A History of Ancient Israel and Judah.* Philadelphia: Westminster.

Montet, Pierre. 1928. *Byblos et l'egypt, quatre campagnes de fouilles a Gebail 1921, 1922, 1923, 1924.* Paris: Paul Geuthier.

Moore, J. R. 1979. *The Post Darwinian Controversies.* Cambridge, UK: Cambridge University Press.

Moulton, W. J. 1928. "The American Palestine Exploration Society." *AASOR* 8: 55–78.

Noth, M. 1938. "Grundsätzliches zur geschichtlichen Deutung archäologischer Befunde auf dem Boden Pälestinas." *Palästinajahrbuch* 34: 7–22.

———. 1960. "Der Beitrag der Archaologie zur Geschichte Israels." *Vetus Testamentum Supplement* 7: 262–82.

Parrot, Andre. 1952. *Decouvert des mondes ensevelis.* Neuchatel, Switzerland: Delochaux and Niestle.

Petrie, W. M.Flinders. 1891. *Tell El Hesy.* London: Alexander P. Watt.

———. 1894. *Tell El Amarna.* London: Methuen.

———. 1901. *Diospolis Parva.* London: Egyptian Exploration Fund.

———. 1904. *Methods and Aims in Archaeology.* London: Macmillan.

———. 1932. *Seventy Years in Archaeology.* London: Sampson Low, Marston.

———. 1931–34. *Ancient Gaza.* Vols. 1–4. London: British School of Archaeology in Egypt.

Phythian-Adams, J. 1923. "Report on the Stratification of Askalon." *PEQ:* 60–72.

Pritchard, J. B. 1962. *Gibeon. Where the Sun Stood Still.* Princeton: Princeton University Press.

Rainey, Anson. 2001. "Stones for Bread: Archaeology versus History." *NEA* 64.3: 140–49.

Reisner, G., C. S. Fisher, and D. Lyon. 1924. *The Harvard University Excavations at Samaria I.* Cambridge, MA: Harvard University Press.

Renan, M. E. 1864. *Mission de Phenicie.* Paris: Imprimerie Impériale.

Rian, E. 1984. "Theological Conflicts of the 1920s and 1930s in the Presbyterian Church and on the Princeton Seminary Campus." *Princeton Seminary Bulletin* 5.3: 216–23.

Robinson, Edward. 1841. *Biblical Researches in Palestine.* 3 vols. London: John Murray.

———. 1852. *Further Biblical Researches in Palestine.* London: John Murray.

Rogerson, J. 1984. *Old Testament Criticism in the Nineteenth Century.* London: Society for Promoting Christian Knowledge.

Ruby, Robert. 1993. *Jericho: Dreams, Ruins, Phantoms.* New York: Henry Holt.

Running, L. G., and D. N. Freedman. 1975. *William Foxwell Albright: A Twentieth Century Genius.* New York: Two Continents.

Saghieh, M. 1983. *Byblos in the Third Millennium B.C.: A Reconstruction of the Stratigraphy and a Study of the Cultural Connection.* Warminster, UK: Aris and Phillips.

Sandeen, E. 1970. *The Roots of Fundamentalism.* Grand Rapids, MI: Baker Book House.

Sasson, Jack. 1993. "Albright as an Orientalist." *BA* 56.1: 3–7.

Sauer, James. 1986. "Transjordan in the Bronze and Iron Ages: A Critique of Glueck's Synthesis." *BASOR* 263: 1–26.

Sayce, A. H. 1884. Preface to *Troja,* by Heinrich Schliemann. London: John Murray.

———. 1890. *Fresh Light from the Ancient Monuments*. London: Society for Promoting Christian Knowledge.

———. 1894. *The "Higher Criticism" and the Verdict of the Monuments*. London: Society for Promoting Christian Knowledge.

———. 1895. *Patriarchal Palestine*. London: Society for Promoting Christian Knowledge.

———. 1904. *Monument Facts and "Higher Critical" Fancies*. London: Society for Promoting Christian Knowledge.

———. 1918. "The Date of the Amarna Letters." *Proceedings of the Society of Biblical Archaeology* 40: 101–17.

Schiffer, M. B. 1983. "Toward the Identification of Formation Processes." *American Antiquity* 48: 675–706.

Schliemann, H. 1880. *Ilios*. London: John Murray.

———. 1884. *Troja*. London: John Murray.

Schumacher, G. 1908. *Tell el-Mutesellim I*. Leipzig: Hinrichs.

Sellin, E. 1904. *Tell Ta'annek*. Vienna: Genhold.

Sellin, E., and C. Watzinger. 1913. *Jericho, die Ergebnisse der Ausgrabungen*. Leipzig: Hinrichs.

Shanks, Hershel, ed. 1999. *Ancient Israel*. Revised ed. Washington, DC: Biblical Archaeology Society.

Silberman, Neil A. 1982. *Digging for God and Country: Exploration, Archaeology and the Secret Struggle for the Holy Land, 1799–1917*. New York: Knopf.

———. 1989. *Between Past and Present: Archaeology, Ideology, and Nationalism in the Middle East*. New York: Henry Holt.

———. 1991. "Desolation and Restoration: The Impact of a Biblical Concept on Near Eastern Archaeology." *BA* 54.2: 76–87.

———. 1993. "Visions of the Future: Albright in Jerusalem, 1919–1929." *BA* 56.1: 8–16.

Sinclair. 1976. "Gibeah." In Encyclopedia of Archaeological Excavations in the Holy Land. Ed. M. Avi-Yonah. Englewood Cliffs, NJ: Prentice-Hall, 444–446.

Smart, J. D. 1979. *The Past, Present, and Future of Biblical Theology*. Philadelphia: Westminster.

Smith, W. 1884. *A Dictionary of the Bible*. New York: Parker and Coates.

Stager, L. E., A. Walker, and G. Ernest Wright. 1974. *American Expedition to Idalion, Cyprus*. Cambridge, MA: American Schools of Oriental Research.

Stern, E. 1982. *Material Culture of the Land of the Bible in the Persian Period 538–332 B.C.* Warminster, UK: Aris and Phillips.

Stinespring, W. F. 1939. "The Critical Faculty of Edward Robinson." *JBL* 58: 379–87.

Thomas, P. 1984. "The Success and Failure of Robert Alexander Stewart Macalister." *BA* 47: 33–35.

Thompson, T. W. 1974. *The Historicity of the Patriarchal Narratives*. Beihefte zur Zeitschrift für die alttestamentliche Wissenschaft 133. Berlin: De Gruyter.

———. 1978. "The Background of the Patriarchs: A Reply to William Dever and Malcolm Clark." *JSOT* 9: 2–43.

Tufnell, O. 1958. *Lachish IV: The Bronze Age*. Oxford: Oxford University Press.

————. 1969. "The Pottery from the Royal Tombs I–III at Byblos." *Berytus* 18: 5–33.

Tufnell, O., C. H. Inge, and L. Harding. 1940. *Lachish II: The Fosse Temple*. Oxford: Oxford University Press.

Uruquart, J. 1915. *Archaeology's Solution of Old Testament Puzzles: How Pick and Spade Are Answering the Destructive Criticism of the Bible*. London: Society for Promoting Christian Knowledge.

Van Seters, J. 1975. *Abraham in History and Tradition*. New Haven: Yale University Press

Viviano, Benedict T. 1991. "Ecole Biblique et Archéologique Francaise de Jérusalem." *BA* 54.3: 160–67.

Watzinger, C. 1929. *Tell el-Mutesellim II*. Leipzig: Heinrichs.

Wellhausen, Julius. 1885. *Prolegomena to the History of Ancient Israel*. Edinburgh: T and T Clark. Originally published as *Prolegomena zur Geschichte Israels*.

Wheeler, Mortimer. 1954. *Archaeology from the Earth*. Harmondsworth, UK: Penguin.

Wilkinson, J. 1978. *Jerusalem as Jesus Knew it: Archaeology as Evidence*. London: Thames and Hudson.

Willey, Gordon. 1974. "A Summary of the Complex Societies Colloquium." In *Reconstructing Complex Societies, An Archaeological Colloquium*. Ed. C. B. Moore. Supplement to *BASOR* 20. Cambridge, MA: American Schools of Oriental Research.

Willey, G. R., and J. A. Sabloff. 1980. *A History of American Archaeology*. Revised ed. San Francisco: Freeman.

Williams, D. D. 1941. *The Andover Liberals*. Morningside Heights, NY: King's Cross.

Wright, G. Ernest. 1936. "The Chronology of Palestine in the Early Bronze Age." *BASOR* 63: 12–21.

————. 1937. *The Pottery of Palestine from the Earliest Times to the End of the Early Bronze Age*. New Haven: American Schools of Oriental Research.

————. 1938. "Chronology of Palestinian Pottery in Middle Bronze I." *BASOR* 71: 27–34.

————. 1940. Review of Barrois, *Manuel d'archeologie biblique*. *AJA*. 44.3: 400–401.

————. 1941a. "Archaeological Observations on the Period of the Judges and the Early Monarchy." *JBL* 60: 27–42.

————. 1941b. Review of Glueck, *The Other Side of the Jordan*. *JBL* 60: 189–94.

————. 1941c. Review of Rowe, *The Four Canaanite Temples of Beth-Shan, Part I*. *AJA* 45.3: 483–85.

————. 1941d. Review of Avi-Yonah, *Map of Roman Palestine*. *AJA* 45.3: 485–86.

————. 1941e. Review of Tufnell, Inge, and Harding, *Lachish II, The Fosse Temple*. *AJA* 45.4: 634–35.

————. 1941f. Review of Ehrich, *Early Pottery of the Jebeleh Region*. *AJA* 45.4: 635–36.

————. 1942a. "Two Misunderstood Items in the Exodus-Conquest Cycle." *BASOR* 86: 32–35.

————. 1942b. Review of Ingholt, *Rapport preliminaire sur sept campagnes de fouilles a Hama en Syrie (1932–1938)*. *Journal of Bible and Religion* 10.3: 173.

————. 1944. *The Challenge of Israel's Faith*. Chicago: University of Chicago Press.

————. 1946. "Neo-Orthodoxy and the Bible." *Journal of Bible and Religion* 14.2: 87–93.

————. 1947. "Biblical Archaeology Today." *BA* 10: 7–24.

————. 1950a. *The Old Testament against Its Environment*. Studies in Biblical Theology No. 2. London: SCM Press.

————. 1950b. "The Discoveries at Megiddo." *BA* 13: 28–46.

————. 1950c. Review of Loud, *Megiddo II, Seasons of 1935–1939*. *Journal of the American Oriental Society* 70.1: 56–60.

————. 1952. *God Who Acts: Biblical Theology As Recital*. London: SCM Press.

————. 1958. "Archaeology and Old Testament Studies." *JBL* 77: 39–51.

————. 1959. "Is Glueck's Aim to Prove That the Bible Is True?" *BA* 12: 101–7.

————. 1961. "The Archaeology of Palestine." In *The Bible and the Ancient Near East: Essays in Honor of William Foxwell Albright*, ed. G. E. Wright. Garden City, NY: Doubleday, 85–139.

————. 1962a. *Biblical Archaeology*. Revised ed. London: Gerald Duckworth.

————. 1962b. "Archaeological Fills and Strata." *BA* 25: 34–40.

————. 1963. "The Fourth Campaign at Balatah (Shechem)." *BASOR* 169: 1–60.

————. 1965. *Shechem: Biography of a Biblical City*. London: Gerald Duckworth.

————. 1969a. "Archaeological Method in Palestine: An American Interpretation." *Eretz Israel* 9: 120–33.

————. 1969b. "Biblical Archaeology Today." In *New Directions in Biblical Archaeology*, ed. D. N. Freedman and J. Greenfield. Garden City, NY: Doubleday, 149–65.

————. 1969c. *The Old Testament and Theology*. New York: Harper and Row.

————. 1970. "The Phenomenon of American Archaeology in the Near East." In *Near Eastern Archaeology in the Twentieth Century*, ed. J. Sanders. Garden City, NY: Doubleday, 3–40.

————. 1971. "What Archaeology Can and Cannot Do." *BA* 34: 70–76.

————. 1974. "The Tell: Basic Unit for Reconstructing Complex Societies in the Near East." In *Reconstructing Complex Societies: An Archaeological Colloquium*, ed. C. B. Moore. Supplement to *BASOR* 20. Cambridge, MA: American Schools of Oriental Research.

————. 1975. "The 'New' Archaeology." *BA* 38: 104–14.

————. 1978. "Shechem." In *Encyclopedia of Archaeological Excavations in the Holy Land*, ed. M. Avi-Yonah and E. Stern. Englewood Cliffs, NJ: Prentice-Hall, 1082–94.

Wright, G. Ernest, and Robert Boling. 1982. *The Anchor Bible Joshua*. Garden City, NY: Doubleday.

Wright, G. Ernest, and R. D. Fuller. 1957. *The Book of the Acts of God*. Garden City, NY: Doubleday.

Wright, G. Ernest, and E. Grant. 1938. *Ain Shems Excavations, Part IV (Pottery)*. Biblical and Kindred Studies No. 7. Haverford, PA: Haverford College Press.

————. 1939. *Ain Shems Excavations, Part V (Text)*. Biblical and Kindred Studies No. 8. Haverford, PA: Haverford College Press.

————. 1970. "Megiddo of the Kings of Israel." *BA* 33.3: 66–96.

Yadin, Y. 1972. *Hazor: The Head of All Those Kingdoms*. London: Oxford University Press.

————. 1977. "Megiddo." In *Encyclopedia of Archaeological Excavations in the Holy Land*, ed. M. Avi-Yonah. Englewood Cliffs, NJ: Prentice-Hall, 830–56.

Zorn, Jeffrey. 1988. "William Frederic Badè." *BA* 51.5: 28–35.

ARCHIVAL COLLECTIONS

Palestine Exploration Fund (PEF) Files

Palestine Exploration Fund archival material is abbreviated as PEF followed by the file name and accession number.

Macalister: Gezer expedition and Robert Alexander Stewart Macalister
Petrie: Sir W. M. Flinders Petrie Papers
Schick: Letters from Jerusalem correspondants to the secretary, George Armstrong
WS: Warren Survey File

University Museum of Archaeology/Anthropology (UMA), University of Pennsylvania Files

Record Group: Expedition Records
Subgroup: Syro-Palestine/Beisan
Syro-Palestine/Ain Shems
Record Group: Biography
Subgroup: C. S. Fisher

Index